No Longer Strangers

Hi

from Ray Whitehill

No Longer Strangers

SELECTED WRITINGS
OF BISHOP K. H. TING

Edited with an Introduction
by Raymond L. Whitehead

ORBIS BOOKS

Maryknoll, New York 10545

Second Printing, December 1989

The Catholic Foreign Mission Society of America (Maryknoll) recruits and trains people for overseas missionary service. Through Orbis Books, Maryknoll aims to foster the international dialogue that is essential to mission. The books published, however, reflect the opinions of their authors and are not meant to represent the official position of the society.

Manuscript editor: Joan Marie Laflamme

Library of Congress Cataloging-in-Publication Data

Ting, K. H.
   No longer strangers: selected writings of Bishop K. H. Ting/
edited with an introduction by Raymond L. Whitehead.
      p. cm.
   Bibliography: p.
   Includes index.
   ISBN 0-88344-653-7
   1. Christianity—China.   I. Whitehead, Raymond L. II. Title.
BR1285.T55   1989
275.1′0825—dc20   89-15989
                                                   CIP

Today . . . there is in China a Christianity to which revolution is no longer a stranger, and a revolution to which Christianity is not such a stranger either.

K. H. Ting

Contents

Preface

The purpose of this book is to make accessible to the general reader the writings of Bishop K. H. Ting (Ting Kuang-hsun). The corpus of his work includes over one hundred essays, sermons, speeches, articles, and informal talks. Some have never been published before, and many of the published articles are not easily accessible; additional material has been published in Chinese but not in English. Many of the other articles were written in English, the language in which K. H. Ting first studied theology at St. John's University in Shanghai.

The material has been edited extensively, including excerpting, abridging and making stylistic changes. Gender-inclusive English was introduced or expanded but not all male-exclusive usages were eliminated; of course, problems of gender-inclusive language are quite different in Chinese. Some references to events, organizations or persons not relevant to this collection were removed from the text where the essential meaning was not affected. Editing has been done in consultation with Bishop Ting. The agreed-upon goal was not to re-create the texts as they originally stood, but to provide a window into the work and thought of one Chinese Christian. Although Bishop Ting had access to the edited material prior to publication, I bear responsibility for any errors or misrepresentations. The preparation of Bishop Ting's complete works is underway and will be available in electronic format, microform, or hard copy.

The Introduction and the notes preceding the parts and subsections are intended to give a context for the reader who may be unfamiliar with China and events and persons there. My intent has not been to give an interpretation of K. H. Ting's thought but to set the scene so that his writings can speak for themselves. Again, distortions or biases that may appear in the explanatory material are my responsibility. Not all questions are addressed, obviously, in the Introduction and notes. The reader is directed to suggestions for further reading listed at the back of the book.

The Introduction describes some aspects of Ting's life. He provided me with very little biographical information, responding that he is not important as an individual, and that this book should simply be some thoughts of one Chinese Christian, reflecting the collective experience of the church in that context. I admire this modesty, but readers of the manuscript continued to ask for more background on the author. From old friends of

K. H. Ting and from archives and letters, I was able to glean the few details that appear in the Introduction.

Rather than use a chronological sequence I arranged the selected writings by themes. This served better the goal of presenting Ting's theological views in a systematic manner. In each subsection, however, the articles on a specific theme are grouped in chronological order, with one or two exceptions where clarity was served by altering the sequence.

There are many thematic divisions that could have been used to organize the materials. The one I chose seemed to arise naturally from the writings themselves. The works selected are divided into four parts, with three subsections in each. At the beginning of each part the theme is explained, and before each subsection, notes give the context of each article and explain terms and names where necessary.

The first part, "Embodying Christianity," discusses the need to find a form and expression of Christianity that is Chinese, not foreign. The second part, "Serving the People," focuses on the pastoral care and service that the church is called to provide, including the tasks of preaching and evangelism. Much of the life of the church in China in the past half century has been caught up in the currents of domestic and international politics, making it possible for us inadvertently to overlook the ongoing ministries of support and healing that are integral to its work.

The third part, "Confronting the World," shows how K. H. Ting and the church in China have had to face difficult political and cultural issues, including problems of imperialism, the search for justice and peace, the encounter with various worldviews, and the relationship of the church to socialism. In the last part, "Affirming the Church," we turn to Chinese Christians' faithfulness to the church. The part starts with articles on the struggle against attempts to lead the church astray or to impose foreign control. Subsequent selections affirm the new course charted by Chinese Christians toward selfhood, community, and hope in the Holy Spirit's empowering of the church in China.

Nearly fifty articles have been selected for this book. The earliest is from 1947 and the most recent from 1986. There is a long hiatus between 1961 and 1979, when no articles appeared. Ting's output of sermons, speeches, and essays in the 1980s is beginning to make up for that dearth. It has been difficult for me to bring this project to closure, although I now feel I have included the main currents of Bishop Ting's thought.

References to the Roman Catholic Church in China are infrequent in this collection. Relations between Catholics and Protestants in China have been cordial in recent years. It is important to remember, however, that Catholic and Protestant Christianity are considered different religions in China. This is partially the result of conscious rivalry between the missionaries of each group at an earlier period. It also reflects decisions made by missionaries on the translation of names. The Catholic missionaries chose to call God *Tianzhu* or Lord of Heaven, and their religion came to be known as *Tianzhujiao*, Lord of Heaven religion. When the Protestants arrived in China, they adopted the name *Jidujiao*, Christ religion, often rendered back into English simply as Christianity. This means that when Christian or Christianity appears in an article it is probably a translation of a word that could be rendered alternatively as Protestant or Protestant Christianity. The context does not always make clear which is intended. Other problems of translation are noted in the explanatory comments preceding the subsections.

In his student days Ting Kuang-hsun adopted "K. H. Ting" as the international form for his name. In the contemporary Chinese romanization (*pinyin*) it would be rendered as Ding Guangxun. Although some English-language publications in China today use that form, Bishop Ting himself has never adopted it. This book uses his preferred form for the name. His wife also continues a traditional spelling of her name, Kuo Siu May, and that form is followed in this book. Kuo is her family name, which appears first in Chinese usage. The adoption of initials by K. H. Ting follows a style that was intended to avoid confusion about the surname.

Some other personal names and place names retain the traditional style of spelling in this book: for example, Hong Kong, Y. T. Wu, Chiang Kai-shek. Names that have been used extensively in the foreign-language press in China and are now familiar in their new form appear in this book in that new form: Mao Zedong (for Mao Tse-tung), Zhou Enlai (for Chou En-lai), for example. Most Chinese place names appear in the new form also: Beijing (for Peking), Nanjing (for Nanking). The new *pinyin* spellings are generally easier for the foreign reader if it is remembered that "q" is pronounced as a slightly softened "ch," and "x" as a mildly slurred "s."

Bishop Ting is steeped in the Bible, familiar with the Chinese version and both the King James and modern English versions. Biblical references and allusions abound in his writing. I decided not to standardize the biblical references by using one English translation, since to do so would sometimes confuse the sense of his allusion. References are most frequently rendered in the Revised Standard Version.

In 1977, on a visit to Nanjing, I met K. H. Ting in person for the first time, though we had corresponded and exchanged materials for some time. He and Siu May invited me to their home for dinner. It was the same house from which they had been expelled by Red Guards a decade earlier in the Cultural Revolution. A highlight of the meal was ice cream, topped with fresh strawberries from their tiny garden, their first crop since moving back in. The sharing of the precious strawberries was an act of graciousness that stays in my memory. The setting provided small signs of hope. The political situation was changing.

When K. H. Ting visited Toronto in 1979 and 1981, we spoke of the value of collecting and publishing his writings. In succeeding years we met from time to time and with his help and concurrence I was able to gather most of his written work. We collaborated in a general way on questions of editing, style, and format although he did not become involved in details. The friendship of K. H. Ting and Kuo Siu May has continued to encourage and inspire me to complete the work.

The quotation on the title page from which the title of this book is derived is from K. H. Ting's Foreword to *James G. Endicott: Rebel Out of China* (by Stephen Endicott, University of Toronto Press, 1980, p. x). The words, written in tribute to James Endicott, could also apply to K. H. Ting himself.

The project of collecting and editing these writings stretched over several years and involved the help of many people. Initial input of the data, sometimes from very unclear copies, was done by Kathleen Copeland Hummelen. Ms. Cheng Musheng of Qinghua University in Beijing, the Reverend Ng Kam-yan of Toronto, and Mr. Yao Niangeng of Dalien Foreign Languages Institute translated articles for this volume.

Audrey Douglas did major work editing, abridging, and excerpting articles. Carolyn Sharp researched sources and gave critical suggestions on conceptual and theological clarity, as well as carefully proofreading the text. Terry Thompson gave me access to archival material from the Canadian Student Christian Movement and the World Student Christian Federation that filled in biographical details on K. H. Ting's years abroad. Stephen Endicott read the manuscript and provided many helpful corrections and guidelines. Cyril Powles also made many useful suggestions after reading the entire text.

Funding came from the Presbyterian Church in Canada, the United Church of Canada, the United Board for Christian Higher Education in Asia, and the Foundation for Theological Education in South East Asia. Susan Perry of Orbis Books gave patient and practical assistance to the final production work.

I am deeply grateful to these individuals and organizations, and to many others left unnamed, who made the completion of this project possible. Lastly, I thank my family for their patience and support as "free time" was continually consumed by this task, and especially my wife, Rhea, for her help and encouragement all along the way.

May 15, 1989

Introduction

THE LIFE AND WORK
OF A CHINESE CHRISTIAN

In a small private dining room in the Parliament Buildings in Ottawa in the autumn of 1979 Prime Minister Joe Clark along with a few other Members of Parliament and Canadian church leaders gathered to meet Bishop K. H. Ting. Three fateful decades had passed since Ting was last in Canada. After the meal several of those present stood in turn to speak a few words. Except for some closing remarks, Bishop Ting was the last to speak. Through our window, high above the Ottawa River, we could see stars and city lights sparkling in the chill autumn air, but Ting's words were warm and elegant. He spoke of the thirty-three years since he and his wife, Siu May, had ventured from Shanghai to Canada to work with the Student Christian Movement. The intervening decades were marked by war, cold war and broken relationships, but also by lasting friendships. A time of renewal seemed about to begin. None in that room could have guessed the extent of the change in China and the Chinese church that the 1980s would witness.

THE ORIGINS AND DEVELOPMENT OF CHINESE CHRISTIANITY

Chinese culture can be traced back long before the rise of Christianity. Confucius was teaching in the sixth and fifth centuries B.C.E. and although clear historical information is not available from much earlier than that, the civilization in which Confucius lived was obviously centuries old. Archeological information indicates civilization developing perhaps two thousand years earlier than Confucius. China was first unified in the third century B.C.E. by the Emperor Chin, who was followed by the four-hundred-year Han Dynasty.

There were modest contacts between the Chinese Empire and the Roman Empire (our name for China is presumed to derive from the name of Emperor Chin), and at various times trade along the "Silk Road" through

1

central Asia. However, China remained for the most part mysterious and inaccessible to the developing European civilization of the medieval and renaissance period. Marco Polo's thirteenth-century adventures in China indicate both the possibility and the rarity of contact. Franciscans established missions in China at this period, but their work did not survive dynastic change. Nestorian Christianity existed in China for a time but also did not endure.

Chinese considered the borders of their empire also to be the limits of civilization. They developed a complex and beautiful writing system, invented printing, devised paper-making, made advances in astronomy, discovered the magnetic compass, produced beautiful porcelains, invented gunpowder, and led the world in many other ways. This is all familiar information, but it shows why some contacts with Europe were not fruitful; Europeans also tended to see their own culture as the only or the highest civilization.

Jesuit missions started in China in the late sixteenth century. Matteo Ricci (1552-1610) had notable success in the seventeenth century, winning considerable support from the emperor for a time. Reports from Jesuit and other missions back to Europe were quite favorable. Chinese arts and crafts, pagodas and gardens were adopted by wealthy Europeans. Enlightenment scholars admired Confucian philosophy.

When Robert Morrison, the first Protestant missionary to China, arrived in 1807 things had already begun to change. Catholic mission work suffered from disputes among various religious orders and European powers such as Portugal and Spain. Controversies about Chinese culture and rites resulted in setbacks. The Qing (Ching) Dynasty was in a state of decline and the Chinese, rather than receiving the praise of the Europeans, were looked down on. The increasing military and industrial power of Europe and North America led to Western expansion. Mission work became increasingly entangled with imperialist policies. The proud Chinese suffered humiliation and became the victims of Western drug trafficking when opium from India was used by the British and North Americans as a way to secure Chinese silver and other products such as tea.

From the mid-nineteenth until the mid-twentieth century the problem for China was how to achieve national salvation: keeping the country unified and free of foreign intrusion; and achieving a renewed cultural identity that would form a base of support for these goals. England, Germany, France, Portugal, Russia and eventually Japan, all had taken property or gained control of aspects of Chinese life. The United States concentrated on economic invasion. The memory of these attempts to carve up China governs the attitudes of Beijing today toward Tibet, Taiwan and Hong Kong.

Sun Yat-sen (1866–1925), the first modern leader of China after the overthrow of the last imperial dynasty, left his home village near Macao at age 18 to study in Hawaii and later in Hong Kong, where he was baptized and received a medical degree. He never gained effective control of the country, much of which had fallen into the hands of regional leaders (warlords). His successor, Chiang Kai-shek (1887–1975), was also baptized a Christian. It was a rival Western worldview, however, Marxism, which captured the minds of more capable revolutionaries. In 1949 Chairman Mao Zedong (1893–1976) led a peasant army to a victory that unified most of the country and restored pride to the Chinese people. As leader of the Communist Party he declared the establishment of the People's Republic of China with the words, "The Chinese people have stood up."

The year 1949 was a fateful juncture for Chinese Christianity. Missionaries almost universally opposed the Communists. And both the Protestant and the Catholic churches were still heavily dependent on missionaries. The great majority of Catholic bishops in China were foreign. Protestant churches had developed slightly more Chinese leadership, but they had many large medical and educational institutions that required a steady flow of foreign funds and personnel. The People's Government allowed missionary work to continue, though many missionaries departed of their own accord. The Korean War broke out in 1950, and soon resulted in United States, European, Australian, Canadian and other forces under the United Nations flag fighting against Chinese "volunteers," who moved in to help North Korea when threats were made to cross the Yalu River and march into China. Under these circumstances Western missionaries in China became a liability and an embarrassment to the Chinese church. Those who had remained now left, bringing to a close four hundred years of more or less continuous Catholic missions and one hundred fifty years of Protestant missions in China.

From the viewpoint of many Chinese Christians the change in 1949 represented not a closing down but a beginning, albeit a painful beginning amid harsh ideological conflicts and bitter warfare. Christians were not well-prepared to deal with Marxism and the meaning of the victory of socialist revolution. There was a need for exceptional leadership at this crucial turning point. K. H. Ting, who was abroad at the time of the Communist victory, eventually joined his mentor, Y. T. Wu, and others in providing leadership.

K. H. TING AND CHINESE CHRISTIANITY
BEFORE LIBERATION

When K. H. Ting was born in Shanghai in 1915 the Qing Dynasty had just ended, as much fading away in corruption and incompetence as being overthrown by the Sun Yat-sen revolutionaries. China was in disunity and foreign governments controlled various parts of its territory. Shanghai itself was divided into various administrative regions: the French Concession, which was administered by the French Consul General; the Foreign Settlement, which was a combination of the British and American Concessions and operated under a Municipal Council essentially British in style; and the Chinese area under the Chinese Municipal Government. The foreign concessions began in the nineteenth century as a result of the treaties forced on China after its defeat in the First Opium War (1839–42). In Ting's childhood the foreign-controlled areas of Shanghai had a population of about thirty thousand foreigners and about one and a half million Chinese. It was China's leading port city, a center of manufacturing, and a center of church administration and education.

There were a million Catholics in China in the early decades of this century, most of the priests and bishops being foreign (predominantly French). Protestants (that is, all non–Roman Catholic Christians) numbered one hundred thousand, with three hundred Chinese clergy and thirty-five hundred foreign missionaries. The French Concession in Shanghai was a center of Roman Catholic administration and education, and a major seminary was adjacent to the cathedral there. Protestant publishing and educational work were also concentrated here. K. H. Ting's father, in the banking profession in Shanghai, worked to make Chinese churches self-supporting. Ting's maternal grandfather was an Anglican priest. K. H. Ting recounts that his mother prayed that he would enter the priesthood.

The Shanghai of K. H. Ting's childhood was also a place of political and social ferment. In 1919, when Ting was 4 years old, demonstrations broke out in Shanghai and other cities in response to the Treaty of Versailles, which gave German concessions in China to Japan instead of returning them to China (even though China had sent labor brigades to Europe after declaring war on Germany). The demonstrations started on May 4, and the name May Fourth Movement came to be applied to a range of reform movements that included anti-imperial politics, the reform of the written language, a literary renaissance, educational restructuring and radical social policies. The October Revolution in Russia (1917) brought Marxism to the attention of many Chinese intellectuals. The Communist Party of China traces its origin to an underground conference of a dozen representatives held in Shanghai in the summer of 1921. The 28-year-old Mao Zedong was one of the twelve.

Although not aware of all these things, obviously, a child in Shanghai in the 1920s could hardly be sheltered from the sense of ferment. Ting was 12 in 1927 when a great struggle for the city of Shanghai began. Communist leaders, including Zhou Enlai (1898-1976), organized the workers of Shanghai to take the city from foreign and anti-revolutionary Chinese control in anticipation of Chiang Kai-shek's "Northern Expedition" reaching the city. As soon as Chiang Kai-shek's forces entered the city, they turned against the Communists with whom they had been allied and began a purge from which Zhou only narrowly escaped. Shanghai returned to the control of foreign and Chinese conservative business interests, but Chinese antipathy to foreign imperial power continued to smolder.

K. H. Ting attended St. John's University in Shanghai. He studied engineering but later turned to theology at the urging of his mother. St. John's had excellent academic standards, but as a mission of the American Episcopal church it was known also for its "foreignization" of Chinese intellectuals. All classes were in English except courses in Chinese language and literature. Ting received a sound, Western-style, undergraduate education in one of the few lulls amid China's continuing upheavals. Not that the rest of the country was quiet. Battles were continuing between the Nationalist and the Communist armies. While Ting was a university student in the mid-1930s Chiang Kai-shek's Nationalist forces were chasing Mao and the Communists across the vast rugged terrain of inland China. The Communists called this strategic retreat "The Long March" and were able to assemble enough troops and leadership in the isolated hills of Yanan in Shaanxi province to continue to fight against Japan and to prepare for the eventual showdown with Chiang.

Japan's all-out invasion of China began in 1937 just as K. H. Ting was finishing his B. A. His theological studies were carried out under wartime conditions and the Japanese occupation of Shanghai, but he completed the B.D. degree in 1942. He was ordained deacon, then priest, in that same year. Subsequently he worked as student secretary of the YMCA, served as curate at the Church of the Saviour, and served in the International Church, all in Shanghai.

During the mid-1930s Ting came into contact with Y. T. Wu (1890–1979). From his description of their earliest encounters we get a glimpse of the kind of education he had received at St. John's. While listening respectfully to Wu's theology of involvement Ting says, "I had in one pocket my lexicon on New Testament Greek and in another my textbook on the Thirty-Nine Articles of the Church of England." He was moved by Wu, however, to set out in a new, more meaningful direction. Y. T. Wu "opened a sluice-gate for many Chinese Christians to take their place in the movement for national salvation with their faith intact" (see "A Pioneering Theologian").

In 1942 K. H. Ting married Kuo Siu May, who was born in Wuhan in central China in 1916. She studied at St. Mary's Hall, an Anglican high school in Shanghai, began her university studies in Beijing at Yanjing (Yenching) University and completed her degree at St. John's. During the later war years she taught at both St. Mary's Hall and St. John's University.

After the war Ting responded to an invitation from the Canadian Student Christian Movement (SCM) to serve for a year in Canada as mission secretary, with provision for Siu May to accompany him and share in the activities. The position was usually filled by a Canadian but organizers hoped that a Chinese Christian leader would help restore an international missionary interest among students. In September 1946 the couple arrived to start a year's work, which had an impact that is still talked of today. They were viewed by friends as a close working team who touched the lives of many students who were looking for a socially responsible Christian faith. The Canadian SCM was a progressive organization whose membership included many future leaders of Canadian church and society.

The academic year following their stay in Canada was spent in New York. K. H. completed a master's degree at Union Theological Seminary and Columbia University, while Siu May earned her master's degree at Columbia University Teachers College. Their first son, Stephen, was born in the summer. K. H. Ting, now 33 years of age, accepted an assignment to work as secretary of the World Student Christian Federation (WSCF) in Geneva, Switzerland, while his wife and son stayed on in New York.

In addition to his experience in Canada and the United States, Ting was now immersed in the life of Western Europe, traveled to Latin America and Eastern Europe and had contact with Christian leaders from Africa and Asia. In May of 1949 the Communist victory in China was imminent. Many North American and European Christians were caught up in the cold war rhetoric of "the loss of China." Ting himself was struggling to define his role. He visited Prague as WSCF secretary and renewed his acquaintance with Y. T. Wu, who was there to attend a peace conference. Their long talks in Prague helped him to see that the success of the socialist revolution did not mean the church would have no function. The problem was how Chinese Christians were themselves to respond to the new situation. Ting reflected later that even Y. T. Wu was not completely aware at that time of the immensity of the task of reforming a still mission-dependent church and enabling it to stand on its own (see "A Pioneering Theologian").

K. H. Ting and Siu May planned to return to China in the summer of 1950 after completing his two-year contract with the World Student Christian Federation. Some Western friends warned or worried, but the Tings' clear conviction found understanding and support among WSCF colleagues. After visiting Latin America Ting proceeded to Canada to prepare for a WSCF conference in Whitby, Ontario, which had been the site of an historic consultation of the International Missionary Council in 1947. He planned to meet Siu May and Stephen in New York and then proceed to San Francisco to embark for China. The outbreak of the Korean war in the summer of 1950 upset all plans.

The Korean War, however it may have begun, became one more element of the United States' "containment policy." The strategy of aggressively containing Chinese communism came in response to the fear that the Chinese Peoples' Liberation Army, victorious in mainland China, would sweep over Korea, Taiwan, Indochina, Malaya and Thailand. If communism were not contained, according to this reasoning, soon the fighting would be in our backyards. The Nationalist Chinese forces under Chiang Kai-shek, which had fled to Taiwan, claimed to be the official government of all China, a fiction accepted by many Western powers until the 1970s. The United States simultaneously began its buildup in Korea and moved the Seventh Fleet into the Taiwan Straits to prevent reunification of Taiwan with the rest of China.

Between the victory of the People's Liberation Army in China in 1949

and the start of the Korean War in the summer of 1950 it was still possible
to take a ship from San Francisco to north China, but Ting and his family
missed this chance and ended up stranded for a time. Canada would not
give Siu May and Stephen visas, and the United States would not give Ting
a visa. British Hong Kong was not immediately willing to give them visas
either. Their national status was in question because of the fluid situation
in China, and it was unclear when and how they could return home.

Eventually Siu May and Stephen received Canadian visas, and in August
of 1950 a relieved Ting went from Toronto to the United States border to
meet their train from New York. The WSCF extended Ting's appointment
by one year, and the family travelled by ship from Montreal to Le Havre
and settled into Geneva for another year's work. Hong Kong visas were
finally secured, and in August 1951 the family went by plane from Europe
to Hong Kong with overnight stops in Karachi, Calcutta and Bangkok. In
Hong Kong they stayed in the Church Guest House, courtesy of Anglican
Bishop R. O. Hall. On August 29 they boarded a morning train for Canton,
where they transferred to the famous Canton-Shanghai Express. The couple, in their mid-30s, with their 3-year-old son, arrived home in Shanghai
five years after their international sojourn had begun. Their world had
changed.

THE CHURCH IN NEW CHINA AND THE ROLE OF K. H. TING

K. H. Ting speaks often of all he had to learn in China's great transition.
He did not return to Shanghai as a hero or savior but as an important young
leader ready to do his part. Y. T. Wu is the person described by an anon-
ymous missionary in the early 1950s as "the man who saved the church in
China."[1] But other leaders, male and female, also played crucial roles in
the period of adjustment in the 1950s.[2]

Many saw the China to which Siu May and K. H. returned as under a
thoroughly evil Communist regime. Scathing language was used to describe
Chairman Mao and the Chinese Communists in the 1950s and 1960s by
journalists, scholars and missionaries. Conservative Christian journals
talked of "red rape," and "red murder." Even middle-of-the-road journals
called Mao "psychotic."

Before the Vietnam War not many people in the West viewed Washington's policies as possibly dangerous and wrongheaded. In fact, ideological anti-communism was so strong that few people saw through it. In 1953
the *Christian Herald* published an editorial supporting congressional investigation of clergy who wanted a policy of recognition of the People's Republic of China (PRC). The editorial stated that such people were enemies
in a fatal struggle and should be rooted out.

Red lies, red murder, red rape, red slavery, and red atheism are over
half the world today. . . . In the United States there are a few . . . "red

deans," red educators, red labor leaders, red politicians, red journalists.[3]

Later the same year the journal continued its attack on those who wanted relations established with the PRC:

Even as I write, this sadistic, obscene, atheistic Red scourge continues to enslave and destroy the bodies, minds and souls of uncounted ... men, women and children over the whole earth. Lies, murder and rape are its trusted weapons.

After listing alleged atrocities committed by the Chinese against Americans in the Korean War, the editorial continues:

We must sit now in armistice talks with the evil men who have done this, but shall we make them presently or ever our chosen comrades? Shall we give them the honored places of that most loyal ally, Nationalist China? Shall we accept them as partners in the UN? ... Specifically, shall we who worship the "One God and His Christ" support a co-equal compact with this government which is infinitely worse than infidel?
NO! ...
Christians of America must unite and join with all other men and women of good will to strengthen American Freedom, to help save the world from political and moral anarchy and from the last deluge which would be atheism.[4]

More liberal Christian journals used saner language, but they also displayed the same ideological anti-communism. In 1963 the *Christian Century*, for example, condemned China for "wanton attacks on Korea, Tibet and India" and for intervening in Southeast Asia. After earlier criticizing China for its alliance with the Soviet Union it now criticized Beijing for breaking with Moscow and making China the "the most isolated nation in the world." Mao's denunciation of policies of Western nations was interpreted as racism:

[Mao's] call for worldwide racial war reflects a degree of hatred and desperation which can only be described as psychotic. ... Mao and the other leaders of China have been isolated so long and so completely that they have lost touch with the realities of the modern world.[5]

From within China things looked quite different. The anti-Communist propaganda of the Western churches felt anti-Chinese, an expression of the continuing desire of imperial powers to control China. Christians in

China responded to a revolution that was at once nationalistic, socialist and determined to change the social and cultural ethos in a direction that supported China's continuing independence from all outside powers and moved the country toward industrialization. Many Chinese Christians struggled to overcome their "foreignization," their elitist separation from ordinary workers and peasants, and their cultural and theological dependency.

The transition within the Chinese church was not without conflict and pain. Christians drew up a document called the *Christian Manifesto* that set out their critique of the missionary past and called for a renewed and independent Chinese church.[6] Breaking the bonds of dependency created controversy and bitterness. The *Christian Manifesto* looks rather mild in retrospect, but at the time it caused considerable anguish among former missionaries. Public-spirited Christians denounced some Chinese church leaders and Western missionaries who were involved in imperialist policies.

The spirit of the *Christian Manifesto* required the development of a church not only independent of missionary control but also Chinese in its theology and self-understanding. Chinese Christians who had adopted Western-style fundamentalism lacked the flexibility of thought to deal with the new situation in China. Some of them refused to support the *Christian Manifesto* or make any attempt to adapt church life to the socialist context. Wang Mingdao (b. 1900) was one of the most famous of such fundamentalist preachers. He opposed attempts at church unity and efforts to work with the new government. Wang refused to cooperate with anyone who did not follow his own narrow theology. He spent many years in prison when his approach put him in conflict with the government.[7] Some Christians in the West made him into an anti-Communist hero, forgetting the atmosphere of war created by the containment policy. Wang's actions aided the enemy, in the view of the new government. K. H. Ting sharply criticized Wang in 1955 (see "Truth and Slander").

The movement that developed the *Christian Manifesto* continued among church leaders and grassroot Christians and led to the creation of the Chinese Christian Three-Self Patriotic Movement (or simply the Three-Self Movement—TSM). The concept three-self goes back to nineteenth century missionaries such as Henry Venn of the British Church Missionary Society and Rufus Anderson of the American Board of Commissioners for Foreign Missions (and further back to the apostle Paul). Missionaries should help create churches that are self-supporting, self-administering and self-propagating. The idea had a long history in China but the rise of imperialism thwarted its expression. The creation of the Three-Self Movement was crucial for the development of the church in China in the latter half of the twentieth century.

Through the Three-Self Movement Christians established their identity as Chinese. One motto Christians used was *"ai guo, ai zhu,"* "love the country, love the Lord." The simple but significant idea here was that it is possible to love God and church without becoming foreign, without being alienated from one's own people. That this was so important a point to be made is an indication of the depth of the missionary error that identified Christianity with Western culture, consciously or subconsciously.

The Three-Self Movement provided the structure for Chinese Christians to come into a self-confident ability to participate in the larger society and the tasks of social reconstruction. In April 1951 church leaders met with Premier Zhou Enlai to discuss their plans to make the church truly Chinese. A committee started preparatory work for a National Conference, which convened in 1954. This conference established a National Three-Self Committee. By 1956 the churches moved toward a unification of Protestantism. Protestants celebrated in common worship and created post-denominational structures by 1958. A second National Conference in 1961 assessed progress.[8]

Ill-equipped as they were to deal with the new situation of socialist China, Protestant Christians had some of the best leadership of any religious group. The core of leaders around Y. T. Wu, an excellent team to carry Chinese Protestantism through a most difficult transition, included not only senior leaders but young talent in K. H. Ting and others. The period of transformation was a long one. Unfortunately Y. T. Wu did not live to see the flowering of his efforts, which came about only in the 1980s.

International tensions remained high in the 1950s and 1960s. The United States Seventh Fleet in the Taiwan Straits effectively prevented Chinese unification. The truce in Korea in 1953 did not result in a reduction of United States military involvement in Taiwan and the Taiwan Straits. Shooting incidents continued over islands in the Straits held by Chiang Kai-shek's forces, but which lay within sight of the mainland. Eventually only two, Quemoy and Matsu, remained in Nationalist hands. The names of these tiny islands were household words in the West in the 1950s. They were also debated in the 1960 United States presidential election campaign, with Richard Nixon vowing not to give up one square inch of the "free world" and John Kennedy opposing US military risk for anything other than Taiwan itself (and the Pescadore Islands, which lay close to Taiwan).

In this period China was viewed as a puppet of Moscow. The Sino-Soviet split, which came in 1959, eluded Western interpretation for a few years because such a split did not fit the stereotype of monolithic communism. After the election of Kennedy as president, many observers expected the diplomatic gulf with China to be bridged. Kennedy's assassination and Lyndon Johnson's headlong plunge into war in Vietnam postponed hopes for new contact for another decade.

In China massive social developments took place. Municipal organizations cleaned up the problems of drugs and prostitution. Urban and rural life was reorganized. The government brought inflation under control and made food supplies available on an equitable basis. Mass trials of landlords accused of merciless exploitation resulted in many executions. Land reform programs gave farm land to the peasants. Cooperatives, and later communes, became the order of the day. The social and economic policies effectively restored national unity and order. A new marriage law changed feudal practices that were detrimental to women. The system supported day-care for children, women's rights and more nearly equal pay for equal work. The Chinese Communist Party had wide-based support and prestige among the people; this secured a position of leadership that remained firm for two to three decades.

K. H. Ting and Siu May went on with their work in the midst of all the momentous changes in and out of China. Siu May was appointed head-mistress at her old high school, St. Mary's Hall, later changed to the Second Girl's Middle School of Shanghai. K. H. served as secretary to the Christian Literature Society. In this time of revolutionary excitement in China some of his friends wondered why he stayed on as a preacher in the church, which seemed so backward in comparison with the social change all around them (see "Why Be a Minister?"), yet his commitment to the church remained firm. The Tings' second son, Heping (meaning "peace"), was born in 1951 in Shanghai.

In the Protestant movement toward unity a newly organized theological college brought together several schools from quite different denominational backgrounds. Ting was given the difficult task of principal of this new venture, the Nanjing Theological Seminary. In 1955 he was consecrated a bishop of the Anglican Church in China, while continuing as principal of the theological school. After their move to Nanjing Siu May secured a position as associate professor of English at the University of Nanjing and was later promoted to full professor, a position she held until her retirement.

International travel continued to be part of Siu May and K. H. Ting's life. In 1955 Siu May attended a conference in Zurich. She and K. H. travelled together to Europe in 1956, where K. H. attended the Lambeth Conference preparatory meeting. They went on to Budapest to meet with the Central Committee of the World Council of Churches and visited Christian leaders in Russia on their return to China. Relations were tense between the Chinese churches and the World Council. T. C. Chao (1888-1979) had resigned as one of the presidents of the WCC in 1950 in protest to the WCC's support of United States intervention in Korea. In the 1954 Evanston Assembly an American and former missionary to China, Charles West, was invited to speak about the situation of the church in China. Chinese Christians were livid. In the atmosphere of hostility that existed in this period and in the new selfhood the Chinese church was experiencing, the move was seen as continued imperialist involvement in the internal affairs of the Chinese church. K. H. Ting told WCC leaders in no uncertain terms that this was unacceptable. For years after, the WCC hesitated about uttering a word on the Chinese church.

Bishop Ting visited Europe in 1957 and 1961 and other Chinese Christian leaders also travelled internationally. Soon after, however, internal

struggles in the Chinese Communist leadership led to a much more restricted situation for everyone. The struggle between groups representing
different approaches to China's development came to open conflict, at
times bordering on civil war or anarchy, in the Cultural Revolution from
late 1965 until 1969. A Canadian agricultural delegation met K. H. Ting at
the theological school in 1965,[9] but once the Cultural Revolution started
there were no foreign contacts for several years. From 1961, when Ting was
47, until 1979, when he was 64, he did not travel abroad, nor do we have
any published materials for this 18-year period. He did remain in correspondence with friends outside China until the Cultural Revolution started
in late 1965 and was in touch again by 1973.

DEATH AND RESURRECTION: THE CULTURAL
REVOLUTION AND AFTER

The Cultural Revolution had as its stated goal the revival and renewal
of the spirit of revolution and commitment to socialist goals. Prominent
mottoes such as *Serve the people* aimed at overcoming selfishness and elitism. Very quickly, however, a kind of political fundamentalism also surfaced, often referred to today as ultra-leftism. The terms are inexact, and
little hard analysis has been done on the social sources of this phenomenon.
Social conditions were such that millions of people and thousands of leaders
in all spheres of life were ready to enter the movement with great enthusiasm.

Factions developed, each trying to show itself publicly more revolutionary than the others. Behind the scenes some opportunistic leaders manipulated the emotions of the people in attempts to protect their own positions
or attain greater power. Many people sincerely sought to overcome dispar-
ities in society by moving into remote areas to bring skills and modern ideas
to traditional peasant life.

The dogmatic side of the movement was intolerant of other worldviews.
In this regard it took on characteristics not unlike fundamentalist Islam or
fundamentalist Christianity in other contexts. But also like other funda-
mentalisms the movement contained ideas that represented values vital to
the worldview of which it was part.

The Cultural Revolution was a time of struggle for Christians, for
Chinese religions in general, for intellectuals and professionals, and for
many of the Communist Party elite. Activists criticized "old thinking" as
an impediment to social progress and in a rather simplistic way attacked
all religion as outmoded. Virtually all public practice of religion ceased
from 1966 until 1980. Groups of young Red Guards moved about the countryside rooting out old ideas, replacing old religions with a new one, dogmatic Maoism. Political leaders and administrators went along with the
Red Guard campaigns. Actual shooting battles took place in some areas.
Behind the scenes old scores were settled and innocent people suffered

humiliation, beatings, deprivations and cruelty. By 1969 the army had to be brought in to restore order. It was an uneasy peace, however, and struggles continued.

All institutions of higher learning were closed down. One Red Guard group took over Nanjing Theological College as its headquarters. Red Guards searched K. H. Ting's house several times; then they expelled him and his family from their home and confiscated all their belongings. Christian friends found them space to live. Ting was not jailed, but he was not allowed to leave Nanjing. He and other faculty members took part in growing vegetables on a nearby farm.

The Beijing government restored order by 1971 and achieved a series of international diplomatic advances. The People's Republic of China assumed its proper seat in the United Nations; until then the Nationalists still held the UN seat from their Taiwan provincial base. Canada and China established diplomatic relations. "Ping Pong Diplomacy" began in April 1971 when the United States' table tennis team accepted an invitation from the Chinese team at a tournament in Japan. Change was in the air. Later in 1971 the United States' Secretary of State Henry Kissinger made a secret trip to Beijing to arrange President Richard Nixon's historic visit early the next year.

One or two religious institutions were open in 1971, including a mosque in Beijing. In Nanjing visitors were told that Nanjing Theological College was one of the institutions of higher education in the city, although no visits were possible. It had been closed for some time, but the closure was seen as temporary. Occasional visitors to China reported hearing of private meetings of Christians.

Near the end of 1972 names of Christian leaders began to appear occasionally in the Chinese press. In 1973 the Reverend Ted Johnson from Canada and one or two others visited K. H. Ting, and by the next year Ting corresponded with several friends outside China and received a few more foreign visitors. A delegation of American church leaders visited Nanjing in 1976 and talked with Siu May and K. H. Ting. At this point Ting hoped Christianity would develop in China in a non-institutional form. He envisaged a Christianity without paid clergy, perhaps without the practice of ordination, with little formal theological education, and without elaborate structures.[10]

In 1976 Zhou Enlai, Mao Zedong and Zhu De, all old revolutionary leaders, died. The Gang of Four, a faction that included Mao's widow and used political fundamentalism to gain power, was overthrown. Celebrations in the streets greeted their downfall. The wine shops of Shanghai sold out all their stock in a matter of hours. A few months later, in February 1977, Ting wrote in a letter:

Life here is literally exciting everyday. People seem to experience a new liberation. It was quite impossible to foresee that a new vista so full of promise would open itself up so soon after the unretrievable loss of Chairman Mao with all its sadness and foreboding. It is not hard for our people to visualize what state of affairs we would be in if the foursome gang had succeeded in usurping state power.[11]

In 1978 the entire theological faculty became staff of a newly-created Center for Religious Studies and part of the University of Nanjing. K. H. Ting became a vice-president of the university. The hard work of creating the Three-Self Movement in the 1950s began to bear fruit after a barren spell. In an earlier period the Theological College was tolerated and re-spected — and ignored by people outside the church. Now, at the end of the 1970s, Chinese intellectuals had a different attitude toward Christianity. As a part of the University of Nanjing the theologians met other scholars on an equal footing.[12]

In a sense K. H. was back in his old milieu of student work again. He found it exhilarating:

Our Center for Religious Studies is a much busier place than Nanjing Theological College. We have truly broken through our isolation. Time and again I feel myself once again an SCM secretary chatting with all sorts of students and teachers. Five of us were televised yes-terday by some Frenchmen as we spoke to colleagues on why we thought religion an important subject. These opportunities for making the Christian presence felt . . . would be unthinkable without two things: (1) the downfall of the policies of the Gang of Four . . . and (2) the upholding of the principle of selfhood and independence on the part of Chinese Christians since 1950.[13]

Further changes were in the wind. In the autumn of 1979 K. H. Ting and three other Protestant Christian leaders, along with Buddhist and Is-lamic representatives from China, attended a meeting of the World Con-ference on Religion and Peace held at Princeton, New Jersey. The development of international contacts and mutual recognition that began in 1971 made such a visit possible. It was K. H. Ting's first visit outside China in eighteen years. The previous had been a peace meeting also, the Christian Peace Assembly in Prague (see "The Call to Peace"). After the Princeton meeting Ting visited Canada. On September 30 he arrived in Montreal, the city from which he and Siu May and Stephen had sailed for Europe in the summer of 1950. Now at age 64 he was a distinguished world figure. The Chinese delegation in the United States had been invited to the Carter White House. In Canada Bishop Ting was invited to dinner at Parliament with the prime minister, the meeting described at the beginning of this Introduction. Ting spent several weeks in Canada, renewing contacts with old SCM friends in Toronto and across the country.

The unexpected continued to take place. The mood and style in China changed completely. The revolutionary confidence of the Communist Party in the 1950s was gone. The bout of political fundamentalism and the strong reaction against it left people confused and uncertain. Many people were disillusioned by the shifts in policy and changing social conditions, leading some to a new interest in religion. The singleminded desire for modernization became the most important national goal, still roughly within some kind of socialist framework. Exactly what socialism meant no one was trying to say. There was a new openness to the West and Western technology and ideas. Thousands of students went to Europe and North America to study. Unfortunately many "old ideas" such as intellectual elitism and male chauvinism surfaced with new strength. Communes were dismantled, private initiative encouraged, and provision made for limited capitalist development.

China did not return to a pre-Cultural Revolution status. Indeed the 1980s have been a whole new era. The United Front policies of the 1950s, in which a strong Communist Party solicited the cooperation of other citizens such as religious groups, was replaced by a United Front policy in which the Party no longer assumed it had the answers. In the area of religious policy this has meant not only tolerance but encouragement for religious groups to take initiative in many areas.

Hundreds of churches have been reopened throughout the country, some of which had been closed long before the Cultural Revolution. Churches have been compensated for rental value on confiscated space and money has been provided to restore buildings that had been put to other use. The Nanjing Theological College opened its doors again in 1981 and has grown into a major center of theological education for the whole country. About twelve other Protestant theological training centers have been created in various parts of the country.

In 1981 K. H. Ting was elected chairperson of the National Three-Self Movement and president of a newly-constituted China Christian Council. That same year K. H. Ting, along with other Protestant and Catholic leaders, attended a major international conference held in Montreal, Canada, a meeting that looked to "a new beginning" of international Christian relations.[14]

In 1985 K. H. Ting took the initiative in establishing the Amity Foundation, an organization for cooperative social service and educational work with Christian impetus but community based. A modern printing press associated with Amity Foundation has been established; it provides for printing Bibles and other Christian literature.

Finally, as president of the China Christian Council Bishop Ting has travelled with church delegations to renew contacts in many parts of the world, including India, Europe, Australia, Hong Kong, Africa and Japan.

In 1989 K. H. Ting and Siu May accepted an invitation from Victoria University in Toronto, in cooperation with Canadian churches and friends, to visit Canada together to receive honorary doctorates. At the Convocation

of Emmanuel College, the theological faculty of Victoria and members of
the Toronto School of Theology, the Doctor of Sacred Letters was con-
ferred on Siu May and the Doctor of Divinity on K. H. Ting. The visit
brought Siu May back to Toronto for the first time since 1950, fulfilling a
long-standing wish.

Retirement is not mandatory in China, and the dearth of experienced
leaders in the churches puts demands on senior leaders. Ting has served
as a representative from religious circles on the National People's Congress,
and on the important citizens' organization called the Chinese People's
Political Consultative Conference, of which he was elected vice-chairperson
in March 1989. He continues as principal of Nanjing Theological College,
as president of the China Christian Council and as national chairperson of
the Three-Self Movement.

The historical shifts and social conditions of the present have made the
policy of Christian selfhood adopted by Protestant Christians in the 1950s
more effective than they ever could have imagined. After the period of
political fundamentalism when the church seemed about to disappear, the
renewal of the church was experienced as "resurrection" (see "A Chinese
Identity"). No one knows what the future will bring, but Protestant Christianity in China today is firmly established.

K. H. TING AS AN ACTIVIST-THEOLOGIAN

The writings of K. H. Ting gathered in this volume span four decades.
They reflect the "occasional" nature of his writing, that is, written work
that responded to specific events and occasions. An activist in the Student
Christian Movement and in the life of the church, he never wrote comprehensive or systematic theology. His continued activism and unwillingness
to take time to rewrite his theology, especially for a foreign audience, influenced the decision to bring his work together in this book.

Although Ting's thought responded to developments in church and
world, it shows consistent themes and patterns and a strong biblical orientation. Bible study in relation to social justice issues was a hallmark of
the Student Christian Movement. Ting was nurtured in this style and is
constantly in dialogue with the world and the Scriptures. The story of the
prodigal son and the jealous elder brother is a favorite passage. Jonah, the
grumpy but faithful missionary, appears more than once. The "Cosmic
Christ" of Ephesians, Colossians, and the Gospel of John informs his Christology, and the worldly Jacob at Peniel wrestling with the angel of Yahweh
provides images of prayer and spirituality.

The selections very properly begin with reflections on the simplicity of
the gospel and end with thoughts on the empowering Holy Spirit. Ting is
insistent that the gospel has a directness and simplicity that should not be
clouded by theological statements. Confidence in the guidance of the Holy
Spirit is evident in his writings.

Bishop Ting often reflects on the enigma of an all-loving and all-powerful God in a world with so much suffering and evil. The problem is an old and persistent Christian dilemma. Ting believes that movements and activities that reduce people's suffering make it possible for them to be open to an understanding of God's love and grace. The themes of God's graciousness and the new life of the resurrection experience are prominent in K. H. Ting's thought. He believes that in response to God's grace Christians need to serve others; thus a strong pastoral concern is evident in his theology.

Justice and peace issues receive a great deal of attention. Some of his articles in the late 1940s take a clear stand on imperialism and exploitation. He makes a sharp analysis of international problems. A sensitivity to any lack of respect of the Chinese in general and Chinese Christians in particular lies behind the Chinese nationalism (love of country) so prevalent in his writings. He commented, for example, that he did not like to see the Chinese church as just a dot on somebody's missionary map. Finally, his passion for peace is evident not only in his writing but in his international peace activities.

Critical to an appreciation of K. H. Ting's theology is an understanding of his views of Christ and the church. Throughout his writings Ting is careful to segregate theology from politics. He does not find political theology or liberation theology useful for China, for example. Yet he supports socialism in China and values the contributions of atheists to human good; he finds precious insights in traditional Chinese religion. How does his faithfulness to church and to Christ relate to this valuing of that which is not Christian?

To answer this we can look first to the nature of his faithfulness to the church. The problem for the church in China in the 1950s was how to survive and develop under a socialist system that did not have any particular appreciation of the church. Christians needed to find a theological basis for unity and selfhood in order to overcome their identity with Western imperialism. Since denominational differences reflected Western historical developments, it made sense for the churches in China to move away from these foreign designations. The Three-Self Movement in the 1950s provided a common structure from which to work as the churches in China moved toward post-denominationalism.

The Three-Self Movement provided a context in which Christians began to study, understand and participate in socialist reconstruction. Was this simply "selling out" to the Communists and collaborating with the enemies of God as some Western missionaries and a few Christians in China believed? We need to look at K. H. Ting's Christology to see that he understood cooperation in a much different vein.

Ting did not turn to a liberationist Christology. That would have contradicted his own deeply held theological beliefs about Christ and worked against his ecclesiological commitments. Unity of the church in China could never be maintained on the basis of a liberationist Christology because of the strength of Christian fundamentalism among many ordinary believers.

As long as unity of the church is a primary goal, and as long as the mentality of ordinary Christians remains at a fundamentalist level, any move toward a more radical theology for China would be difficult.

Ting appreciates the radical theology based on a preferential option for the poor but does not feel this is a useful theological approach for Christians in China. There is a continuing fear of the pseudo-radicalism that became widespread in the Cultural Revolution period, using political fundamentalism and ultra-dogmatism to extoll the poor as born revolutionaries. The option for the poor mistakenly may make the poor, as such, the bearers of salvation. He writes:

> But the poor are not the Messiahs of the world, as if it were only necessary to liberate the poor and they would then liberate the world. . . . We must not idealize or absolutize the poor. . . . If the poor are liberators because of their poverty . . . those who had been poor to begin with and had now benefitted through their labor and become rich would then become targets of revolution. Is this not the same old doctrine of "perpetual revolution under the dictatorship of the proletariat?" We have had a taste of this during the ten years of the Cultural Revolution. Society was thrown into chaos.

Nevertheless Ting reiterates his appreciation of liberation theology:

> Although Chinese Christians, situated politically in a post-liberation situation, have these reservations about liberation theology, we yet believe that liberation theology is a great and new thing in the history of Christianity. It is without peer, surpassing many traditional systematic theologies. I treasure it greatly, and have little sympathy for certain people who oppose it.[15]

Elsewhere Ting has explained that China can be described as in a post-liberation position only in the sense that power went from Chiang Kai-shek's Nationalist Party to the hands of the people in 1949. The process of liberation is long and continues in the struggle against feudalism and backwardness. There is a need for revolutionary dedication to the cause of the people's greater liberation.

K. H. Ting's understanding of Christ is informed by the Gospel of John and other writings with which the idea of the "Cosmic Christ" is associated. This is the understanding that all things were created through Christ, the Word of God. Therefore Christ can be found in creation far beyond the places where missionaries and church structures have penetrated. On this topic Siu May said, "As Chinese Christians we do not see Christianity and socialist China as opposed to each other. It is God working, whether in his name or not." K. H. added:

For two thousand years the Christian church has faced the question of how to account for things that are good and beautiful which are found outside the churches. Very few Christians would say that all these things are done by the devil in the garb of an angel. Christians have always appreciated good things that have appeared outside the churches, in science and art. What is happening in China is only one of these things, on a larger scale.[16]

Bishop Ting frequently speaks of the Incarnation as God's affirmation as well as redemption of the human. The image of God in humanity redeemed by Christ, he writes, is surely stronger than the fallen image symbolized by the sin of Adam. God's embodiment in the human context shows something about all humanity, not just Christians. The sharp dichotomy between believers and unbelievers is not as important as God's love for all humanity.

From this understanding of Christ some Christians may move to a theology that incorporates the stories and experiences of people in a way that would restructure many traditional theological formulations. Others may move toward a political or liberationist theology. Ting does not do this. Even though there is good in the world outside the church, there is something precious in the gospel, in Christ, in the church, which "the world" can never fully grasp. It is this limitation of the world that provides the grounds on which Ting segregates theology from politics and maintains a church-centered perspective.

For Bishop Ting it is only in the Christian community and the Christian revelation that the fullness of the gospel is found. The power of God is at work in all creation, true. Revolution may restore human dignity. Chinese traditional spirituality may provide some movement toward God. Unbelievers may have some glimpses of the divine. Christians can therefore appreciate, stand in solidarity with and learn from all kinds of peoples and movements. But such movements can never reveal the fullness of Christ. The church-centered and Christ-centered nature of K. H. Ting's theology emerges at this point. Revolutions may aid human dignity, but they cannot overcome spiritual poverty — only the gospel can do that. Chinese religion may move toward God, but only to a "slight" degree. (See "The Cosmic Dimension" and "Theology in Socialist China.") Ting's writings evince a Christian self-confidence, sometimes bordering on Christian superiority, based on this theological understanding of a cosmic Christ active in creation combined with a Christianity that alone has access to the full revelation of God. Christians do not have to be against the world, and can in fact affirm and benefit from all kinds of things in the world, but the world can never offer anything approaching the gospel of Christ.

This approach allows for a maintenance of church and theology in one compartment, and cooperation with socialist nation-building in another compartment. In Ting's words,

Christianity is not something political and socialism is not something theological, though outside there are discussions about the theological implications of the new China. China has not posed a new theological problem for the church.[17]

Unlike liberation theology, feminist theology, black theology, minjung theology, political theology and similar developments in other parts of the world, this approach does not involve a reshaping of theology on the basis of insights derived from the cultural and social context, nor from the stories and experiences of the people.

This has proved to be a most effective theology for the long period of transition in China. It has preserved unity in the church and established the selfhood of Chinese Christianity. It set out a basis for Christian cooperation in socialist nation-building and secured a space for the church in Chinese society, laying a foundation on which the next generation of Chinese theologians may build, a garden in which they may cultivate.

No one knows what new and beautiful things may be cultivated in this space that has been preserved for a "theological garden." Ting himself continues to participate in the cultivating done by the Chinese churches. For example, the Protestant Church in China consecrated two new bishops in 1988, the first in thirty-three years. In a sermon delivered at the consecration, Bishop Ting reflected on the new and different situation of the Chinese churches. An ancient civilization has entered into socialist reconstruction, raising new challenges for the self-understanding of the church. The church survived a period when many thought its fate in China would be extinction. Not only has it survived, it has won new respect:

Today our society in general takes a much more favorable attitude towards our church. More and more people think that Christianity and socialism are compatible. We welcome this point of view. Insofar as our faith permits, I prefer to see greater compatibility between our church and socialism. But what the church does must be compatible first of all with God's loving purpose, with the teaching of the Bible, with the nature of the church as church, and with the rightful wishes of the masses of our Christians.[18]

In deciding to elect bishops, the church in China is cultivating an approach firmly based on the biblical understanding that bishops were an early phenomenon, but remaining open on the question of exactly how the bishops are to function:

This much is clear, we will have bishops but we are not choosing the episcopal system of church government. Our bishops are not diocesan and not administrative. They have their authority but their authority does not base itself on any written constitutional stipulation or on any executive position, but on their spiritual, moral, theological and pastoral ministration, on their service to others.[19]

Ting also says that bishops are to depend on the power of love and example, not on the power of rank and position.

Another area for the cultivation of new ideas is in the relationship of church and state. In December 1988 K. H. Ting delivered an address to church leaders in Shanghai in which he summed up recent changes in thinking in this sphere. The Three-Self Movement was developed in the 1950s to help Christians adjust to living independently of foreign support and to re-assert their Chineseness and participate in socialist development. It achieved notable success in guiding the church through a long period of transition. It also promoted unity among Protestant traditions, exposed the colonial and imperial dimensions of the missionary movement, represented a model of church development for Third World churches, and in general received world-wide attention among theologians and church historians. By the end of the 1980s, however, the time had come for a reassessment of the movement.

Although the Three-Self Movement made many achievements, it also made mistakes. Although the original agenda of the movement was to promote love of China and independence of the church from overseas domination, in the course of time leadership of the church in some areas came to be centered in Three-Self organizations. The situation in which the Three-Self leads the church, or the Religious Affairs Bureau becomes responsible for any area of church administration is unacceptable to Christians, Ting claims. Some people do not understand that the church is not just a social organization in the eyes of Christians, but is a divinely inspired community that Christ loved and for which Christ gave himself, cleansing the church with water and the word (Ephesians 5). The purification of the church in China was necessary, but after the cleansing it is the church that will endure and not the water with which it was cleansed.

A time for re-ordering relationships has arrived. Some Christians fear that any adjustment will open the way again for foreign interference or subversion. Ting argues, however, that the church is now able to run its own affairs. Although hostile forces from Hong Kong and abroad will continue to attack and denigrate the Chinese church no matter what the church or the Three-Self Movement do, it will be healthier for the churches to develop their own structures and leadership, always adhering to the Three-Self principles.

The same is true of the Religious Affairs Bureaus of the government. They have been of great help in the transitional period, and will continue to help in the future. But the time has come for the principle of separation of church and state to receive greater emphasis. According to Ting, the government and the church should develop a style of relationship for the long term that is based on mutual monitoring and equality. The government should implement policies of religious freedom and carry out its legal responsibilities. But the work of the church in areas of finance, personnel, property, and organization needs no government involvement. This separation of church and state does not arise from any antipathy on the part of the Christians to the Communist Party or the People's Government, but arises from their faithfulness to Christ.[20]

A final area where new thought is being cultivated in China's theological garden is in the study of religion. The church in China has had to deal with doctrinaire Marxists who have argued that religion is always and only an opiate. K. H. Ting and others responded to this challenge in the past and again more recently as the discussion has re-emerged in academic circles. In 1988 an article written jointly by Ting and another theologian, Wang Weifan, argues that religious studies must not be bogged down in Marxist dogmatism. Ting and Wang show how publications in China have sometimes praised certain scholars of the past but have purposely left out any reference to their religious adherence. They also show that Marx and Engels never reduced religion to simply an opiate. The dogmatic scholars in power in some research centers, according to their article, never look at religious phenomena in China in an analytic way but only argue from abstract doctrines.[21] Young scholars in China have watched the older Marxists and Protestants contend over whether or not religion is an opiate and have jokingly dubbed the debate the Second Opium War. Reports indicate that Protestants are making it understood that religion and particularly Christian theism play a positive role in Chinese society.

Bishop Ting emphasized this vital role of Christianity in a convocation address at Emmanuel College of Victoria University in Toronto in May 1989:

> The aspect of human growth that concerns us Christians most has to do with the human search for transcendence, for surpassing what we can see and touch and taste and read in our daily newspapers. There is a universal dissatisfaction with staying where we are, a universal desire to transcend, to reach for something higher and deeper. . . . These days we may not be certain of many things. But one thing certain is that human beings cannot be long in resting contented in their day-to-day living, that there is an irrepressible human need to transcend, to break limits and barriers, to transform one-dimensional to multi-dimensional living. "God, you have put a restlessness in my heart, so that it can find no rest until it finds it in you." That is not only a prayer of St. Augustine, but also the yearning of men and women of all ages living with all sorts of social systems. It is this fact that makes Christian communities needed to bring people face to face with the transcendent God.

NOTES

1. Quoted in Mary Austin Endicott, *Five Stars Over China* (Toronto: Canadian Far Eastern Newsletter, 1953, p. 433).

2. Robert Whyte, *Unfinished Encounter* (London: Collins, 1988), pp. 228f.

3. *Christian Herald*, Vol. 76, No. 5 (May 1953), p. 16.

4. *Christian Herald*, Vol. 76, No. 10 (October 1953), p. 16.

5. *Christian Century*, Vol. 80, No. 37 (September 11, 1963), p. 1091.

6. The full text of the *Christian Manifesto* is included in Francis P. Jones, *The Church in Communist China: A Protestant Appraisal* (New York: Friendship Press, 1962), pp. 53–55.

7. For an excellent scholarly interpretation of Wang see Ng Lee-Ming, "Wang Ming-tao—An Evaluation of His Thought and Action," in *Ching Feng: Quarterly Notes on Christianity and Chinese Religion and Culture,* Vol. 16, No. 2 (Hong Kong, 1973), pp. 51–80.

8. Wallace C. Merwin and Francis P. Jones, eds., *Documents of the Three-Self Movement: Source Materials for the Study of the Protestant Church in Communist China*, Introduction (New York: National Council of Churches, 1963), pp. iii-v.

9. *Canadian Far Eastern Newsletter*, No. 182 (July 1965).

10. Eugene Stockwell, a member of the delegation, prepared a transcript of his notes for publication. Excerpts appear in Raymond L. and Rhea M. Whitehead, *China: Search for Community* (New York: Friendship Press, 1978), pp. 46–49. This positive view of non-institutional Christianity contrasts with the rapid re-institutionalization in the 1980s. Chinese theologians' further reflection on this contrast would be instructive.

11. Letter, K. H. Ting to Raymond L. Whitehead, 8 February 1977.

12. These comments were taken from my notes of K. H. Ting's 1979 visit to Toronto, at meetings on October 21 and 22, 1979.

13. Letter, K. H. Ting to Raymond L. Whitehead, 30 April 1979.

14. See Theresa Chu and Christopher Lind, eds., *A New Beginning* (Toronto: Canada China Programme, Canadian Council of Churches, 1983).

15. K. H. Ting, "Inspirations from Liberation Theology, Process Theology and Teilhard de Chardin," in *Chinese Theological Review*, 1986, pp. 53-54.

16. Whitehead, *Search*, p. 49.

17. Ibid.

18. "Taking a New Way" (a sermon preached on the occasion of the consecration of two new bishops), Shanghai, June 26, 1988 (English translation by K. H. Ting).

19. Ibid.

20. "Re-Ordering the Relationships" (an address by K. H. Ting to the Joint Meeting of the Standing Committees of the National Three-Self Committee and the National Christian Council, Shanghai, December 13, 1988), in *China Notes*, XXVII, 1, Winter 1988-89 (translation by Jean Woo).

21. K. H. Ting and Wang Weifan, "Recent Developments in the Study of Religion," translated by Janice and Philip Wickeri, *China and Ourselves* (Toronto, China Programme, Canadian Council of Churches, Spring 1989.)

Part 1

EMBODYING CHRISTIANITY

Bishop Ting's lifetime covers the period in which Protestant Christianity first takes on a Chinese form. There were important lay Christians and clergy prior to the twentieth century, but the life and thought of the Chinese Christian community remained in a relationship of dependency with European and North American mission structures until the 1940s. Christian faith is only becoming embodied in a Chinese form in recent decades.

The material collected in Part 1 illustrates the struggle to find forms for expressing Chinese theology, a goal at times self-conscious and at other times rather nebulous. There are ups and downs in K. H. Ting's thinking about foreign influence, for example. A love of China is always present, but criticism of foreign interference varies in emphasis. Of course internal and international conditions also change drastically. In 1948 Ting spoke of the need for foreign missionaries as links for newer Asian churches with the whole body of Christ ("A Vital Vocation"). At the same time he expressed the expectation that "in coming years Christians in India, China, and Japan . . . will begin to communicate their own expressions of Christ, unfettered by Western tradition" ("The Simplicity of the Gospel"). This use of the future tense in 1948, a century and a half after the beginning of the Protestant missions in Asia, is a poignant reminder today that just a few decades ago the gospel was still in bondage to European and North American cultural expressions.

The victory of the socialist revolution in China in 1949 brought the added task of expressing Christianity in a way that made sense to people in a radically new social setting. Not only did traditional Chinese thinking need to be taken into account, but also Marxist socialism in its Chinese form. Marxists were much more confident than Christians that their system had taken on a Chinese identity. Mao Zedong's thought was seen to be a Chinese form of Marxism. Christianity suffered from being identified with

Western imperialism and from being identified with capitalist and landlord oppression within China. Theological development required new ways of describing human nature, sin and the tension between belief and unbelief ("The Cosmic Dimension"). Christianity had to overcome the stigma of being merely another Western import, which was an evil in the eyes of Marxist Chinese fresh from the struggle to emancipate China from foreign control.

Building up the church in a Third World socialist country was a task for which there were no precedents. Not to support socialism would make the church hypocritical, since socialism was overcoming many of the evils of poverty and inhumanity that Christians had struggled to end. Ting expected the church to be both "participatory and critical" ("The Cosmic Dimension"). This required a search for unity within the church in spite of strong initial theological differences ("The Spirit of Wisdom"). In this search for unity the study of the Bible played a crucial role, especially study that emphasized an "epistemology and hermeneutics of practice" ("Changing Relationships").

K. H. Ting's writing is firmly rooted in a biblical faith informed by biblical imagery. Two images stand out in the selections in Part 1: the elder brother from the story of the prodigal son (Lk 15:11-32), and Jonah, the reluctant emissary. Ting uses the images to warn against arrogance toward non-Christian spirituality. The elder brother image warns against self-righteousness toward other Christians as well.

This set of essays gives us an unsystematic but powerful taste of an emerging Chinese theology. The gospel is central. There is a call to return to the simplicity of the gospel in order that it may speak to China: "Lay aside your biblical criticism and exegesis—even your theological assumptions—and enter into the spirit of the New Testament for the first time" ("The Simplicity of the Gospel").

Ting's theology has a high Christology. The gospel is identified with Christ himself ("Realizing the Gospel"). Christ shows us what God is like ("The Cosmic Dimension"). Christ is also the new human person, "sinless in the midst of the universal sinfulness of humanity." In Christ "was established a center of perfect order, a focus of restored creation, which now began to emerge within the surrounding disorder of the fallen world" ("Realizing the Gospel"). Christocentrism to this extent in Chinese theology is surprising.

Ecclesiology is described in terms of separation and identification, "in but not of the world" ("Christianity in Tension"). The church historically has failed to manifest God. It is called continually to correct itself so that the liberating strength of the gospel may be made known and people brought to repentance and the confession that Christ is Lord ("Challenges to Faith"). This understanding of sin does not, however, blot out the essential goodness of creation or the image of God in human persons. The prodigal "does not cease to be a son, even as he tends the swine. By virtue of the image of God latent in all people, human misery cannot destroy human dignity" ("New Life").

1

FAITH AND REVOLUTION

Four sources are drawn from in this subsection, all originally in English. The first, "The Simplicity of the Gospel," is from a 1948 article in *The Canadian Student*, the journal of the Canadian Student Christian Movement (SCM). K. H. Ting and his wife, Siu May, first visited the Western world in 1946 when he was invited by the Canadian SCM to be international secretary (see the General Introduction). The journal was intended for student members of the SCM. This article, among the earliest writings we have from K. H. Ting, was written after he had completed his term with the SCM and had moved to New York City to study at Union Theological Seminary. It is appropriate to begin with his words about commitment to the gospel, as this spirit pervades his writings through all the twists and turns of China's fortunes over the decades and helps us to understand his contribution to the attempt to embody Christianity in revolutionary China.

The second segment, "If Christians Speak Rightly," is from a sermon delivered in Sweden in 1982. It includes a reference to "the ten years of the Cultural Revolution," from the 1966 call to mass campaigns by Chairman Mao Zedong to 1976 when Chairman Mao died and Hua Guofeng rose briefly to power. During the Cultural Revolution "criticism and self-criticism" were "weakened." In other words, political leaders were not subject to the reviews that were normal earlier, nor was there expectation of the self-criticism that had become the norm during the building of socialism. This resulted in arbitrary use of power. Christians believe that their unjust suffering in the Cultural Revolution period, and their continued loyalty to socialist China through it all, left them in good stead in the succeeding period, with a church stronger than at any previous historical period.

In 1984 Ting visited Japan where he delivered a lecture from which the third excerpt, "The Cosmic Dimension," is drawn. The opening reference to "the time of liberation" refers to the victory of the socialist revolution in 1949, when China was freed from outside interference and from internal control by landlord and capitalist classes.

The fourth selection, "New Life," is from an unpublished sermon given in India in 1985 on Luke 15:32, the story of the prodigal son and the elder brother.

THE SIMPLICITY OF THE GOSPEL (1948)

Where Christianity is taken for granted—where it is only immanent as some vague cultural atmosphere—it is difficult to catch the simplicity and force of the New Testament. No sooner have you opened it than you are perturbed by the complexity of its queer ways of saying things and its bold ethical demands. You wonder whether certain passages are to be taken literally, puzzle over miracles and question the meaning of certain words. Intellectually and emotionally, you and the biblical writers seem to be in two separate worlds.

The typical Chinese experience on entering the world of the New Testament is quite different. In this case it is not the complexity but the simplicity—the obvious truth—that strikes the reader.

The New Testament was the product of a small community of people living in circumstances of desperate spiritual struggle. Through their experiences they came to grasp the truth of Christ's words and the reality of his person at deeper and deeper levels. As Christians in various parts of Asia and Europe struggle and suffer for their faith, they too enter the fellowship of those who suffered in the first century, and the words of the New Testament become alive and relevant to their own situation.

It is above all the simplicity of the gospel that captures the imagination of people in China. For the average Chinese, religion is typically an agglomeration of primitive beliefs: in spirits and punishment, in a complex hell, and in some form of afterlife of which ancestor-worship is one indication. Confucianist ethical requirements, difficult to fulfill, add to feelings of fear and frustration and the sense of a crushing moral burden and inner conflict. In this situation the Christian message is truly one of release and freedom, bringing to life itself assurance and meaning. The way of life it advocates is also obviously good. To be "converted" then is to throw away frustrating and unavailing crutches, so that standing up one discovers the hitherto invisible landscape in all its simple coherence. "Lo, in Christ the new has come" (2 Cor 5:17).

To the early disciples the message of Jesus was similarly a breath of fresh air. They were entangled in an impossible system of rules and laws, precepts and traditions. The yoke was heavy. When Jesus spoke, however, people could not only understand him, but knew that he was speaking "with authority" and heard him gladly. Proclaiming the freedom of "the acceptable year of the Lord," Jesus thanked God, saying, "Thou hast hid these things from the wise and prudent, and hast revealed them unto babes" (Mt 11:25, Lk 10:21).

In writing the epistles Paul communicates the new sense of freedom and simplicity that he experiences as he steps out of the frustration and slavery of his Pharisaic religion into the religion of grace. His purpose is not to obscure truth but to help people understand it. We may get at his meaning if we gradually build our understanding of him on the basis of his conversion experience and his discovery of the liberty of the order of God as contrasted with the slavery of the disorder of humankind.

Then, in reading 1 Corinthians 1:18-31, we find Paul telling us how futile it is to expect Christ's gospel to be another "system" (even a less complicated "system") for "disputation."

Theological discipline should come only after we have been captured by the reality and simplicity of the New Testament message. Lay aside your biblical criticism and exegesis—even your theological assumptions—and enter into the spirit of the New Testament for the first time. It is then a living book with a message; as gospel, it is good news of freedom. It is only this experience, constantly maintained and enriched, that gives content to your theological pursuits.

None of this means of course that it is simple to live as a Christian. Since this is a complicated world, where we are required to use all our efforts to make the gospel real to the people around us, it is all the more important that we should constantly go back to the reality of the New Testament message in order to continually fortify ourselves for the task.

Over the centuries the gospel has taken upon itself the imprint of various philosophies and social patterns encountered throughout its journeying. Our knowledge of God is enriched through that process. In the coming years Christians in India, China and Japan—each community in its own way—will begin to communicate their own experience of Christ, unfettered by Western tradition. They will tell of the simplicity of the gospel, of its power to set us free. The Western world must welcome and encourage this contribution.

IF CHRISTIANS SPEAK RIGHTLY (1982)

One of the officers standing by struck Jesus with his hand, saying, "Is that how you answer the high priest?" Jesus answered him, "If I have spoken wrongly, bear witness to the wrong; but if I have spoken rightly, why do you strike me?" Annas then sent him bound to Caiaphas the high priest (Jn 18:22-24).

Here we have an account of Jesus' trial before Annas, in front of a big crowd. Some were onlookers, dismayed by their lost dream of a victorious king. Many were emotionally worked up, ready to be manipulated by demagogues. The various political and religious leaders could not have cared less for the fate of Jesus—they were trying to make the right moves so as to reap benefits for themselves. In that crowded scene Jesus' response to the officer was a very weak one indeed. No one seemed to take his words seriously or tried to meet his challenge. The answer was to bind him and send him to Caiaphas.

But the voice of Jesus was a conscientizing voice. Down through the ages the echoes of the question he asked there and then have resounded in every land and among every people. It is also the voice of reason. "If I have spoken wrongly, bear witness to the wrong; but if I have spoken rightly, why do you strike me?" No one except a believer in the human capacity to distinguish between what is right and what is wrong could raise such a question as this. This is the voice of one who asserts the ultimate triumph of what is right.

There is nothing dogmatic here either. Christ does not say that he, being the son of God, cannot err and therefore must be obeyed. He says, "if" — "if I have spoken wrongly," and "if I have spoken rightly" — encouraging other people to make a judgment about him for themselves. He does not even assert that to strike is necessarily wrong, but simply invites people not to strike in haste. He respects human judgment.

Now the power of words depends not on how loudly they are uttered but on their correspondence to the ultimate principle by which the whole universe is governed. In the outskirts of Nanjing, where I come from, there is a spot where the oppressive Kuomintang regime under Chiang Kai-shek killed tens of thousands of patriots and revolutionaries who dared to oppose its misrule. Many were cut short even as they cried out patriotic slogans. Yet the message survived and proved to have great mobilizing power, bringing into being wave upon wave of the struggle for liberation that culminated in the emergence of the People's Republic of China. It is still an inspiration today as we build a new life for ourselves and for our children.

During the ten years of the Cultural Revolution in China our churches suffered a lot of repression, as did many intellectuals and high government personnel. For, with criticism and self-criticism weakened, leaders may turn a revolution into its own antithesis, making enemies of those who are properly its supporters and allies. This is what happened under the name of the Cultural Revolution. Yet, today, with the return of religious freedom, we find that many of our fellow citizens have been quietly watching with a big "if" for themselves to see whether Christians spoke wrongly or rightly. A number of them have chosen, entirely on their own, to commit themselves to faith in the Christ we witness to. As Paul said, "For the sake of Christ then, I am content with weaknesses, insults, hardships, persecutions and calamities; for when I am weak, then I am strong" (2 Cor 12:10).

History has shown that however small the voice of reason, of truth, or of justice, it is never really weak. It is backed up by the risen and ascended Christ. It is full of power to set people thinking about dividing the right from the wrong. The world's Annases and Caiaphases and Pontius Pilates can never quite shut the people's ears to such a voice. For us, this is all the proof we need that Christ is not dead, but risen, sitting at the right hand of God and upholding the universe by his word of power.

THE COSMIC DIMENSION (1984)

At the time of liberation there were two circumstances that greatly affected us as Chinese Christians. First, as we came into contact with revolutionaries we found that they had ideals, serious theoretical interests and high ethical commitment. They took from ancient Chinese teaching the notions that they were to be "severe in making demands of themselves," and "sad before the whole people are sad and happy only after the whole people are happy." Many practiced mutual criticism and relentless self-criticism in order to become useful to the revolutionary cause. While they had no high regard for religion, they did not demand its persecution or liquidation. Christians, however—though happy to see in these revolutionaries the hope for the country's future—were still faced with the question whether there was still any place in China for their religion.

Second, there were those in the church who stubbornly refused to be impressed by new developments; they argued forcibly, both on theological and political grounds, against the validity of liberation and of the establishment of new China. We may briefly summarize their argument. The world is the realm of Satan, they said, condemned to imminent destruction (it was even claimed that the two-horned beast and the red horse, depicted in the Book of Revelation, represented the Communist Party). The Christian is not to love the world—or whatever is in it—even if it appears worthy of love. Those who accept Christ and those who do not are absolutely opposed, sharing no common language; hence belief in Christ is prerequisite for doing good. The doctrine of the security of the believer ensures those elected by Christ freedom of action, while the rest are condemned no matter how good their work may seem. This antinomianism was the main theological weapon used in the early fifties by those who were determined not to be reconciled to the fact of New China. It had a temporary attraction, but in the end drove some away from the church for good.

The two sets of circumstances outlined above set Chinese Christians thinking. On the one hand, while impressed with the conduct of revolutionaries, many of us found it impossible to take leave of Christ, choosing to say with Peter, "You, Lord, have the word of eternal life, to whom can we go?" (Jn 6:68). On the other, antinomian reactionaries wanted us to work against the people's liberation movement, with all its goodness and beauty, certainly an ethically indefensible alternative. As a result, Christians all over the country were engaged in a spontaneous study movement, looking at the Bible in relation to social change. With discussion and written papers theology emerged from an academic context to become a tool in the hands of lay people. Struggling to keep the vitality of their faith, they were still able to relate positively to the new reality, using the Bible as their main resource, and re-reading it for the new lights or new insights that we so commonly refer to nowadays.

Much of the early discussion was concerned with the world itself, and with human life and its relationship to goodness (or depravity), to truth and beauty. Many conscientious revolutionaries, practicing serious self-criticism, would feel at one with Paul when he says that he fails to do what he ought to do, yet tends to do the very thing he ought to shun (Rom 7:15). We like to point out to our humanist revolutionary friends that people are not in the state that God means them to be in—as Christians we say that sin is responsible for this failure, and only God's help will enable us to change our condition. For China, it is true, the change from a feudal and capitalist society to socialism has been all-important for human dignity, but that change has not alleviated spiritual poverty. That the number of Christians has actually increased in the last thirty-five years is witness to this fact. We pray that the day will come when Christians will have the love, light and language to communicate with revolutionaries on matters of basic conviction, thus strengthening mutual understanding and national unity.

To understand Chinese Christians it is important to know that for thousands of years no sage or scholar ever dealt with the idea of inborn perversity in human nature. Mencius, for instance, widely regarded as second only to Confucius himself, taught that human nature is essentially good. Compassion and humility, discrimination between right and wrong, a sense of shame—all are innate "beginnings of goodness." Chinese folklore also affirms people's natural strength and goodness: Traditionally, it was a human being who mended the broken heaven and set up pillars to support it when it became crooked, a conception of the relation between the celestial and the human that is vastly different from that found in much Western philosophy. Down to this century a pupil learning the first Chinese characters would study the "Three-Character Rhyme," which opens with the sentence, "At birth, a person is good by nature."

In spite of all the suffering they have borne, the Chinese are thus fundamentally an optimistic people. Even in time of war they affirm that what is demonstrated in life is not just evil and brutality but fortitude and friendship. In the course of the revolution, as during the reconstruction period, countless men and women of courage, ingenuity and self-sacrifice have emerged.

It is easy to see, therefore, why Christians in China, who do recognize the fact of sin and human finiteness, still find it impossible to ignore the latent image of God in each human being and the indwelling of the Holy Spirit in the world. So, in making these comments, we do not want to discount all tradition outside the church. More than two thousand years ago, Lao Tse wrote:

> There is already begotten before
> Heaven and earth came into being:
> serenely silent, peacefully alone,
> eternally faithful,

the Immovable Mover, like
the caring Mother of all things. I do not know its name
And describe it as Tao (*Tao te ching,* ch. 25).

Can we say that this is worthless because it emerged outside the Christian tradition? In our attitude toward non-Christian spirituality we certainly should avoid the arrogance of the elder brother in the parable of the prodigal son, and that of Jonah toward Nineveh. We should affirm any and every move, however slight, that is made in the direction of God.

Sin has affected creation, but the created world after all is still under God—it is not the devil's occupied territory. Otherwise in what sense can we honestly say, "God so loved the world that he gave his only begotten son to the world" (Jn 3:16) or that God became flesh in Jesus Christ? Martin Luther said that all creation is the most beautiful book or bible; in it God is described and portrayed.

Chinese Christians have moved on from debating creation and the indwelling of the Holy Spirit to establish a solid Christological foundation. Many intellectuals from a social-gospel background have claimed the Christ of John's gospel and of Ephesians and Colossians as their own; his incarnation is not an intrusion into an alien world but a divine yes to creation, a means for human redemption and renewal. They listen with joy to Paul's words of adoration of the Christ as the image of the invisible God, the firstborn of all creation. "For in him all things were created, in heaven and on earth, visible and invisible; whether thrones or dominions or principalities or authorities—all things were created through him and for him, and in him all things hold together" (Col 1:15-17). Christians in China find this passage liberating, with its sense of the ascended Christ, like sunshine, filling the universe, bringing out every latent spark of color. Reality is one gigantic process, one in which matter and simple organisms achieve higher and higher expressions of existence, with the loving community as the ultimate human attainment, just as the triune God is a community of love.

"If by the offense of the one man all died, much more the grace of God and the gracious gift of the one man, Jesus Christ, abound for all" (Rom 5:15). In the new light of our re-reading the words "much more" take upon themselves a meaning previously unseen. The verse assures us that our human solidarity with Christ is more universal, more decisive and more efficacious than our solidarity with Adam. The greatest word in the New Testament is not sin—it is grace.

Thus we shift away from the belief-unbelief antithesis as the sole demand Christianity makes upon humanity to an appreciation of the unity of God's creative, redemptive and sanctifying work in the universe and in history. In the process we see many contemporary thoughts and movements, not in contrast with the divine revelation or as destructive of it, but rather as aids in glimpsing the way of Christ.

Since God is love, events and undertakings in nature and history cannot end in total destruction. They will be sifted, some to be destroyed, but others to be transfigured and subliminated in Christ and by Christ, to be received by God at the final consummation. A deepening understanding of Christ allows us to put historical movements into cosmic perspective. Then we can glimpse not only the historic but also the ultimate value of what we do with nature and with the world, and what we make of ourselves.

> The end of all our exploring
> will be to arrive where we started
> and to know the place for the first time.
> (T. S. Eliot, "Little Gidding" in *Four Quartets*)

Chinese Christians value liberation theology for the way it mobilizes Christians in Latin America to join with the masses in their struggle for independence, democracy and a more humane socio-economic system. We also appreciate its emphasis on context and praxis. Biblical hermeneutics as a result is eye-opening, morally impelling and politically conscientizing. Liberation theologians are our friends and fellow pilgrims.

Now, if European theology helps believers with the reality of world hunger, and if liberation theology moves them to share in the struggle to overcome hunger, we in new China are pursuing the evangelistic task of showing our fellow citizens—for whom hunger is no longer the prime concern—that we do not live by bread alone, but by the word of God's mouth. In China our church is small, still trying to live down the stigma of being a Western import. In the last thirty-five years our experience as a nation, as a church and as individual Christians tells us that strength is found in weakness and life in death. Resurrection is not something that happened only to Christ, but a principle that governs nature and history. An old Chinese poem aptly expresses this conviction:

> With mountains and waters all around
> We wondered whether there was a way out.
> Flowers brightened us up in the dark shades of willows,
> And we soon found ourselves reaching another village.
> (*"You Shanxi Cun"* by Lu You, 1125-1210 C.E.)

We have come to know the risen Christ more intimately. We realize more surely now that between alpha and omega there is no straight line but many zigzags and curves. Creation is a process as yet incomplete and subject to frustration. Birth pangs are antecedent to the emergence of creatures who will eventually respond to their creator and cooperate among themselves lovingly, intelligently and voluntarily. They will then be truly daughters and sons, not slaves.

Our Christology does not dwell only on the God-like-ness of Christ but tells also of the Christ-like-ness of God. As Hosea says, he leads us with cords of compassion and bands of love; he is like one who eases the yoke on our jaws, bending down to feed us (Hos 11:4). The disclosure that God lives with the kind of love that is embodied in Christ crowns and corrects whatever else that may be said about God. In the end every chain of cause and effect returns to God, the loving one at the heart of reality. Everything that is of some good is not going to be lost but is safe in God, to be preserved and transformed for the kingdom, where love will be supreme. That is essentially what is meant when we say that God is sovereign. This theological orientation denotes a longer view of history than any humanly possible, and yet makes sharing in the day-to-day struggle for renewal of life worthwhile. The Christian role is at once participatory and critical.

Of course there are still theological differences among Christians in China, but we co-exist in mutual respect within a fellowship that holds to the historic creeds. A Christology true to the New Testament and to the tradition of the church, evolving in common and shared by all, provides the theological ground for wide-ranging post-denominational unity.

NEW LIFE (1985)

> This your brother was dead, and is alive;
> he was lost and is found (Lk 15:32).

The parable of the prodigal son has prompted many sermons. Today I want to consider the parent who tells us something about God; the prodigal son who tells us something about people in general; and the elder son who tells us something about ourselves as Christians.

The parable tells us that the most important attribute of God is love. A Chinese Christian once criticized the story for its portrayal of God as too lenient, too permissive. But God *is* permissive. There is a seeming impotence and powerlessness in divine love — it craves fellowship, but to be itself, fellowship must be free. And freedom is not freedom if one is incapable of making wrong choices; God allows men and women to err — as in the parable — so that they may come to fellowship freely, as the perfect community. As Paul puts it, love bears all things, believes all things, hopes all things, endures all things (1 Cor 13:17). God chooses to suffer, to wait, to heal and educate, to transfigure through his saving work of creation, redemption and sanctification. God's image is one of community and mutual love among the three persons of the Trinity. The destiny of humanity, likewise, is to attain the community of perfect love.

Alfred North Whitehead said that Christians too often hold to one of three wrong notions, seeing God either as the ruling Caesar, the ruthless moralist or the unmoved mover. Our parable shows clearly that God is supremely love — not an imperial pharaoh who enslaves life, a forbidding taskmaster, or a static being unresponsive to the doings of creation. In the story the father is moved first to sorrow and then joy. Anxiously he awaits his son's return, then runs to embrace and kiss him, ordering in celebration that the best clothing be brought out and a feast be prepared. So God is love—a love that hungers for loving responses from women and men, a love that impels God to enter into our humanity.

What does the parable tell us about men and women? It tells us that, while we are capable of sinking to the lowest depth, we can also rise to the highest destiny as children of God. Humankind may live in the shadow of original sin, but it is encompassed by universal grace. When we depart from God's ways we are not in our proper state, the state for which we were created. We need to come to ourselves, as the prodigal son does. Yet there is no ground for self-hatred or misanthropy. The in-dwelling and the enabling of the Holy Spirit turns the escapades of the young man into a spiritual pilgrimage back to his proper home; he does not cease to be a son even as he tends the swine. By virtue of the image of God latent in all people, human misery cannot destroy human dignity. We must see human life not only as being, but also as becoming. In this sense, as unfinished products in the hand of God, we are all in the making, on the way to our destiny. Our destiny is to be freed from preoccupation with self so that, returning to God in penitence and adoration, we may be welcomed in love and given God's work to do.

Finally, we learn from the parable something about ourselves as Christians. The elder brother has always remained at home. But if we take him as a paradigm of the Christian then we must take into account that he has no love for humanity, that is, for all those who make up the family of God. He does not rejoice in his brother's new life; he refuses to go into the house and join the celebration. To his father he speaks of "this son of yours." He has to be reminded, "This is your brother."

Over the years Christians in China have been learning to do away with this "elder brother" mentality and to celebrate the new life of our people. We do this with the whole family of God, even with those members who do not themselves acknowledge God. For only as we grow in love can God use us as channels through which the saving message of Christ is mediated to those around us.

2

A GOSPEL FOR CHINA

The World Student Christian Federation (WSCF) headquartered in Geneva is an international umbrella organization bringing together various national Student Christian Movements. K. H. Ting worked closely with the WSCF while in the SCM in China and Canada and served on the WSCF Geneva staff. It was in *Student World*, a publication of the WSCF, that the first two articles in this subsection originally appeared. "Christianity in Tension," which appeared in 1948 under the title "Power and Its Denial on the Cross," shows how Ting understood power and powerlessness from the perspective of the cross. Reference in the last paragraph to an incident during the Japanese occupation of Shanghai reminds us of the extensive reach of Japanese power into China in World War II. "Realizing the Gospel," which appeared in 1951 under the title "Behold the Man," shows how Ting struggled with questions of Christ's uniqueness, on the one hand, and the need to understand "non-Christian language and culture" on the other.

The third excerpt, "Challenges to Faith," was originally given as an address to the students of Nanjing Theological Seminary on 12 June 1957, when Bishop Ting was president. The talk was published in the *Nanjing Union Seminary Review* in August of the same year (*Documents of the Three-Self Movement*, p. 156). A translation was also done abroad at the time, but Ting was not very satisfied with it. This excerpt is based on an unpublished translation by K. H. Ting himself in 1985. The Three-Self Chinese Church mentioned in this selection is an allusion to what is more properly called the Three-Self Patriotic Movement, or simply the Three-Self Movement. This was an effort by the Protestant churches to break away from foreign identification by emphasizing self-support, self-administration and self-propagation by the Chinese church itself. (See the Introduction for a discussion of this movement.)

The last selection, "Resurrection and Liberation," is from a 1985 sermon delivered in India when K. H. Ting visited with an official church delegation from China. The sermon was given in English and has not been previously published.

CHRISTIANITY IN TENSION (1948)

"He came into his own"—that was the incarnation; "and his own received him not"—that was the tragedy of the incarnation and, more important, the tragedy of humanity (Jn 1:11). The son of God became one of us. He lived and worked and ate with his fellows. He shared in their joys and sorrows, bore their burdens and sufferings. He understood their yearnings and took upon himself their humiliations. "And, being found in human form, he humbled himself and became obedient unto death, even death on a cross" (Phil 2:8). But Christ identified himself with men and women only to redeem them, not to condone them. He cannot, therefore, have anything to do with sin. Otherwise his identification would be completely meaningless and amount only to indulgence.

Thus there are two modes of existence for the Emmanuel: identification and separation. They are the mystery and the tragedy of messiahship, and at the same time its scandal and glory. We find them enacted again and again in the gospels, finally issuing in the cross. And we find the impact of Christ's nature no less acute in the personal life of a Christian, who knows only too well how Christ is at once both intimate and yet uncompromising, understanding and yet demanding; how he loves intensely and yet judges penetratingly.

Now just as Christ identified himself with people in their needs, but separated himself from them in their sins and thus redeemed them, so the church carries out the same role and task, sharing the fate and glory of its Lord. The politician gains power by manipulating people's desires with abundant promises aimed at their complete satisfaction. When promises prove difficult to carry out and tensions mount, the politician manufactures scapegoats to divert people's pent-up emotions. But the church, by virtue of its commitment to the power of the cross (which is "weakness" in human terms) deals with power differently. The church chooses rather to identify with people in their real needs and offer what God sees as their salvation, though always accepting their freedom to reject it. This of course puts the church in a difficult position. If it were completely to identify itself with the world, then the powers of this world would be only too glad to acquire ecclesiastical sanction and blessing for their desires. But if the church were to seal itself off from the world—as the hermit is confined to "spiritual" things—the world would again be overjoyed, because then church and world would each be "minding its own business."

The church, therefore, must be both in the world and not of the world. It must keep its own independence and initiative, saying with its Lord at one moment that "all those who are not against us are for us" (Lk 9:50); but at another that "all those who are not for us are against us" (Mt 12:30). There is in the nature of the church an absolute identification with God and an absolute repudiation of sin that forbids its other identifications and separations to be absolute. This means that nowhere in the world will a Christian find a moral atmosphere to call home. Perpetually a stranger, perpetually engaged in revolt against the human world as it is, a Christian finds suffering the rule rather than the exception.

The moment that the church takes on the world's standards, it has nothing left but its weakness and powerlessness. Of all things in the world it becomes the most miserable, because now it makes claims that sound fantastic. It has put itself also in the position of being judged by the world. But, on the contrary, the church is meant to judge the world. And the only way it can do so is by the power of God. "For the word of the cross is folly to whose who are perishing, but to us who are being saved it is the power of God" (1 Cor 1:18). Power as the world knows it is denied by the cross because the cross is power itself, the power of an entirely different order.

At a meeting of Christian representatives called by the military authorities in Shanghai early in 1942, a Chinese pastor was called upon to open the meeting with a prayer of thanksgiving to God for the victory of the Japanese imperial army, which had just occupied eastern China. This demand was not only a test for the church of its patriotism but of its fundamental character, of its real identification and separation. The pastor stood up and offered a prayer for peace instead. (And let us remember that in those days to advocate peace was treason itself.) The offering of that prayer tells us that the church has a resource of power that the world does not understand. The church calls on its people to abandon the only power that common sense knows and to rely on the power of God to "lift the drooping hands and strengthen the weak knees, and make straight the paths for your feet, so that what is lame may not be put out of joint but rather be healed" (Heb 12:12–13). It is a declaration that identification has a limit, that the limit has been reached, and that the time has come to say, "Here stand I— I can do no other."

REALIZING THE GOSPEL (1951)

Often we think that we have understood something if we succeed in categorizing it. If, on the other hand, we cannot fit it into some known pattern or classification, we regard it as wrong or out-of-place. This attitude is by no means new. But in this age of science, in which wisdom, knowledge and classification are almost synonymous, it has become an ideal that we consciously pursue.

Our faith in science may amount to nothing short of forbidding ourselves to recognize the new unless it happens within known boundaries. Instead of revising our old categories in face of the new fact that defies them, we try to pretend that they are adequate to contain the new fact and should not be changed or discarded. The old categories even try to claim the new fact as integrally their own so as to receive new life from it. Thus we try to annihilate the new and disagreeable phenomenon by refusing to reckon with its existence, by misrepresenting and distorting it, and by pronouncing a death sentence upon it. We refuse to see that there are moments when the old must make its contribution to truth by a willing acceptance of death in order that the new may have room to flourish.

In the New Testament we find many who fail to understand Christ simply because they only entertain Christ in familiar and expected forms. They measure his size with conventional yardsticks and contain him in traditional jargon: "He came unto his own, and his own received him not" (Jn 1:11). Human sensitivity to the unique is dulled by the desire to classify and systematize. Christ's appearance in the synagogue in Nazareth could have opened the eyes of many people, but the shock was absorbed by a typically irrelevant question: "Is this not Joseph's son?" (Lk 4:22). Similarly it was asked, "Art thou also of Galilee? Search, and see that out of Galilee ariseth no prophet" (Jn 7:52), and "Can any good come out of Nazareth?"(Jn 1:46).

Think of the dead weight in the mind of Nicodemus as he tried to assess Christ, asking, "How can a man be born when he is old?" (Jn 3:4). It takes a child, with no intention to fit truth into human categories, to know the answer to this question.

"Who do men say the Son of God is?" (Mt 16:13). Tragically the best guesses all had to be done in terms of figures from the past—John the Baptist, Elijah, Jeremiah, one of the prophets. For one moment Peter seemed to have gone beyond the familiar to recognize the Christ. But the next found him still bowed down under a stereotypical view of Christhood. Christ himself characterizes this condition as one of minding the things of humans and not the things of God.

This limiting of perception was by no means only a New Testament characteristic. Every age and every people have forbidden Christ to come to them as the judge of their basic assumptions and as their redeemer. Instead Christ is pictured in images that best suit their selfish views of what he should be like. Thus we have caricatures of Christ: We have the Christ who belongs to a particular civilization; the Christ who, like a Rotarian leader, is always active in service and social welfare; or the Christ, impatient with reform, who champions world revolution. Sometimes Christ is the great pacifist; at other times his blessing is invoked in time of war. He may be depicted as a genial member—perhaps at the head table—of the fellowship of the world's great religions. Others remind us that he is "the forgotten factor" in family and industrial discord and in the struggle against international totalitarianism. In some of our "religious emphasis" weeks Christ is introduced by classroom speakers as a relevant and helpful influence in home economics, personality development and banking.

It seems that while men and women cannot afford to obey the Christ of the New Testament, they cannot afford to leave him alone either. What they do is try to do business with him, absorb him into their own systems, and harmonize him with their own interests so as to ride on the bandwagon of his name and authority.

But Christ cannot be fettered by us. Just as the stone was rolled away from the sepulchre that had enclosed him, and the linen clothes that his body had been wrapped in were discarded, so the living Christ is still free from all our attempts to contain him. He breaks unharmed through the clamor and confusion about him and reveals himself to us in all his splendor and otherness. We cease to cling to our bankrupt maps and diagrams and charts, and instead, traversing the dark, wide spaces of the ocean of life, we look to Christ as our only light.

To behold the incarnate Christ is to see with eyes of faith his unique position at the center of history. Behind and through human history we discern another history, that of God's persistence in working toward the realization of a loving purpose.

Christ is the new person, sinless in the midst of the universal sinfulness of humanity. In him there was not only continuity with the common stock of humankind in that he was born of Mary, but also discontinuity in that there was a new creative act of the Spirit, which alone gave the chosen mother power to conceive and bear her son. In thus taking humanity into God the incarnate Christ became a new creation of God. In him was established a center of perfect order, a focus of restored creation, which now began to emerge within the surrounding disorder of the fallen world. Because of this unique position Christ becomes our only source of humanity, the way for the realization of the true nature of the destiny of us all.

But we are not merely to be onlookers. We are also participants in this history, as members of the living and acting body of Christ in this world. To behold Christ is to participate in God's action of reclaiming the world by ourselves proclaiming the gospel of Christ. In bringing about the ultimate triumph of this purpose, God counts on the church to contribute its witness in the world.

Here we are in a seemingly impossible situation. The uniquenesss of Christ obliges us to call our fellows to behold him; yet the fact that he is unique also means that his quality cannot be proclaimed by any human means without distortion. So the proclamation of Christ necessarily has to be an act of the Holy Spirit through the church. Evangelism or witness is only done in obedience to the Holy Spirit.

The evangelist — and every Christian is an evangelist — does not just witness in order to give vent to some strong urge to speak of Christ. He evangelizes with a strong sense of responsibility to God and to his listeners. He knows that he must speak to individuals whose backgrounds, aspirations and ways of thinking are all different. Nevertheless, for its full revolutionary impact to be made on each individual, the unchanging truth of the gospel must be made real to women and men in terms of their own environment.

We are not here advocating syncretism, or the harmonization of the gospel with secular ideologies. Far from it. We must realize that for the

Christian evangelist in a town in Asia to refuse to adopt forms natural to the people there is to try to preserve forms in which Christianity has been introduced from the West. For an evangelist living and working among proletarian workers in Europe to make a similar refusal is to present them with a Christ in bourgeois clothes. We would then be calling people to become respectively second-class Westerners and second-class bourgeoisie.

The uniqueness of Christ is no justification for intransigent attitudes on our part, attitudes that attempt to isolate and lock him into one situation. The uniqueness of Christ and our eagerness to guard against distortion and syncretism should be the very reason that we seek to give the proper interpretation to our people. This we shall be able to do only as we learn to be conversant with non-Christian language and culture.

CHALLENGES TO FAITH (1957)

Christian belief in God is not so much the result of reasoning or persuasion as of spiritual insight. This is not surprising. We know our mother not because we have been persuaded by some argument or demonstration, but because from childhood we have felt her love. Many a carpenter who has never heard the formula *Pi* equals 3.1416 still knows that the circumference of a circle is a little more than three times its diameter, and this is enough for the practical needs of his work.

But for a theological student or church worker just to believe in God, and not know how to give a reasoned explanation of this belief, is not enough. Theological understanding is too important to be neglected. We do not subscribe to the various atheistic theories, but we must know wherein they are wrong and, still more, what the right view is. When we go out to preach the truth of the gospel our words should carry weight because of their reasonableness. In 1 Peter 3:15 we read, "Always be prepared to make a defense to any one who calls you to account for the hope that is in you, yet do it with gentleness and reverence."

Is Christianity idealist or materialist? Many people both within and without the church are interested in this question. Some Christians try to deny that Christianity is idealist, equating that stance with political backwardness; some try to prove that Christianity is materialist because to be materialist is assumed to be politically progressive.

But the question itself does not correspond with reality. To answer it simplistically is to adopt a scheme or framework imposed on us from outside our Christian understanding. Paradoxically, while idealism and materialism stand opposed to each other, they also interpenetrate each other; they are mutually exclusive and mutually influential; they share points of disagreement and points of agreement. There is some idealism in a materialist, and some materialism in an idealist.

It is still more impossible to classify Christianity as either idealist or materialist because, although it is in form a product of history, it is in essence not an ideology, not a structure built upon an economic base. Its true substance—the incarnation—is revelation; thus it transcends all human lines of reasoning. Some Christians accept the line between idealism and materialism and say, "We are not idealist," or even say, "We are materialist." This is all unnecessary because we do not need to accept the dichotomy itself.

In its organization, its thought and its ceremonies Christianity has of course been deeply influenced by human history, but in essence it is not a fruit of history. The gospel comes from the free revelation of God. This gospel is Christ himself, through whom all things were made. A theologian of Western Europe has said, "The greatest danger facing Western theology today is that of reducing Christianity to an ideology and thus of placing it in opposition to another ideology—communism." This is true. We must always remember that what we preach is Christ; it is the gospel, something in nature entirely different from an ideology, something that moves in a different orbit from any mere system of thought. Then we clearly understand that all talk of a comparison of Christianity with communism, of likenesses or differences, is superfluous.

"Religion is the opiate of the people." We should note, first, that this critical judgment is relative only to the religion of certain times or of certain persons, and not to religion itself. Let us grant, furthermore, for argument's sake, that the religion of certain individuals has indeed had a narcotic effect upon them. This discovery, however, does nothing to prove that the universe is without a creator. The mental state of some believers may be chaotic, so that in seeking for an anesthetic they use religion as opiate. But what does this prove one way or another about the existence of God? Similarly, the fact that they do not resort to an opiate is neither an argument for nor an argument against the existence of God. Whether God exists is a different and independent question.

Some preachers even take pride in presenting religion as a form of opiate, and of course this is not good. In Matthew 27:34 we read that when our Lord was hanging upon the cross a well-meaning individual, wishing to relieve the pains of Christ's death, offered him a cup of some opiate, which, when he had tasted it, he would not drink. Did he not have the right to drink it? Why did he refuse? Our Lord at the end of his human life, at its most important moment—when he was bearing the sins of all humankind upon the cross—wanted to keep a clear mind to the very end. He was not willing to go with a drugged and benumbed mind to the completion of the work God had given him to do. Without hesitation he refused the opiate. If he had consented to drink the drug, he might have escaped the pain, but then he would no longer have known what was going on around him, the seven great words from the cross would have been left unsaid, and the meaning of the cross itself would have remained dark and unclear to posterity.

What Christ gives us is forgiveness, consolation and strength, not a benumbed spirit. We pray, "Thy will be done on earth as it is in heaven." Where is there any opiate in that prayer? This is the highest religion, the religion of revelation. St. Ambrose once said, "You rich, when will your greed end? Will it continue until there is nothing left on earth but your-selves? How do you dare to take all nature as your own? The world was made for all, how can you claim it as your private property? Nature does not recognize the rich, it produces the common person. The products of nature are for the use of all, and God wants the world and all it contains, to be for the use of all" (Ambrose, *De Nabuthe Jezraelita*, 1, PL 14:732). The saint who said this certainly was not benumbed by some opiate. In the National Museum of Literature at Prague there is a statue of John Hus, under which is carved his own words: "Woe unto me if I remain silent. For it would be better for me to die than not to take a stand against great wickedness, as this would make me an accomplice to sin and hell." Who dares to say that a man who talks like this had been drugged with opiate? People do not take the primitive conditions of early Communist society as a reason for distrusting the future of the Communist cause; they do not, because of the absurdities of alchemy, look down upon modern chemistry, nor because of the superstitions of ancient astrology despise modern as-tronomy. In the same way we must not judge the gospel of Christ by evi-dence of narcotic religion.

The Bible does not lay down arguments for belief in the existence of God. We know that God is invisible, infinite, indefinable. To lay down a definition implies limitation. But God is infinite, and anything we can define is not God. Everything in the world is subject to definition; only God es-capes every definition that we make. St. Anselm said, "God is that than which nothing greater can be imagined" (Anselm, *Proslogion*, Chapter 4). Clement of Alexandria said, "We cannot know what God is, but we can know a little of what he is not." If the existence of God were as plain to us, say, as the existence of this table, what place would there be for faith? Faith is higher than scientific demonstration. Faith is the only thing in the world that will call us to great achievements and great sacrifices.

Someone said, "Religion is betting your life on the existence of God." Yes, religion is exploration, fellowship, love, deep calling unto deep. Fel-lowship can be established only upon the basis of mutual trust. Take the parable of the prodigal son. The elder brother was living a life without faith, hope and love. Although he daily saw the face of his father, his father's existence meant nothing to him; much less was there any real fellowship. But when the younger brother found himself in serious trouble, his one thought was to return to the bosom of his merciful father. You may call it adventure, or the great decision. Certainly it was a venture of faith. And so he returned. And what he found was really the love of a father, and not the cold sentence of an impartial law. He truly became the son of his father. And after this experience his knowledge of his father, and his relation with his father, was something different from what it had been before. The father's love transcended scientific reasoning and became the experience of faith. This relationship, and this experience, not even the older brother could understand.

How far can we go in understanding God on the basis of our own reason and observation? The Roman emperor and philosopher Marcus Aurelius — he was not a Christian—once said, "This world is either a haphazard miscellany or an ordered unity. If it is the former, what is there for me to consider except how I myself will ultimately return to dust? But if it is the latter, then I am in the presence of the mind that created that order; I am filled with awe, and have a ground on which to stand" (Marcus Aurelius, *Meditations*, Book 6, No. 10).

If you are walking through a trackless desert and come upon a wristwatch lying on the ground, you will at once conclude that someone has been there before you. The wristwatch in itself is an indication of a mind, an intelligence, a purpose. Now the universe is much more complicated than a wristwatch, and its workings much more exact. How could it possibly be the result of an accidental concurrence of phenomena without a mind or intelligence behind it? We cannot deny that behind the manifestations of nature there must be a mind, an intelligence, a purpose. Of course, to make this affirmation does not solve every problem, but to fail to make this affirmation leaves still greater problems unsolved.

Anyone who views the universe only in the light of reason will not be able to proceed further; from natural observation he will not be able to perceive more than this about God, for God transcends nature.

But on the basis of human reason how much can we know of this God? We can know something of the creator's activity, but what of God's purity and righteousness, love and redemptive purpose? We cannot but recall the Old Testament words, "Canst thou by searching find out God? Canst thou find out the Almighty unto perfection?" (Job 11:7). So it is not surprising that Paul presents another side to the picture: "After that in the wisdom of God the world by wisdom knew not God, it pleased God by the foolishness of preaching to save them that believe" (1 Cor 1:21). The foolishness of preaching is no less than the revealed truth of God. The mystery of nature can only be unfolded by revelation. Only after we have accepted the revelation, and come to know the Lord of revelation, can we understand the mystery of nature. But from that moment on, we can see in every part of nature the handiwork of God.

Let us take an illustration. Some of you are graduating this year. Suppose you think to yourself, "I have been away from home for a long time—I must go home and see my mother before reporting for work." When you get home she is not there. But you know her and love her, and as you go in and look around everything in the house reminds you of her. But now suppose you had one of your classmates with you, one who did not know your mother. As she looks around the room it will not remind her of anything; to her it is just a room.

We are like this with nature. Unless we have come to know God through revelation and faith, nature itself will only be space and mystery, and not much else. But if after receiving the revelation we again look at nature, all is now new. We now perceive that all the truth, goodness and beauty of the world proclaim the glory and working of God.

Modern thinking has a tendency to attribute all the ills of society to a bad social system, as though there could be no other source for them—for instance, humanity itself. For Christians this tendency is an important corrective. In the past we thought little about the social order. Our bias was simply to attribute all evil to our sinful nature. We said that once the question of sin was solved any social system would be good; if it were not solved, no social system would be good. Today we must acknowledge our mistake. It is true that the question of sin is fundamental. But we cannot expect everybody to repent at once—or once and for all—and thus solve the problem of sin. What kind of society will be best for our common life? The difference between socialism and capitalism is very great. Our studies during the past few years have shown us the superiority of socialism. We certainly cannot think of the two systems as having equal value for China.

In new China the level of morality has been greatly raised. Does that mean that the question of sin has been solved? Decidedly not. Consider your old grandmother, crippled with rheumatism so that she cannot move around much in winter. Then, with spring and summer, she becomes more lively. Does that mean she is now well? No, it only proves the weakness of the body. The fact that people must come into a good environment (as in new China) in order to manifest a better standard of behavior does not mean that we are without sin; rather, it is a demonstration that humanity is carrying a heavy load of sin, so that we are not free from the influence of environment.

I once studied in a school that had in its gymnasium a ball about the size of a basketball, but much heavier, and with an off-center weight in it. The result was that no matter how you tried you could not roll it straight. It was very exasperating. Is not our life like that? Yesterday, today and tomorrow men and women can still be described in the words of Isaiah: "All we like sheep have gone astray; we have turned every one to his own way" (Is 53:6).

In today's society the level of moral behavior has been raised, and this is a fact Christians should welcome. We should not go around looking for flaws, as if the only way to vindicate our faith is to discover that things in the world are as bad as ever. We should welcome a social system that is able to raise the level of moral life. But changes in the social system can only limit the effectiveness of sin, they cannot solve the fundamental problem of sin. Sin can only be healed by love, forgiveness, salvation and grace. It is not a matter of social progress.

From the beginning of the world there have been people who would not believe in God. There are two reasons: the first is spiritual and universal; the second is rooted in history.

To believe in God and to believe in life on Mars may seem to be identical acts of belief, but they are vastly different. Whether you do or do not believe there is life on Mars makes no difference to you morally or spiritually. Your life, your thinking and your actions will be the same.

Belief in God is a different thing. If you don't believe, that is all there is to it, but if you do believe, the consequences are great. Adam sinned, and then when God drew near, he hid himself in the trees because he did not dare to look upon the face of God. We can imagine how relieved he would have been then if there had not been within or without the universe any such person as this God. And if he had remained hidden for a long time, would not he and his children have come to believe that God after all did not exist?

Peter knelt at Jesus' feet saying, "Lord, depart from me, for I am a sinful man" (Lk 5:8). Since he knew Jesus to be Lord and himself to be a sinner, should he not instead have repented? Why would he ask Jesus to depart? Yes, we have all had these experiences of both wanting Christ and not wanting him. Christ is what we want, yet he demands that we repent. If we are not willing to repent, if we are unwilling to pay the moral and spiritual price, we can only ask this Christ to leave us. We might even wish that he did not exist.

Now we come to the second point, and that is the church's historic failure to manifest God. Jesus said, "Let your light so shine before men that they may see your good works, and glorify your Father which is in heaven" (Mt 5:16). But we do not do this. People are not able to see God, full of love, justice and purity, in the life, the thought and the work of Christians. What people see in the church instead is a God in whom their own sense of morality and justice does not allow them to believe. This is an important reason why people today do not believe in God.

In his book *The Origins of Russian Communism* Berdyaev, a Russian theologian, writes:

> Christians, who condemn the Communists for their godlessness and anti-religious persecutions, cannot lay the whole blame upon these godless Communists; they must assign part of the blame to themselves, and that a considerable part. They must be not only accusers and judges; they must also be penitents. Have Christians done very much for the realization of Christian justice in social life? Have they striven to realize the brotherhood of man without the hatred and violence of which they accuse the Communists? The sins of Christians and the sins of the historical churches have been very great, and these sins bring with them their just punishment (Berdyaev, New York: Charles Scribner's, 1937, pp. 207-208).

We need not agree entirely with this view. But because of its sins, and especially because politically it was often on the side of the people's enemies, the church lost its ability to show forth God. The Chinese church in particular can appreciate this point. The Three-Self Patriotic Movement is calling the whole church out of its bondage to imperialism and to all sorts of reaction. This makes it a movement of great significance to the future of Christian witness in China.

Criticism of religion has mainly centered attention on some of the evil results of religion in personal and social life, such as its inhibiting influence on human development, its harmful effect on health, and its upholding of private ownership of means of production; it has not touched upon the substance of our faith. Some of the things criticized are foreign, perhaps now a thing of the past, while others are Chinese in origin, and thus still problems. These should rouse us to greater vigilance and self-examination, amending what is wrong and strengthening what is right.

We should recognize the right of all shades of atheism and agnosticism to exist and become accustomed to living with them. We must learn how to profit from their criticism of religion, and how to present the gospel to people who have been influenced by these views. Theism and atheism are matters of personal faith and worldview, not matters of the state or government. A state or a government cannot hold to either theism or atheism. But in the West there are those who try to make this question an issue in the cold war, and of this we do not approve. We know that neither cold war nor hot war will change an atheist into a theist. The West has published many books on the subject of Christianity and communism, but they are not of much value to us, because their authors have been too much influenced by the anti-Soviet, anti-communist spirit of their own milieu, so that they speak not with the loving spirit of an apostle, but with the self-righteousness of an elder brother. We know that only as the church corrects itself and becomes really the church can the gospel radiate the liberating strength of its own truth and bring people to a knowledge of sin, repentance and confession of Christ as Lord.

Faith is personal. The two Chinese characters for faith both have the character for person on the left-hand side. Only an individual person can believe or not believe in God. Now a nation or a government is not a single individual; it can neither believe in God nor not believe in God. Christians need not take it seriously when a particular nation calls itself a Christian nation. We see that its leaders appear to be very devout, but their purpose might well be only to advance their own political ends and get support for their actions. They call their nation a Christian nation and their government a Christian government. But Christ has said that his kingdom is not of this world. How then shall a nation or government dare to call itself by the name of Christian?

We know from history that those who make a pretense of religion can appear very devout. Even Herod, who wanted to kill the Christ child, pretended that he wanted to worship him. So Christians must be wary. In regard to the political leadership of any nation, it is not what the leaders believe but the content of leadership that is the important factor. Do we approve of the government's principles? How do the ruling party and people join together to carry out those principles? We do not approve of the Communists' atheism, but we welcome their political leadership, and we welcome their frank attitude regarding questions of belief too. They tell the world openly what they think about religion, and so there is less danger of their trying to use religion for their own purposes.

The building of the church in a socialist country is a task never before faced. In self-government, self-support and self-propagation we face a difficult responsibility. Why does God give this responsibility to us and not to someone else? Is it because we are better? No, God has his own purpose, one that we cannot fathom. But because our Chinese church is a weak minority group, we can at least demonstrate how the church of God in weakness shows forth strength, we can show the workings of God's might, and thus we can give glory to God.

RESURRECTION AND LIBERATION (1985)

He is the image of the invisible God, the first-born of all creation; for in him all things were created, in heaven and on earth, visible and invisible, whether thrones or dominions or principalities or authorities—all things were created through him and for him. He is before all things, and in him all things hold together (Col 1:15-17).

There exists one person whose presence makes men and women feel ill at ease, but they cannot get rid of him, much as they might like to! We have tried to distort him, condemn him, explain him away, write him off, streamline, ignore and suppress him—even silence him by crucifixion—but all to no avail. The grave could not contain him. He rose from it victorious. Impelled by love he pleads, "Come to me all who labor and are heavy laden, and I will give you rest. My yoke is easy and my burden is light" (Mt 11:28, 30).

During the first half of this century there were many in China—Christians and non-Christians—who classified Christ as a great moral teacher. Jesus, who gave us the sermon on the mount, drew much respect among conscientious intellectuals. Their attitude to Christianity was positive but did not do justice to the fullness of the New Testament Christ. During that time there were also Christians in China who treated Christ as a means of attaining bliss in heaven. They deserve our sympathy because for many life on earth was then so hopeless that they could only resort to religion as a shelter from their misery. But this too was a limited perception of Christ.

Thirty-five years have passed since 1949 (the establishment of the People's Republic of China). In those years we think we have come to know a

Christ who is much greater than we dared to think. The livelihood of millions of our formerly marginalized and spiritually mutilated people has changed for the better. No longer starving, they do not need to earn their living in ways that violate self-respect. Chinese Christians do not think lightly of these changes. If in the past our religion was strongly marked by despair and hopelessness, we now find that thanksgiving has become an important factor in our spirituality. In Paul's words, "As grace extends to more and more people, it may increase thanksgiving, to the glory of God" (2 Cor 4:15). As we increase our thanksgiving, we come to an enlarged and higher view of Christ. He is not just a great moral teacher, not just a plane trip to heaven for you and me, not just Lord of those who confess him, but the firstborn of the whole creation, elder brother of all humanity, shaper of our history and mover of all life—in short, the Christ of the whole universe. There is something cosmic in the nature of the Christ of our love and adoration.

Life in China is now more humane. Since, as Psalm 16 says, we have no good apart from God, it is only right that we offer to God a larger portion of thanksgiving. But China is not paradise. The so-called Cultural Revolution [1966-1976] was a time of testing. We had our Peters, who in their weakness wavered and denied Christ, and our Judases, who sold him for their personal gain. Our losses were great. It was a real experience of dying for the Chinese church. But as we come out of that period, we find the faith of most Christians not only intact but steadier and warmer. Today we have more Christians than ever before. We are also more united than ever before. Churches are being reopened or built at the rate of one a day for the whole of China. Bibles are being produced. Large numbers of young Christians are offering themselves to the ministry of the church; in my seminary alone there are over 180 students, both men and women. As we look at the experience of our nation, of our church and of ourselves as individual Christians, resurrection comes up as the most appropriate word. From our own experience we have been led to see more clearly the reasonableness and the logic of Christ's rising from death after his sufferings. So we have come to know the risen and ascended Christ more intimately as the one who through all vicissitudes upholds the universe by his word of power. He is sovereign over principalities and powers. This is liberating. We are not in the grip of an almighty fate. To be free from fatalism and futility is true liberation.

3

CREATIVE MISSION

The theme of Part 1, "Embodying Christianity," refers to the attempt to find a Chinese form for Christian faith. This contextualization of the faith is not intended to compartmentalize it. The three articles in this subsection, from quite different periods in K. H. Ting's life, all deal with the mission of the church and especially with the creative role churches in Asia were being called to play in this mission. The first, "A Vital Vocation," from the World Student Christian Federation journal *Student World*, was published in 1948 under the title "Does God Call Us?" while Ting was studying in New York. In this article Bishop Ting speaks of the gospel inviting all human beings — "it will take the whole of humanity to embody the Christ that is yet to be."

"The Spirit of Wisdom" is taken from a two-part bible study published in 1954 in *Tian Feng*, a journal of the Protestant churches in China. The study was entitled "The Spirit Who Grants Wisdom and Revelation to Humankind." The bible study was originally given at a retreat for church workers in Nanjing. This excerpt is based on an unpublished translation done recently by the Reverend Ng Kam-yan of Toronto. The study reflects the attempt to explore the depths of Christian faith to find the basis of unity so necessary for the Chinese church at this time. K. H. Ting had returned from abroad, where he lived when the previous article was written, and was now immersed in the concerns of the Chinese church as it struggled to find its mission in the early years of Communist rule.

In 1982, almost three decades later, Bishop Ting visited Sweden, where he lectured on the situation of the church in China. "Changing Relationships," the final article in this subsection, is taken from that lecture which was given in English. His comment on "the hermeneutical disadvantage of privilege" states from the opposite side the more usual liberation theology formula of the "preferential option for the poor," or the "epistemological advantage of the oppressed." His closing statements on particularity and universality attempt to deal with the problem of how the former mission churches of the West are to relate to a Chinese church, that has found its selfhood.

A VITAL VOCATION (1948)

It is most natural for Christians to want to tell others about Christ. My friend Chuan Wen is a typical example. How quickly after his conversion he went about not only selling insurance policies—which was his occupation—but trying to convert people to his new way of life. To be sure, he committed many blunders. We felt it was dangerously quick. We doubted whether he was not doing much more harm than good to himself, to others and to the church. Perhaps, from the standpoint of common sense, our worry and doubt and fear were all warranted. But his new life in Christ simply defied all human common sense. It was we who had to learn anew to relax, allowing the Holy Spirit, who escapes our inclination to "pattern" things, its full freedom. Converts like Chuan Wen may be said to be natural missionaries, right from the moment the seed of the gospel takes root in their hearts.

If this is true of individual converts, it is just as true of those communities we know as the "younger churches." They quickly discover that evangelism is the lifeblood of the church. It is only in reaching out into the world that the church can keep the gospel vital for itself. Nothing can really kill the church unless it is induced to forget its missionary task.

The truth amounts to this: If Christ has become anything at all to you, he must be everything to you. And if indeed he is everything to you, how anxious you must be that he should be made to mean everything to all people everywhere. That anxiety in you corresponds in a small way to the eternal divine longing that all humanity return to God. Thus the missionary vocation is not something that is debatable, as if the force of our arguments were necessary to prop it up. The conquest of the world by God's love allows no alternative.

If people do not seem to want Christ, we may reason that the principles of politeness and tolerance forbid us to "impose" our religion upon others. But tolerance, a doubtful Christian virtue, may be a convenient coverup for spiritual exhaustion. Everybody seems happy, but issues are blurred. A drowning person who calls for help needs not your tolerance but the salvation of a tried and trusted lifebelt.

As to places like India, China and Africa (among others), they both do and do not want Christ. They are aware of an uncomfortably challenging and demanding call. But they know that it is Christ who summons them, and that the call must be heeded to obtain God's grace and deliverance from sin. Only in this way will they obtain full status and liberty as children of God. To Christ, then, we not only say, "Depart from me, for I am a sinner" (Lk 5:8), but we are also driven to confess, "Lord, to whom shall we go? Thou hast the words of eternal life"(Jn 6:68).

Missionaries from older churches are certainly needed by younger churches, and for reasons that will largely hold good even when the latter grow strong. Missionaries bring us the experience and heritage of older and stronger traditions; they link us with the reality and the richness of the whole body of Christ; they bring us tried methods useful in our own lands; through their life and deeds they help us gain access to people otherwise difficult to reach; as fellow-students in Christ, they use their learning in the teaching and training of youth, preparing us to tackle the big untouched areas. They themselves receive inspiration when they see people accepting Christ for the first time and realize the tremendous impact that the New Testament makes on the life and minds of new converts and their communities. This in itself is an experience that, properly interpreted, spreads out to enrich the spirituality of the universal church. Last but not least, missionaries are important to the mother churches as active communicators keeping the missionary torch burning and invigorating the whole of church life.

Missionary work among other peoples enables us to gain a fuller understanding of the gospel itself. It is only in evangelizing that you really start to evangelize yourself. In the gospel there is such a deep, unplumbed and hidden treasure that it cannot be fully explored by anything less than the whole human race. We shall not know the eminence of the gospel — and our worship is bound to be incomplete — until it comes to include all for whom it was meant. It will take the whole of humanity to embody the Christ that is yet to be and to bring to full expression the unsearchable riches of Christ. We might very well remind ourselves that the New Testament, which is so essential to our faith, came to be written only as a result of the missionary work of the apostolic church.

Then think of the oppression and injustice wrought, even now, by powerful nations in those countries that are at the receiving end of missions. In great humility and penitence Christians must go there, at least with some intention of undoing the wrong that has been done. It is up to Christians to give positive testimony and counteract the negative ways in which their own countries' interests may have made themselves felt.

We are hesitant to greet a missionary who is obsessed with the idea of self-sacrifice. He reminds us of Jonah. Poor Jonah, surviving his three days in the stomach of a whale, lives on incarnate (in a more refined form) in the duty-bound, unhappy and self-pitying missionary!

Like Jonah, an unwilling missionary, while doing some good, can cause a lot of trouble. A sense of duty impels a response to God's call that is intellectual rather than a response of the whole person. There is no joy and no deep love, a lack that cannot be hidden for long. Such a missionary feels the need to be ministered unto rather than to minister — the assumption is that self-sacrifice is a good bargaining counter in the relationship with God. Forgotten is the knowledge that a Christian's vocation, in God's eyes, is really the highest self-fulfillment.

We must take our vocation seriously so that God may use us. Yet in another sense we must not take it seriously so as to leave enough room for the Holy Spirit to work in us. What we do is extremely important because it is God's work. At the same time, what we do is extremely unimportant for exactly the same reason. Just as a physician of the body only establishes certain conditions in the patient and in his environment under which God, who is the God of health and wholesomeness, restores the physical well-being in the patient, so a missionary merely establishes certain conditions under which the Holy Spirit can work to restore the health of the soul. I wonder in fact whether much of the fruit of missionary work has been reaped in spite of the missionaries rather than through them. Even Jonah, though he fell short of the missionary ideal, could be instrumental in bringing about repentance in Nineveh.

And do not let us forget the life-transforming power of our vocation. The power that works through us also works in us; in spite of our unworthiness it transforms our lives in ways as significant as the transformation of the lives of the people to whom we are sent. We are called by God not because we are good, but because we have heard the gospel. As we respond to that call, we are upheld and made into God's fellow workers.

THE SPIRIT OF WISDOM (1954)

That the Gentiles—and not just the Jews—were to share in Christ's salvation is a profound mystery. Paul said that the mystery of Christ was not made known "in other generations as it has now been revealed to his holy apostles and prophets by the Spirit; that is, how the Gentiles are fellow heirs, members of the same body, and partakers of the promise in Christ Jesus through the gospel" (Eph 3:5-6). Without the revelation of this mystery, Christianity would have remained a religion of the Jews. From this we can see the tremendous significance of what is recorded in the tenth chapter of Acts: It was not only an important event in Peter's own experience and in the history of Christianity—it also assumed a definite place in God's scheme of salvation.

Today, however, we are not here to study the whole question of how the Gentiles received salvation but to seek to see how the Holy Spirit leads us step by step, getting rid of our pride and arrogance so that through faith we can reach a place of understanding.

It appears that sometimes God's will is shown not by direct revelation, but through the arrangement of various circumstances in our lives. Let each one of us think back for a while. How did we arrive at where we are today? Was it through our own foresight and plans made years ago? Or was it not rather by the convergence of numerous coincidences that one after another shattered our own well-laid schemes? When we were unable to control what was happening around us, did we not complain, or struggle, or try to run away? And yet, looking back from today's vantage point, we have come to see God's hand at work and are left with no alternative but to praise God and admit the excellence of God's plans over our own.

Paul seemed to be faced with a blank wall everywhere when he tried to preach the gospel in Asia. By rights he should have been bitterly frustrated; instead, apostle that he was, he was able to discern that he was "forbidden by the Holy Spirit" to carry out his self-appointed task (Acts 16:6-7). Yet even Paul did not realize that the closing of the door in Asia would result in the gospel being brought into Europe — something we recognize as vitally important in history, but which no one, including Paul, could have understood at the time. Thus we can see that we are "blind and shortsighted" (2 Pt 1:9) to the work of the Holy Spirit, which proceeds according to long-range and holistic plans.

Christ said, "Go therefore and make disciples of all nations" (Mt 28:19). Prior to his ascension he further commanded the disciples to be his witnesses not only in Jerusalem and all Judea and Samaria but "to the ends of the earth" (Acts 1:8). But because of the spiritual pride of the disciples these words did not seem to have much effect. They knew they were God's chosen! They were the descendants of Abraham, possessing the highest and most perfect truth. They knew what was clean, what was unclean. What room had Gentiles in their eyes?

Such a one was Peter. Three times God bade Peter, as he prayed on the rooftop, to eat foods that Jews never touched, and three times Peter refused, saying, "These things are unclean" — in fact he had never touched them. But the Holy Spirit said, "What God has cleansed, do not call common." Peter, however, banged the door shut in the Spirit's face (Acts 11:5-10).

Never eating what has not been eaten before; never thinking what was not thought before, never doing what was not done before — in this way Peter limited the working of the Holy Spirit. By insisting on the standard rite of cleanliness, by allowing the Spirit to act only within the habitual and familiar, Peter restricted the Spirit.

The Spirit, however, is an active Spirit. "The wind blows where it wills, and you hear the sound of it, but you do not know whence it comes or whither it goes; so it is with everyone who is born of the Spirit" (Jn 3:8). How could the activity of the Spirit be confined or circumscribed by human appetites, human habits and human prejudices?

"Now while Peter was inwardly perplexed as to what the vision . . . might mean, behold, the men that were sent by Cornelius . . . stood before the gate" (Acts 10:17). How often, when we are perplexed by a certain problem, do we not wish we could set it aside for a period, and wait there on the rooftop for a gift of insight from God? But questions seek us out — they are already knocking at the door below — and life demands that we make prompt and daring decisions.

The Holy Spirit leads us to the rooftop to pray; the Holy Spirit also leads us down to the door to face the problems that we do not know how to face. Both on the rooftop above and on the ground below the Holy Spirit is with us — helping us as we pray, accompanying us as we encounter different kinds of people, enlarging our understanding through visions and circumstances.

What we should come to understand is this: Because of our shortcomings, our sin and our pride, what God can get through to us on the rooftop is very limited. God sends us downstairs for another lesson. To be sent downstairs is not to be required to leave God, but to obey God. If indeed we insist on remaining on the rooftop we will be hindering the Holy Spirit.

It is only when we begin to act, upon the strength of just one ray of light bestowed upon us, that we begin to understand. "If anyone's will is to do God's will, that person will know whether the teaching is from God" (Jn 7:17). At the moment that Jesus called to the disciples, "Come, follow me," did they have any idea of what would develop from that summons? Resolutely leaving everything else to follow him, they found that the more they followed, the better they understood. When the wise men from the East saw the star, did they fully realize the meaning of the birth of Christ? Yet they did not hesitate, and in following the star they finally found Christ. It is only after the first step has been taken that we can learn more and more as we walk along. This is the life of faith.

> Rise up, my love, my fair one
>   and come away.
> For lo, the winter is past,
>   the rain is over and gone.
> The flowers appear on the earth;
>   the time of the singing birds is come,
> and the voice of the turtledove
>   is heard in our land.
> The fig tree puts forth her green figs,
>   and the vines with the tender grape
>   give a good smell.
> Arise, my love, my fair one,
>   and come away (Sg 2:10-13).

What a tender, loving appeal God is making to us! This day God would have us, disciples living in the new China, rise up like young people in love, and with joy and eagerness go forth to receive all things good that have been prepared for us. Should we lock ourselves up and seal ourselves off from the the Holy Spirit? Do we still hesitate time after time, cruelly making the Spirit wait outside our door, making the Spirit disappointed?

The Spirit is a Spirit that unites. The Spirit led Peter to an all-important discovery: Cornelius, whom he was called to meet in Caesaria, was, like Peter himself, a human being. "Stand up; I too am a man" (Acts 10:26). Is this not something quite ordinary? And yet Peter had to learn this lesson at great cost to himself. He lowered himself from the rooftop; he came to see that a Gentile, one whom he had always looked upon as too "unclean" to associate with, could actually be acceptable to God. In this way the Holy

Spirit bridges the chasm between one person and another. This is not all. Peter soon learned another lesson: Cornelius shared with Peter the same salvation by the same Lord and received the same grace from the same Spirit. A longstanding separation was finally healed, for the Holy Spirit not only unites person to person, but also disciple to disciple.

Through Cornelius the Holy Spirit not only worked on Peter's stupidity, not only built a bridge between Gentiles and the gospel, but also greatly enriched the life of the church. Would the Jews alone have fulfilled God's longing for the world? Would homogeneity have been the church's hallmark? Certainly not. The inestimable length, breadth, height and depth of Christ's love require the acceptance and witness of innumerable disciples from around the world. The complete mystery, the complete potential for beauty, goodness and truth embedded in the gospel require exploration by many Corneliuses of countless eras, regions and cultures.

In the past, however, not only have we not acted in a way that respected or enriched one another, we have hardly tolerated one another. We have dealt in suspicion, ostracism, discord—sometimes even to the point of splitting hairs on a question as fine as a hair. Thankfully, since liberation things have improved considerably. Within the church even those with differing theologies, differing disciplines or differing liturgies have been able to work together as the right hand works with the left. In this way the church can truly fulfill itself, as Paul affirms.

CHANGING RELATIONSHIPS (1982)

"The ends of the earth" are wherever Christians are. It is there that we are to bear witness to Christ and build up his body. We do want, however, to be a part of the universal church and enjoy a give-and-take existence within it. Even so, we consider that being independent would enable us to be better prepared to enter into true interdependence.

When a local church, instead of achieving independence, only sinks deeper and deeper into dependency, a measure of dissociation becomes essential. Paul set us an example when he opposed the apostles in their wish to keep the Gentile converts permanently on the periphery, dependent on the mother church in Palestine. Christianity, a religion based on incarnation, must make room for each new church, each new people, and not run the risk of their alienation.

In our theological work in China we are admittedly at our weakest in the study of the Bible in its original languages and texts. Here we are indeed counting on a lot of help from Western colleagues. The Bible may also be studied, however, as literature or history, and as an embodiment of ethical and philosophical views, especially in relation to Western culture. Here there is a definite and increasing interest. At Nanjing University there is a course on the Bible as literature. The China Christian Council intends to supply bibles to academic libraries all across the country. Chinese Christians have also had creative experience over the past thirty years in theological and devotional studies based on the Bible. We refer to this experience as the gaining of new light on old truths. On the other hand, studying the Bible by comparing individual texts from different books is increasingly unpopular. Christians are interested now in the epistemology and hermeneutics of practice, that is, of actions that transform history.

There has been a traditional dichotomy between theory and practice, with primacy given to theory over practice — and therein lies the danger of gnosticism. Christians are now reading the Bible anew from the standpoint of the people's struggle, with all their joys and sorrows, all their hopes and fears. To a certain degree we are thus sympathetic to liberation theology, insofar as it points out the hermeneutical disadvantage of privilege.

We are less sure today of the original meaning of a biblical passage in the mind of the author, or of some absolute meaning or timeless truth. But this does not mean we are agnostic. Paul Ricoeur says, "The text's career escapes the finite horizon lived by its author. What the text means *now* matters more than what the author meant when he wrote it" (*Interpretation Theory: Discourse and the Surplus of Meaning*, Fort Worth, Texas: Texas Christian University Press, 1976, p. 30). Chinese Christians refer to the manna that is ever fresh and edible if gathered early every morning, but becomes stale and rots later in the day.

In our present post-denominational existence, the China Christian Council can probably be best understood as a form of unity in development, to be located somewhere between a Council of Churches and a United Church. We are thankful to say that Chinese Protestantism has never been united on such a large scale as it is today. We want to guard our emerging selfhood, which is our particularity, but we also know that selfhood is meaningful only as a part of the universality of the whole church — in all the world, in all ages, living and witnessing in all social systems. We like to think of ourselves as an ellipse with two foci, which are not exclusive but mutually strengthening and enhancing — our particularity and our universality. All the good that missionaries of the past have brought to China has not been lost, and we are grateful to them. Today, there are other ways for our church in China to benefit from churches abroad. A relationship of a new kind is not only possible but already emerging. Churches abroad can help us most by understanding our need to keep the two foci in good balance.

Part 2

SERVING THE PEOPLE

What is the church for? There is no one answer and no final answer to such a question. Certainly throughout its imperfect history the Christian church has continually renewed its commitment to serving the hungry, the lost, the lonely sister or brother. In Bishop Ting's writing we again hear the simple stories of serving, nurturing, sharing bread and word with those who suffer, stories that call Christians everywhere back to their roots as a community which is friend and neighbor to all in need.

The pastoring and caring role of the church in China went through dramatic changes during Bishop Ting's lifetime. His own ministry starts in Shanghai under Japanese occupation. The end of the Sino-Japanese war was the beginning of more civil war between the nationalist and communist forces. Student work meant trying to help students maintain body and spirit under adversity, not just with pity but with admiration for their inspiring perseverance ("Hunger, Food and Grace").

The success of the revolution in 1949 under the Communist Party and its Chairman, Mao Zedong, raised new questions. One of Mao's most famous essays was entitled "Serve the People." In Chinese communism there was a movement that sought to relieve the needs of the hungry and to bring dignity to ordinary workers and peasants. K. H. Ting struggled to deal with how the church should respond to this movement. He saw a need to avoid both identification with the old status quo of Chiang Kai-shek and the Nationalists, and romanticizing the new revolutionaries who were coming to power ("The Task of the Church in Asia").

In 1949 Ting saw the revolution neither as a disease nor as a cure but more like a fever, a necessary but passing response to social breakdown. His approach was to give it a chance, to see how it worked out. In contrast to later theological developments in other parts of the world, he did not see the revolution as part of what Christians call salvation. The revolutionary was like the prodigal son, who would eventually return to the waiting father. "If we strengthen our evangelistic purpose we shall be ready to receive with open arms the many tired revolutionaries when post-revolu-

59

tionary despair sets in" ("The Task of the Church in Asia"). It may be that the 1980s are witnessing a fulfillment of this prediction. It should be noted, however, that K. H. Ting did not allow this kind of argument to result in a Christian neutrality in the struggle for justice. He himself left the comforts of the West to return to China after the Communists had taken power, in spite of warnings from Western church leaders that he would be executed or put in a concentration camp by the Communists. He took his stand with new China.

In balancing between the church and various political options some may accuse K. H. Ting of falling into a Christian attitude of being above it all. For example, he praised the Communist General Chu Teh, who, for the sake of unity in the war against Japan, was able to forgive the execution of his wife and children by Chiang Kai-shek's forces in an earlier period. But this forgiveness "has nothing in common with forgiveness between Christians." The believer "has a status in the grace of God and in the church of Christ that no human moral excellence can be compared with" ("The Task of the Church in Asia"). Placing Christian virtue above anything that can be achieved by others suggests an attitude of Christian superiority that Ting may not have intended, or if he did, it was a position from which he later moved. Throughout his writings, but especially in the selections in Parts 3 and 4 below, Bishop Ting speaks of how he continually learned and changed in interaction with Christian leaders such as Y. T. Wu and in response to developments in liberated China.

Serving the people did not only mean relief activities. The contributions of the Asian churches are sometimes surprising to the West. For example, in the 1940s the Anglican bishops from China urged the ordination of women to the priesthood, even though they were functioning in a culture that did not speak of the equality of men and women. It was also from China and India and Ceylon that pressure came for church unity ("The Task of the Church in Asia").

Service means spiritual leadership. Jesus' distributing bread to the five thousand is a sacramental act showing us that in attending to material needs we are agents of the coming reign of God on earth ("The Cry for Bread"). Our solidarity with the victims ("The Sinned Against") both relieves their suffering and is a sign of God's promise. We grow in faith through wrestling with God, as did the scoundrel Jacob ("Wrestling With God"), and we all have a bit of the scoundrel nature in us. We find ourselves as we seek, as did the Magi whose encounter with Christ led them to subvert the authority of Herod ("The Journey of the Magi"). Spiritual leadership needs to be rooted; the selfhood of the Chinese church expressed in the Three-Self Movement is the basis of its active participation in the universal church ("Christian Selfhood").

Service also means evangelism. A humble, repentent church must renew itself and purify itself even as it seeks to take its message beyond itself. Ting's friends find his commitment to the church in the 1950s rather strange since China was embarking on an exciting new course and the church seemed dark and backward. There is a poignancy in their lack of understanding of his faith and his realization that the church had become so distorted by imperialism that its true nature was covered in shame. "Why still be a preacher of the gospel in the new China?" he asks himself, and the answers he finds are particular to his context but still speak universally ("Why Be a Minister?"). The faults of the church are not the last word. Christians must continue to work quietly, search their souls, learn that there is no conflict between loving China and loving God, look to see where the Holy Spirit is leading them and persevere in a new situation ("The Nature of Witness").

There is no sense of Christian complacency in this 1950s period. But echoes of the idea that Christians are somehow above the political fray are perhaps present again in the 1980s when Ting ties together what is called the ultra-leftism of the Cultural Revolution and liberation theology's hermeneutic of the oppressed. He rejects the "preferential option for the poor" on the grounds that to make the contradiction between the rich and the poor the focus of theology is to relativize the biblical revelation. Socio-political liberation is not an adequate expression of theology ("The Church's Mandate").

It is unclear from this just what the Christian's relationship to the struggle for social justice should be, especially in situations of extreme oppression such as Latin America and the Philippines. Ting sees "powerlessness" not necessarily as a bad thing, but as a position marked by its own kind of grace. Evangelism can be done best perhaps, he states, from a position of powerlessness ("The Church's Mandate"). This may make sense in a country like China, where Christians are a tiny minority. But where there is a Christian majority, and where people suffer terrible exploitation, a response that separates the gospel from political struggle may be seen as quietism. Socio-political liberation is not taken by liberation theologians to be adequate in itself, but a view of salvation that does not include such liberation is also inadequate.

The emphasis on incarnational theology in K. H. Ting's thought may provide a clue to his understanding of political questions in relation to salvation. The incarnation of Christ is more powerful in its universality than is the fall of Adam, original sin. "We look at the world in the splendor of the ascended Christ. What human beings do to make love more available to the masses of our people is in consonance with God's work of creation, redemption and sanctification." Humanity is moving toward the recovery of the image of God. "This is how we look at the world and at history, at human aspirations, movement and struggle. And this is the source of our optimism and thanksgiving" ("The Cry for Bread").

4

UPHELD BY GRACE

The World Student Christian Federation publication *Student World* is the source for the first two articles in this subsection, both from 1949. "Hunger, Food and Grace," originally published as "A Creative Experience for Chinese Students," is a reflection on relief work among students, in which Ting had been involved. In the closing paragraph there is reference to the return of ninety thousand students. As Japanese power spread through eastern China during the war, many students and faculty withdrew to the interior to continue their teaching in temporary quarters. After the defeat of Japan these students trekked back to the campuses they had fled. The article is a touching description of grace amid hardship and exemplifies K. H. Ting's consistent understanding of the church as healer.

"The Task of the Church in Asia" is an important theoretical piece on Christian identity and social change. A number of its points have been mentioned in the introduction to this section. Comment on work among the "aborigines" in southwest China refers to the national minorities in that mountainous region. At another point the article makes reference to Nestorian Christianity being uprooted after two centuries in China. Only a few archeological traces remain of this movement, presumably brought into China from Persia, from about 635 C.E.

Bishop Ting mentions that in 1949 the Communists permitted Christian groups to carry on their work. There persists in the West the misperception that missionary work ended with the Communist victory. In fact, foreign Christians continued to work in liberated areas before the establishment of the People's Republic of China at the end of 1949, and even longer. It was the involvement of the United States and other Western countries in the Korean War that made Western missionaries enemy aliens and led to the closing of foreign Christian missions from about the end of 1950.

The other two selections here are from sermons preached in 1979 on Ting's first visit to North America after his return to China in 1951. He preached at a Sunday evening service in Toronto at Timothy Eaton Memorial Church, a sermon later published in *China and Ourselves* as "Give Ye Them to Eat" from which "The Cry for Bread" is taken. The sermon is based on the story of the feeding of the five thousand. "The Sinned Against" is from a sermon preached at Riverside Church in New York. Note again the use of the image of Jonah as the mean-spirited missionary. The phrase "more sinned against than sinning" is, of course, from Shakespeare's *King Lear*.

HUNGER, FOOD AND GRACE (1949)

In the dining hall of a Chinese university, near the big pot from which students help themselves to hot rice, there is a small notice that reads: "Please do not dip the ladle too deep." It is understandable. Rice these days can only be served in the form of thin and watery gruel. The rice particles sink to the bottom of the pot where students, always hungry, instinctively try to scoop them up.

Seeing such a notice we naturally tell ourselves that conditions are desperate. We wish we could do more to help both students and professors. But *desperate* is not the right word for the situation. In reality, there is something inspiring about these conditions. Just think of the fact that knowing how eager students are for food—even tasteless rice gruel—the dining hall authorities can still confidently depend on their restraint and cooperation. An ancient Chinese teacher remarked that people can only understand morality after they are well-fed and well-clad. That expresses the working belief of many a cynic in this age as well. If this were true, however, we should expect some strict rationing system. But that does not seem to be necessary—only a simple reminder not to dip the ladle too deep. The hungry students understand.

A student who comes to a local student relief committee is not merely a hungry human being to be fed, or a cold body to be clad, or an intellectual aristocrat whose privilege as a "scholar" even the struggle for national existence must not disturb. No, each student is a child of God, fulfilled in community with others through cooperative and social undertakings.

The detailed significance of this relief work is manifold. First, thousands of university students have been enabled to continue their education. In China only one in ten thousand people is a student, so that even at the time of the Sino-Japanese war students were asked not to join the armed forces but to continue their education in order to be ready to serve the country in the period of reconstruction. Student relief helped enormously to preserve this leadership strength for new China.

Second, the relief program has demonstrated a positive and constructive role for "charity." In old China people still tend to think of charity—the repair of roads and bridges, for example—as a means to accumulate personal merit. Instead of helping the living, the charitable and feudal rich think it a good deed to provide poor widows with coffins for the burial of their husbands and children. Our student relief work has lifted the people's vision to the realization that there is a public service that has far greater long-range, positive value—helping people to live more abundantly and not merely die less meagerly. Indeed, in spite of currency difficulties, an increasing amount of funds for student relief is coming each year from sources in China itself.

Third, the student relief program has been a powerful instrument in fostering in the student mind the dignity and value of manual labor. Enemy bombardment and the subsequent long march of professors and students shook the foundation of what students today call the "ivory pagoda" of the old scholarship. The work of the student relief program has further helped pull down the pagoda's crumbling walls! The roar of the guns drove students into villages and towns, huts and caves, fields and streets. Through their own hunger and suffering they discovered their fellow citizens for the first time. In consequence, pride melts away, humility opens their minds to learn, shame calls them to identify with the common people. Professors and students now frankly confess they have to revise their ideas about their own country and its population.

Fourth, the program has brought Chinese students and the world student community very close to each other. According to the traditional teaching of Mencius, scholars should starve to death rather than eat food that has been thrown to them. But the spirit in which funds have been raised among students and friends abroad, and the way they are handled, express so much genuine goodwill and love that Chinese students enter into the world family of students, disarmed of suspicion and truly grateful. As token affirmation of solidarity they raise annually a small sum of money—not gathered without hardship—as a gift to students suffering elsewhere in the world.

Fifth, student relief is adminstered in China without any discrimination as to religion, sex or politics, yet the very fact of Christian support and leadership provides significant opportunity for student evangelism. Relief is administered locally through the voluntary service of student YMCA and YWCA secretaries, who maintain close personal contact with students. Student centers are used for religious activities and church leaders play an important part in the program. For Chinese students the last ten years have seen accelerated spiritual reorientation. If the church should miss this opportunity the entire strength and place of Christianity in China in the next few decades will be affected. Let the whole World Student Christian Federation pray with the Chinese SCM that as students leave their "ivory pagoda" and discard old feudal fetters their search for reality may finally lead them to Christ.

Finally, a word about today. The return of ninety thousand students to their old surroundings after a trek of fifteen hundred miles from West China involved adventure for some, but tragedy for others. It was good to be back, in spite of severe shortages—in accommodation, food and clothing—and the threat of tuberculosis. Student needs have if anything increased. For Christians there is much at stake in the whole situation. Can our faith afford not to express itself in deeds of love? Can love afford to be blind to the opportunity of giving a cup of cold water to these brothers and sisters for whom Christ gave even himself?

THE TASK OF THE CHURCH IN ASIA (1949)

When Christianity was introduced to Asia it came face to face with very ancient civilizations, all with highly developed religious and ethical systems and indigenous social institutions. For many years Western missionaries could not convert a single Asian to the Christian faith; they met suspicion, ridicule, even persecution. To be able to speak of the church in Asia now is nothing short of a miracle. We cannot afford to take this mighty act of God for granted.

There are thousands of Asian Christians today who in their own way can say why they believe in Christ. We are not talking of occasional mission stations but churches, universities, schools and hospitals all over the continent, maintaining a close contact with the people themselves. Only a few decades ago Chinese Christians would say that they were members of the Norwegian Lutheran Mission or the American Baptist Mission South (although I presume they knew nothing about the American Civil War). Now they are more likely to say with some pride that they are members of the United Church of Christ in China or of the Holy Catholic Church of China (the Chinese counterpart of the Anglican Church). The churches have given them support, and Christians in turn have sacrificed themselves for the churches, especially since the Sino-Japanese war. So the churches have become their own. There is also the fact of the growth of Asian leadership. Before the Sino-Japanese war the Chinese Anglican Church had fifteen bishops; seven died during the war, an extremely heavy loss. Now, three years after the war, we have twenty-three bishops of whom twelve are Chinese and eleven Western.

While it is essential that we maintain our continuity and our unity with Christ's church in the whole world, Christians in Asia are also determined not to create a mere replica of the church in the West. Consciousness of freedom in the Holy Spirit makes us bold to enter into new experiments — we bring to God, in ways that are natural to us, our prayers and praise, life, work, art and thought.

There are schemes for church union in India and Ceylon. Bishops from China asked the Lambeth Conference to consider the question of the ordination of women to the priesthood. It is interesting to note that this proposal came from China, where for thousands of years women have been considered inferior to men; opposition to it comes mainly from the West, where equality of men and women is a familiar concept.

As yet the church in Asia is still some distance from the creation of its own identity. But there is a growing feeling with regard to theology, worship, art and church life, that if our job is merely to imitate then we are still slaves. We shall be free only if we allow the Holy Spirit to work upon us creatively. This does not mean that Western missionaries must therefore leave the church alone. They are indispensable in helping the church in Asia to grow and find itself.

While relying for the present on Christians in the West for spiritual and material resources and personnel, the church is already conscious of its own missionary vocation. Work has begun among the aborigines in southwest China, and also in northwest China, aimed at the reconversion of an area where the first mission to China, made by the Nestorian Christians, flourished for over two hundred years.

But—a word of caution—let us not romanticize the church in Asia and its achievements. Internally it is weak and cold in many parts, and externally it has barely touched the problems and population of the continent. The most we can claim is that today the foundation has been laid for the building itself. God has given us the miracle of the church in Asia as a sign that the gospel is indeed meant for that part of the world.

Students in the West may say that since things seem to be going well in Asia there is no call to them to be missionaries there. But this is to misread God's sign. God led Peter to come down from the rooftop and showed him how the Holy Spirit descended upon Cornelius and his company just as naturally as upon the Christians in Jerusalem. Peter was helped to see the power of the gospel "unto salvation to everyone" (Rom 1:16); he went on to evangelize the Gentiles even more vigorously.

If Nestorian Christianity could be uprooted after being established in China for over two hundred years, how can we be sure that the church is going to survive the present revolution? Our survival—indeed our revival—depends on the church's striving to be true to its calling as the church. As soon as we begin to be opportunist, we slip into being a mere human society, unable to survive the world.

A revolution is a fever in society, not the disease itself but the result. No matter how we may dislike its terror we must learn to recognize it, once it happens, as an inevitable passing phase. It happens only because of the decadence and evil of the status quo that lags behind the changes demanded by justice. The church cannot easily endorse the romance, the optimism, the method and the tendency to depreciate historic values and cultures in revolution. But it can resist being drawn into the status quo as its partner in decadence.

There is, admittedly, real danger of loss of initiative in our tension with communism. It would be easy for the church to commit itself either to the Communist or to the anti-Communist position. But in either case the church would neglect its obedience to the Holy Spirit—the living Lord in every particular situation—our only guarantee of real freedom. If we make an outright commitment to communism we may succeed in avoiding our responsibility for making frequent moral decisions, but we bar the working of the Spirit in us and through us. Anti-communism, like communism itself, can be made into a religion if it becomes the yardstick of judgment. So then

I must continue to try to judge everything on its merit. In this way I shall be in less danger of obstructing the guiding light of the Holy Spirit. Sincerely but experimentally I must give any act or policy of any person or group, in any moment, in any place or country the benefit of proving its own worth, apart from any pre-judgment that I may borrow from elsewhere. I am sure that this spirit of inquiry represents the attitude of many Christians in Asia.

In China the Communists permit Christian groups to carry on. Two of our thirteen Christian universities are now functioning in Communist areas, reportedly much as usual. The Communists have not substantially interfered in policy or administration. They have even invited the missionaries to stay on. But we do not know what tomorrow will bring. We have no reason, however, to be pessimistic — in any case we have no right to expect kindness from political authorities. We can be sure that Christ was thinking of circumstances such as our own when he said, "Blessed are they that have been persecuted for righteousness' sake.... Rejoice and be exceeding glad" (Mt 5:10; Lk 6:23). But we have no reason to be optimistic either, for the church is under strong but subtle temptation to deny itself: in the last twenty years by identifying too closely with the Nationalist regime, and today by idealizing the new regime. Steering between easy pessimism and easy optimism the church must strive to be itself and to carry on its witness, perpetually in tension with the world.

A revolutionary situation reminds us of the prodigal son, leaving his father's home with dreams of freedom and adventure; the promise of the gospel may look very pale in comparison. Because the non-Christian world, imbued with revolutionary sentiment, is skeptical of Christianity, we are tempted to revise our beliefs in the hope that they may conform to the fashion for optimism. But this opportunistic revision is a fatal compromise. If, rather, we strengthen our evangelistic purpose, we shall be ready to receive with open arms the many tired revolutionaries when post-revolutionary despair sets in. In his suffering the prodigal son will say at last, "I will arise now and go to my father" (Lk 15:14). The church can then offer him hope and a task to pursue.

During the war between the Nationalists and the Communists, the wife and children of General Chu Teh, the Communist commander-in-chief, were captured and beheaded on the order of Generalissimo Chiang Kai-shek. Yet in 1937, as soon as Japan attacked China, General Chu was among the first to send a telegram to Chiang pledging support and obedience to him as national resistance leader. While many of Chiang's own officers surrendered to the enemy and became collaborators, the Communist leaders fought bravely, not one going over to the enemy. General Chu's magnanimity and forgiving spirit challenged many of our student friends to wonder whether there was anything comparable in Christianity's talk of forgiveness. His action as a Communist posed a real temptation to Christians.

Yet however morally glorious a person is, that achievement is still very miserable when set against the criterion of the kingdom. No matter how a child of God fails in forgiveness, that person has a status in the grace of God and in the church of Christ that no human moral excellence can be compared with. The forgiveness between the two generals was without repentance before God, dictated only by expediency. It has nothing in common with forgiveness between Christians, through common acceptance of the forgiving love of God. Eight years later the generals were at war again because this time political expediency, in the name of history, made a different demand.

Communism challenges Christians either to produce the "real stuff" or to give up entirely. Seeing the challenge we see also its inadequacy in being a part of humanity's disorder rather than God's design. The monotonous pattern of history remains, revolution turning into counterrevolution and thesis into antithesis. Only the gospel of Christ gives the world deliverance from this pattern, and a vision in which history (as we have known it) gives way to a new beginning.

Throughout China and Asia there is suffering. People need food, clothes and shelter, all very legitimate needs. Naturally the church wants to relieve this suffering, enabling people to make something of their lives. Jesus fed the five thousand (many of whom could not have heard what he said, or perhaps were only there out of curiosity) just because they were hungry. We too ought to relieve suffering even if there is no hope of conversion. Otherwise evangelism may lead us back to the old unhappy pattern of "rice Christians." Even so, we ought not to condemn a "rice Christian," because the instinct for self-preservation and care for loved ones must drive a person to obtain food under whatever circumstance. Rather than making relief conditional on belief, the church should look into the social system that produces so much hunger.

The greatest temptation to a hungry person in China is to believe that men and women live by bread alone and to blame the environment for all sins committed. This attitude debases human life and encourages the notion that the perfect society may be achieved through material rearrangement. How is the church to bear witness in that situation? Preaching is not enough. Something must be done about the problems of material living. In this way we show the world we understand the importance of bread in people's lives. Only then may we proclaim with authority our point of departure—that we do not "live by bread alone, but by every word that proceedeth out of the mouth of God" (Mt 4:4).

Those Christians in the West who are disillusioned by the abuse of science and technology may think that the kind of feudal agricultural setup that still persists in the East should be maintained. I question if this view—a form of despair—is theologically legitimate. I suspect that it partly reflects the frustration of a decadent culture that refuses to die. While not making false gods of science, Christians must adopt a constructive attitude toward the present industrial movement in Asia. A machine embodies raw material, dug out of the good earth, worked on by mental and manual labor made possible through a complex historical and social network of experience and organization; potentially its use may call forth a larger portion of God's gift to humankind. As matter through which God's grace is made known, it is in an important sense a sacrament. As such Christians in Asia welcome it.

THE CRY FOR BREAD (1980)

There are some thought-provoking aspects to Luke's wonderful story of the feeding of the five thousand (Lk 9:12-17). The disciples, for instance, thought that Christ's work was just to talk about the kingdom—feeding the multitude was none of his business, and none of theirs either. They asked him to send the crowd away to find food on their own. But Christ said, "Give ye them to eat." The disciples were advocating that each look out for himself or herself. Put into practice, as indeed it has been in China, this policy inevitably results in the domination of the powerful over their victims, the common people. It ends up in full-fledged capitalism, defined by John Maynard Keynes as "the extraordinary belief that the nastiest of men for the nastiest of motives will somehow work for the benefit of us all"—and we know it has not worked to that end.

In order to feed the people Christ instructed the disciples to divide the multitude into groups of roughly fifty people; each group was to be seated rather than walking about in disorder. Since it was Christ's command, I suppose it would not be called regimentation or curtailment of individual freedom. It is rather discouragement of individualism, together with a certain amount of program planning and organization. From our experience in China we know that this is necessary.

Christ blessed the food and gave it to the disciples to set before the multitude. My guess is that among the crowd there were all sorts of views and opinions concerning the person of Christ. But Christ respected everyone there. His care was for the whole multitude—all humanity—not just his own friends. God is so great that it would not be true to his nature to confine his love only to those who profess his name. I do not even think he minds that there are those who for some reason cannot acknowledge him, but rather deny his name.

There was no shortage of food. Everybody could eat his or her fill. And that is an important part of the meaning of the word, *liberation*. When I say China is a liberated country, I have in mind the fact that through planning and organization we are able to feed almost one-quarter of humanity with the food produced on only one seventh of the world's arable land. It may not be comparable to Christ's miracle, but it is an achievement for which we want to thank God.

Twelve baskets of food were left over, but we do not know what happened to them. Where did they go? Thrown away? Left to be devoured by animals? Sold to the best bidders, who hoarded the food until there was a shortage and then sold it, so that the rich got richer and the poor poorer? Usually the Christian message is in what the Bible says, but sometimes it is in what is left out. There may be a still small voice in biblical silence. The silence of Luke's gospel at this point perhaps leads us to see that the problem was not really solved by a single feeding of five thousand people. What can twelve baskets of food do to relieve five thousand—let alone five million—poor people of the world of their hunger? This biblical silence symbolizes unfinished responsibility and the unhelpfulness of mere philanthropy in a world that is producing poverty and hunger much faster than philanthropists can keep up with.

The good earth can produce enough for everybody but not enough for everybody's greed. How are we to distribute wealth and opportunities more justly? That is the question raised in Luke's story. When I was in primary school in Shanghai, I knew something of how its wealthy lived. In Yangzhou, some miles away, there were others so poor that whenever there was a drought—and that was often—men and women had to come to Shanghai, barefooted and in rags, to seek work. Bony and lifeless, their very look was frightening to me. They did not expect wages—just food for survival—and they would work. But many could find neither food nor work. They became beggars, sometimes dying on the street, hungry and cold. Girls were sold into prostitution. Boys considered themselves lucky to be apprenticed to barbers. These were the downtrodden, and they constituted the majority of our people.

In 1977 I visited that area. There are no extortionate landlords anymore. There is hydraulic irrigation, and people are living in brick, not mud, houses. Men and women study from kindergarten to university or work in factories or on farms. Many women factory workers wear leather shoes and have watches on their wrists. Some wear woolen trousers and dacron shirts, with pens in their pockets. Hearing their laughter, I was almost in tears, thinking of the plight of their forebears. I longed to tell the young people there what I had seen so they would not forget the past.

In China change has been brought about through social upheaval—the ownership of the means of production has passed from a small section of our population to the mass of the people. That is liberation in the true sense of the word because our people have gained freedom, not lost it, and are now working through organized efforts for greater freedom for themselves and for future generations.

Christians have good reason to be concerned with the question of material distribution. After Christ's resurrection he walked with two disciples on the way to Emmaus. It was only when he took bread and blessed it and gave it to them that their eyes were opened and they knew him to be Christ. Could we not say then that the distribution of bread to humanity has something of the sacrament in it? The way wealth and opportunities are distributed—the way that society is organized—does have a lot to do with the manifestation of Jesus Christ to women and men.

As Christians we insist that God is both loving and almighty, in spite of evil and suffering around us. That is demanding a lot of believers. People find it hard to respond to this conception of God; instead they are attracted to the death-of-God hypothesis. The death of God as a theological fad lasted a short time, but as a working philosophy of life it is spreading. As a Jewish rabbi puts it:

When I say we live in the time of the death of God, I mean that the thread of uniting God and humanity, heaven and earth, has been broken. We stand in a cold, silent, unfeeling cosmos, unaided by any purposeful power beyond our own resources. After Auschwitz, what else can a Jew say about God?

Here in a naked way we see how social, economic and political injustice eats away at faith in a God who is at once almighty and loving. The achievement of a healthier social system and a fairer distribution of the world's goods, with all the prosperity, peace, joy and progress it entails, will enable men and women to see some reasonableness in our Christian conception of God as almighty creator, and to find cause for thanksgiving.

The incarnation has surely made more of an impact on humanity than the fall of Adam. Human solidarity with Christ is more universal, more powerful than solidarity with Adam through sin. We believe in the universality of divine grace. We look at the world in the splendor of the ascended Christ. What human beings do to promote community and to make love more possible and more available to the masses of our people is in consonance with God's work of creation, redemption and sanctification. As Creator, Christ and Spirit, God sparks the image of the loving community. Humanity, created in that image, is moving toward its recovery: Women and men, as God's creation, will be set free from bondage and obtain their glorious "liberty of the children of God." This is how we look at the world and at history, at human aspirations, movement and struggle. And this is a source of our optimism and thanksgiving.

The feeding of the five thousand takes us, then, to an entirely different world—a community of sharing, where life is so organized that men and women can be brothers and sisters to one another. The vision of this coming world sustains us daily in the community of faith, hope and love. For millions today, "Give us this day our daily bread," is not a routine prayer but a desperate cry. We strive to be worthy instruments of the coming reign of God on earth, where this cry will be heard no more.

THE SINNED AGAINST (1979)

During the last thirty years I have had ample evidence to confirm the Christian understanding of each human person as sinner, standing in need of Christ's salvation. For example, I have been moved by many revolutionaries, men and women, who have dedicated themselves to making China a more livable place for their people. They are very sensitive to their own shortcomings and are extremely demanding in self-criticism and self-reform. Yet they would readily agree with Paul that the good they want to do they fall short of, and the evil they do not want to do they do in spite of themselves. If these people, who set such high personal standards, feel that way, then Christians must not suppose that the message of Christ's redemption and of the sanctification of the Holy Spirit is now suddenly irrelevant. If Christ's message is not taken to heart then there are faults in the transmitter rather than in the message itself.

What *is* new to many Chinese Christians is the awareness that people are not only sinners but are also sinned against. The task of evangelism is not only to convince persons of their sin but to stand alongside those who are sinned against in our society. To dwell on sin is not evangelism proper; it does not necessarily move a person to repentance and to the acceptance of Christ as savior. In line with his chauvinism and snobbery, Jonah found it satisfying to pronounce women and men sinners, but his message was one of doom, not compassion and salvation.

In the gospels we often find comments on the compassion of Jesus for others. What we see is not just pity, not just almsgiving or condescension, but identification with the weak and poor and hungry, with those deeply hurt by an unjust system, who as "non-persons" are alienated, dehumanized and marginalized—in short, those who have been badly sinned against. With this understanding we hear Chinese revolutionaries speak of our people's suffering under the oppression of the "three mountains" of imperialism, bureaucratic capitalism and feudalism. Here Christians see eye to eye with other Chinese. This common language enables the evangelist to speak as one with the people, not as an outsider. The Christian speaks free of the misanthropy of Jonah who abhorred the people to whom he was sent.

Evangelism, it is said, is one beggar telling another where to find bread. True, but that is not all. Beggars need to know that their hunger and disease, their sleeping on sidewalks, their infant mortality, unemployment and begging are not God's will, but result from greed on the part of a few and from their own passivity. It is when men and women who are sinned against become our concern that God can put in our mouths the word that witnesses to Christ, the saver of sinners.

In China we have come to realize how lacking we really were in true love for our people. It is not enough to smile and be nice to them. It is to put ourselves in their position, to understand the justice of their cause, to be fellow fighters with them. It is to see how all their revolutionary strivings—industrial, agricultural, educational and artistic—could achieve a deeper grounding and bear better fruit if consciously related to the purposes of God and to the spiritual resources at the base of the whole universe. Love does mean all of this.

For Jonah news that "yet forty days and all Nineveh shall be destroyed" (Jon 3:4) overcame all his reluctance. He had no concern for the people's liberation. But those who evangelize in the spirit of Christ dare not pronounce a message of doom unless they are sure the message is of God and the telling of it breaks their own hearts. Where love exists evangelism happens.

The sinned against of the world are so helpless and loveless that they must form themselves into groups, collectives, fellowships. The evils of fascist and semi-fascist groups should not lead theologians to condemn *all* human collectives. Even those collectives that are not Christian can often be vehicles of the grace of God. To me, an incompletely Christianized intellectual with a sprinkling of traditional Confucianist elitism, it was quite a pilgrimage to come to realize the spiritual potential of human social organization. There is an inspiration in human fellowship enabling comrades to rise to levels unattainable by mere individuals. Common purpose and common enthusiasm transforms and uplifts. The risen Christ urged his friends not to disperse but to stick together in Jerusalem in prayer and expectation; that was the condition for the coming of the Holy Spirit. More and more Christians realize now that the transcendent is encountered not so much "out there" as within the interpersonal relationships of finite beings. We open ourselves to the sacred and to encountering God as we dive into the depths of human relations, no matter how secular they seem.

5

SPIRITUALITY AND STRUGGLE

In a sermon to students at the opening of the 1955 autumn term at the interdenominational Nanjing Theological College, K. H. Ting drew on the story of Jacob at Peniel, wrestling with God's angel, to talk about the prayer life of the students. A brief mention of anti-imperialism is the only break in the spiritual calm of this talk, but it reminds us that 1955 was a period of international storms. In the Western world "McCarthyism," a virulent form of anti-communism, was in the air. Americans were not allowed to travel to China, where a "godless" regime was said to be wiping out all religion. John Foster Dulles, the Secretary of State of the United States, was pursuing a "containment policy" to stop the Chinese "red menace," a policy that included confrontation in Korea, military presence in the Taiwan Straits and on Taiwan, struggle over the offshore islands of Quemoy and Matsu, and the beginnings of American involvement in Vietnam. In the midst of these raging international conflicts K. H. Ting, at a small theological college on the Yangtze River, was serenely discussing with students the problems of their spiritual life.

It is from this sermon that the first selection, "Wrestling With God" is taken. The sermon was published in Chinese in the *Nanjing Union Seminary Journal* in November 1955. This excerpt is from an unpublished translation prepared for this book by Ms. Cheng Musheng of Qinghua University, Beijing, who also translated the following two selections.

"The Journey of the Magi" and "God's Love of Life" are both from sermons delivered at Nanjing Theological College in 1984. The texts were provided by Ting in Chinese. These sermons again convey K. H. Ting's emphasis on the simplicity and directness of the gospel.

The final two articles are from speeches given by Ting in English while travelling as an official representative of the Chinese church. In "The Reality of the Resurrection," from an address given at the Lambeth Palace Chapel in England in 1982, he speaks about the new life that has come to the Chinese church after the shocks of socialist revolution and the attacks during the Cultural Revolution. Part of their new life as Christians is new solidarity with the Chinese people as a whole. A sermon in the Sydney Cathedral in Australia in 1984 is the source of "Christian Selfhood."

WRESTLING WITH GOD (1955)

From childhood Jacob thought only of himself; several times he wronged others. When his twin and elder brother, Esau, returned from the fields, completely tired out, Jacob seized the opportunity to cheat him of his birthright as the firstborn, in exchange for a bowl of lentil pottage. Pretending to be Esau, Jacob tricked his father, in his old age, into giving him the blessing that should rightfully have gone to the eldest son. Jacob employed methods "smarter" than those of his father-in-law to make his own flock of sheep multiply and grow fat, while the other's flock decreased in numbers and grew thin. Jacob was in truth a selfish man, looking after his own interests and "climbing up" in life. In a very slippery and skillful manner he caused others to suffer loss for his own gain.

The root meaning of *Jacob* is "grasp," and this was precisely Jacob's attitude to life. Even at birth he grabbed the heel of Esau, his brother. "Grasp" was Jacob's principle in dealing with others.

There are people today whose approach to life is to grasp everything possible; they grasp at fame, fortune, position, power. Some of them say, "Everyone for himself and the devil take the hindmost." This is going one step further than Jacob. Some go so far as to bring this outlook on life into the church, trying to grasp as much as possible for themselves while ostensibly engaged in spiritual work.

Jacob had been away from his home village for many years; he was about to return and would see Esau the next day. Would Esau treat Jacob as a younger brother or as an enemy? Jacob could not tell; he knew only that Esau had sent out a force four hundred strong to meet him. But Jacob was still the same old clever Jacob. To prepare for any eventuality, he divided his people and his flocks into two groups so that one at least could escape if Esau should attack. In addition, he prayed, "Save me, I pray, from my brother Esau." He showed absolutely no repentance for his wrongdoing against God and Esau twenty years before. Left on his own at Peniel, Jacob now had an opportunity to come face to face with God as he wrestled with an angel—a most singular experience. The bible narrative is simple, but its meaning is not something we can easily elaborate on.

Not long after leaving home twenty years earlier, Jacob had had a dream at Bethel in which he saw a ladder, the bottom resting on the ground, and the top pointing to heaven; angels of God were going up and down (Gn 28:10-17). Bethel represents the sweetest spiritual communion, a closeness with God that knows no barriers, the peak of perfection. Bethel was both "God's palace and the gateway to heaven." At Peniel, however, Jacob had a very different experience. There he met not the sweet acceptance of God, but conflict, struggle and wrestling with God.

First Bethel, then Peniel—what law is at work here? Facing God, should we not first deal with sin at Peniel before we cross the Jordan and enter Bethel to enjoy forever God's presence, grace and love? According to common sense, should not God give us first the bitter and then the sweet? Why is it the other way around here? We can see that although Bethel was good, it did not bring about any great change in Jacob, whereas Peniel did. After Peniel he was no longer called Jacob, but Israel—the man who wrestled with God.

As Christians we like the concept of Bethel, but not that of Peniel; we like God to make us promises but are not willing to face a God who is coming to wrestle with us, to wound our self-assurance and pride. In effect, our idea of what is good and what is bad, what is true and what is false, what is the power of God, what is the expression of our sin—these are all decided by the deep-rooted nature of Jacob within our hearts.

I hope you will see here a ladder leading to heaven, and angels going up and down bringing nourishment from above. In the meantime we must not avoid Peniel. No matter what, the opponent we are wrestling with is none other than the Lord who will on no account harm us. We could close the gate [of the seminary] so that you are isolated from the outside world; we could pursue the sweet "life on the mountain." But in that case you would surely become useless to the church. Christians who love the truth must never fear the necessary wrestling we meet with in ideology and in spiritual life. Only through such struggle can we better understand the Lord, the truth and ourselves. The unity of Christians in loving God, in loving the people, our country and the church, will be made plain. Without Peniel we would still be Jacob, not really understanding Bethel.

True prayer has an element in it of wrestling with God. Unfortunately, much of our prayer is merely a piling up of cliches. But if what we ask for is in complete accord with God's nature, we can ask bravely. The Holy Spirit will come to help us pray. God will surely answer such prayers, so we must dare to give thanks even before they are answered, just as Christ lifted his eyes to heaven while Lazarus was still in the grave: "I thank you, Father, that you listen to me" (Jn 11:41).

We often see another kind of prayer: The mother of James and John asked the Lord to let her two sons sit at his right and his left. This request was for herself, a prayer to "grasp" something, a prayer in one's own interests. It was the prayer of Jacob before the experience at Peniel. The dream at Bethel occurred after the sun had gone down (Gn 28:11). After Jacob wrestled with God at Peniel, the dawn came (Gn 32:31). Peniel does not represent suffering or the blackness of night; it brings forth the glory of God's face and the joy of daytime.

As he wrestled Jacob asked his opponent to bless him and to tell him his name. God agreed to the first request, giving him his blessing, but not to the second, asking "Why do you want to know my name?" If people are interested only in God's name, their spiritual experience in wrestling with

God will be fruitless; it will lead to their forgetting God's blessing and may even produce sectarian infighting. This would be making the important trivial, and the trivial important.

In this seminary anti-imperialism and patriotism are the foundation of the unity we find in our basic faith. Differences exist, it is true, but after all they are of secondary importance. The main thing is that this seminary is your Bethel, God's palace. It is also your Peniel where you can see God's face. We must remember that we have only one Lord, who bestows blessings on us all. We need not ask if a person belongs to Paul, or to Apollo, and so on. We need only ask if God has indeed blessed this person.

THE JOURNEY OF THE MAGI (1984)

> I roamed till peace was to my mind restored.
> The pillar of the earth I stayed beside;
> The way was long, and winding far and wide.
> (Li Sao [*The Lament*], by Qu Yuan, 340-278 B.C.E.)

Human life has commonly been considered a journey. Abraham, a seeker, set out without knowing his destination. The Israelites have long been a wandering people; they went to Egypt, and several generations later wandered in the wilderness for forty years. Even after settling down on the eastern shore of the Mediterranean Sea, they continued to move and wander.

The church has a tradition of praying for its dead. One of our Chinese liturgical texts for the Lord's supper retains the prayer handed down from the early church: "Let them advance eternally in respecting and loving the Lord, and in serving the Lord." This enlarges our understanding of the church to include all Christians who have gone before in history; we are reminded that we are part of a great journey.

When Christ was born a small group of learned travellers came from the East. We do not know exactly how many or which country they came from, but we can be sure they were a group of seekers. They were not satisfied with the status quo and did not want a quiet, comfortable life of leisure. They had an impulse to set out in search of something higher to worship and a more meaningful life.

We can be sure they had fervor, for without it they would not have been able to make a single stride forward in their search. Einstein said, "I never considered leisure and happiness as the goal of life—such ethics I call the ideals of the pigsty." I hope we will not regard the pigsty as a beautiful place; we must always have ideals and fervor, our hearts burning for truth, goodness, beauty, and faith, hope and love. Our Lord was once grieved and disappointed at the apathy he found. He said: "We played wedding music for you, but you would not dance! We sang funeral songs, but you would not weep" (Mt 11:17). Then there were people like Nicodemus, Gamaliel and the rich young ruler, willing to sit and discuss the road to be taken but with no desire to get up and be off. But others were full of fervor. Peter once jumped into the water upon seeing Jesus, and he cursed himself upon hearing the cock crow; Zacchaeus climbed up into a tree to see Jesus and was willing to repay his debts several times over.

Obviously we cannot set rules for worship. People have the right to worship according to their own understanding. Among those who probably worshipped differently were those learned travellers from the East. According to our standards their theological understanding was insufficient and incomplete. Christ, however, accepted their gifts; the Bible records their story; and churches down through the centuries have praised them. This tells us that for a growing enrichment of worship and understanding of Christ the church must adhere to the essential principles of inclusiveness and broadmindedness.

At first the travellers from the East did not see through Herod's plot. They thought Herod really wanted to worship Christ and were ready to report to Herod the whereabouts of the baby once they had found him. After worshipping Christ, however, they were more sensitive to God's righteousness; their moral character strengthened. They resolutely "returned to their own country by another road" (Mt 2:12). They did not—in order to curry favor with Herod—ignore the inspiration they had received from the Holy Spirit through worship. Obeying the dictates of God, they took a different road home. Through worship we too will take a new road, no longer serving but subverting Herod.

GOD'S LOVE OF LIFE (1984)

I am sure you all remember the story of the two women who, only a few days apart, each gave birth to a son—one boy lived, the other died. Which woman was the mother of the live baby? Only the two women themselves knew. Solomon offered to cut the live baby in half with a sword and give one half to each woman. On hearing this the two women had entirely different reactions: The dead baby's mother, filled with jealousy, was quite satisfied to have the baby killed and expressed her approval of Solomon's decision. The real mother, however, had an entirely different attitude—she loved her child and wanted it to live. With life there would be hope for the future. As to whether she could get the child back, that could be decided later. She immediately said that the child must live at any price—let the other woman have him.

So we see that the heart of one woman was filled with jealousy, which made her cruel and hate life. The other mother was entirely different— her heart was filled with love, love for the child and love of life. She was willing to be treated wrongly for a time because her love gave her hope, as well as faith that in the end right would triumph over wrong, truth over falsehood, life over death.

This story came back to me recently when everyone was discussing the question of Britain's planned restoration of Hong Kong to China in 1997. There is a guarantee from both sides of continuing prosperity and stability in the territory. But there are some who feel this agreement endangers their private interests, and so they are against Hong Kong returning to the bosom of the motherland; they want to take so-called "hard-line measures" against China, even if this should cause havoc in Hong Kong and bring good to nobody. Doesn't this bring to mind the cruel, jealous mother in the biblical story?

Turning from Hong Kong to Nanjing and our own school, we find relevance in this story again. Can we allow jealousy, hatred and disparagement of others to exist in our life together? Absolutely not. The worst thing is to tear others down in order to achieve personal goals. What we need is a close relationship with mutual love and consideration, so that we become true brothers and sisters.

Now let us return to the good mother in the biblical story. In her response we can see a reflection of the nature of God's love, which includes protection of life. So that people should not lose life but gain it God went willingly to the sacrifice; the word became flesh and dwelt among us; Christ gave up his life. Our understanding of God's love is still very rudimentary. I hope that through more spiritual nurturing, more bible study, more thinking about God, and more communication, we will receive revelation and arrive at a richer understanding of God's love.

THE REALITY OF RESURRECTION (1982)

The most precious thing that has come out of our experience of the last thirty years is faith in the risen Christ. This does not mean that in China we have some new circumstantial evidence for the empty tomb. It simply means that when we review what China as a nation, or Chinese Christians as a church, have gone through, *resurrection* is the word that best describes it. Our experience of dying and rising up again—in individual lives, in national life and in the life of the church—convinces us that resurrection from the dead is the law by which God carries on the work of creation, redemption and sanctification; it is the principle by which the whole universe is sustained and governed. Many of us are enabled to shed our foolishness and slowness of heart when we see that it was necessary and natural that Christ should suffer before entering his glory. Thus we have appropriated for ourselves something of the mystery of the risen Lord, and we realize his presence and nearness more surely and more intimately.

In 1949, at the time of liberation, many feared the loss of so much that was dear to us as Christians, only to find later that these things were mostly excess baggage. But it was during the Cultural Revolution, which turned out to be quite anti-cultural and not much of a revolution either, that the Chinese people really suffered, and we Christians suffered with them. We felt the gospel to be something precious, but the Red Guards and the so-called rebels thought of it as nothing but a poisonous weed. We had no means of communicating our faith or of answering the attacks in the big-character posters. Not a single church remained open. No government organ was left to protect us from lawlessness. We had no rebel group of our own to support us, nor any bandwagon to ride on. We were lucky if we could just worship in a small group in someone's home. We were very weak indeed—a little flock. By all human reckoning Christianity, perhaps for the fourth time in Chinese history, was again breathing its last.

But as Paul put it, what you sow does not come to life unless it dies. What is sown is perishable, what is raised is imperishable; it is sown in dishonor, it is raised in glory; it is sown in weakness, it is raised in power. After having lost so much, we find there are more Christians in China than ever before, and more dedicated too. And because we have been party to a common suffering, we are no longer so alienated from the Chinese people, but have a much better relationship with them than in the past.

Christians have tried so often to wrap up the remains of Jesus Christ with the cloth we bring to his grave. Others have tried to seal Christ up in the tomb with big, heavy stones. But the living Christ himself cannot be bound or enclosed. He breaks out of any fabricated tomb.

The resurrection truth tells us that the meek are to inherit the earth. I am always reminded of Lao-tse's words about water:

> What is of all things most yielding
> Can overwhelm that which is most hard.
> Being substanceless, it can enter in even where there is no
> crevice.
> That is how I know the value of action which is actionless.
> But that there can be teaching without words,
> Value in action which is actionless,
> Few indeed can understand (*Tao te ching,* chap. 43).

That a person who has died has come to life again is in all common sense an absurd claim. Yet almost a fourth of humankind is more or less committed to the resurrection story of Jesus. This is because as a message of hope it touches the chord in the hearts of so many in the world who simply refuse to accept defeat, humiliation, suffering, darkness and death as having the ultimate say. In the midst of all vicissitudes they grasp this message as the key to comprehend history and reality. It gives them comfort and confidence and strength, and restores their faith in the value of truth, goodness and beauty.

CHRISTIAN SELFHOOD (1984)

We are not three wise men from the East, but eleven not-so-wise people from the North—seven men and four women whose ages range roughly from thirty to seventy. Four of us are from Shanghai, three from Nanjing, one each from Guangzhou, Chengdu, Fuzhou and Beijing. In making this visit we feel we are encircled by the loving care of God at every step, supported by the prayers of our fellow Christians in China and warmly received by the Christians of Australia.

In the second and third chapters of Revelation the risen Christ delivers through John a separate message to each of the seven churches of Ephesus, Smyrna, Pergamum, Thyatira, Sardis, Philadelphia and Laodicea. The individual messages differ because each of the seven churches differs from the rest — in cultural milieu, in problems faced, in strengths and weaknesses. The purpose is not to impose the same pattern on all the churches. Yet all seven messages have the same ending: "He who has an ear, let him hear what the Spirit says to the churches." Each individual message is for Christians everywhere to hear. In this sort of context we can understand why a delegation from the Australian Council of Churches went to China in 1982, and why the eleven of us are here now.

The principle of particularity — or individuality, locality, nationality — belongs very much to the New Testament concept of the church. There is a moment in history when each church must discover its own people and cease to remain a replica of a church elsewhere. We need to be ourselves. Two years ago in Hong Kong the Archbishop of Canterbury said that when Christians in England ended the tutelage of Rome and formed themselves into an independent church, they too established a Three-Self Movement. Since we came to Australia we have learned that the Church of England in Australia has recently changed its name to the Anglican Church of Australia. So you are moving in the same direction, and we feel supported.

We thank God and the Australian churches for all the good things that missionaries from this land did in China. Their deeds of love continue to bear fruits acceptable to God. We know that discerning missionaries worked hard to make themselves dispensable. So we want them to know that the growth of a self-governing, self-supporting and self-propagating church in China is in a real sense their success and their glory, and not their loss or failure.

But at the same time, while rooted in Chinese soil, our selfhood must also be related to the church universal as one of its parts. We cannot afford to remain ignorant of what the Holy Spirit says to other churches. When we say Three-Self, self-isolation must not be one of them, nor self-sufficiency. So we have come here, as it were, to compare notes, and this is desirable from time to time.

We have come to realize that between alpha and omega there is not one straight line but many curves and zigzags. Catastrophe and suffering are but the mother's birthpangs. "When a woman is in travail she has sorrow, because her hour has come; but when she is delivered of her child, she no longer remembers the anguish, for joy that a child is born into the world" (Jn 16:21). This, to us, is history. We know God is not a severe taskmaster.

As Hosea tells us, he leads us with cords of compassion and bands of love; he becomes to us as one who eases the yoke on our jaws, who bends down to us and feeds us. The root attribute of God is not his omnipotence or his omniscience or his self-existence, but his love. Love is not just an attribute of God, but is God. The knowledge that God is one who loves with the kind of love we see in Jesus Christ crowns and corrects whatever else may be said about God. Love is creative and seeks the very best. Everything that is truly good will not be lost but will be preserved and transformed for the coming kingdom in which love will be supreme. That is essentially what we mean when we say God is sovereign.

6

THE TASK OF EVANGELISM

"Why Be a Minister?" is from a 1954 article in the *Nanjing Union Seminary Journal*. Yao Niangeng, of the Dalien Foreign Languages Institute, prepared the translation from which the excerpts here are taken. In Chinese the term *preacher* is a parallel term for clergyperson, priest, or minister, any of which could be used in the question asked here—"Why still be a preacher?" "Why still be a priest?" This essay is one of the few places where Ting speaks of his feelings, of loneliness and depression, and also of joy. The quotation "One who goes on tolling the bell as long as he is a monk," comes from a Buddhist context and is an aphorism about going through the motions even though one's original spirit of commitment is lost. This article speaks eloquently of the purifying task that is necessary in the church in order for evangelism to be possible.

A three-part article, "Spreading the Gospel and Establishing the Body," published in the weekly *Tian Feng* church journal in November 1953, is the basis for "The Nature of Witness." This article was translated by the Reverend Ng Kam-yan of Toronto. There were disagreements in the church over whether to insist on the right to huge evangelistic campaigns or any other one style of evangelism. K. H. Ting asks Christians to be open to the variety of ways in which the Holy Spirit works. When one door closes some other opens. Of more immediate importance than the number of converts was the need for Christians to show that they were in solidarity with the people, loved the country and had broken with imperialism's corrupting influences. There is a comment on the visit of Dean Hewlitt Johnson, dean of Canterbury Cathedral and a peace activist whose visits to Russia and China earned him the epithet "Red Dean" during the Cold War era.

"Toward Unity" is taken from "Chinese Christians: New Prospects, New Unity," published first in *China Reconstructs*, an English-language magazine of the China Welfare Institute in Beijing. It was republished in the World Student Christian Federation journal, *Student World,* in 1956. It provides an interesting snapshot of the life of seminary students and clergy in the mid-1950s as various denominations began to work together in the precursor of the post-denominational Christianity that followed. Reference to the fact that foreign visitors were surprised that China had not given the faith a new look is an attempt to allay fears that somehow a Communist-style Christianity had been developed in China. There were many misconceptions afoot as a result of the propaganda wars taking place.

The last article in this section, "The Church's Mandate," is from a 1982 speech given in Sweden and published in 1983 in both *Missiology* and *China Notes* under the title "Evangelism as a Chinese Christian Sees It." K. H. Ting expressed concern about those China watchers abroad who claim to see something salvific in the Chinese revolution. Such claims are used by conservative observers to condemn the revolutionaries as usurpers of God and to justify attacks on the goals of the revolution. Ting wishes to support the socialist experiment but not see it as a part of Christian "salvation."

WHY BE A MINISTER? (1954)

In the fall of 1951 I was able to meet some of my former schoolmates in Beijing. We talked about the experiences we had had since we last met. One of them said to me, "The church is a dark place; why do you still, even today, want to be a preacher?" I said a few words by way of explanation. There was an unexpected silence. It was only when someone called us to eat that the atmosphere became lively again.

During that moment I was seized by a sense of extreme loneliness and solitude. We were all getting on in years. For courtesy's sake they spared me debate and changed the subject. I asked myself, "Do they want to have nothing to do with the church because it turns a blind eye to its own shortcomings, resigning itself to sinfulness?" The church's prospects are certainly grim if people respond to us with an embarrassed or negative silence.

I could not help being depressed, because the church, which I loved, had been exploited to such an extent that even my former schoolmates thought my involvement with it beyond comprehension. I remembered how I had felt God's loving arm around my shoulders, saying, "Tend my sheep," and how I had gladly obeyed this order and become a worker in the church.

Is there anyone who wants to be the kind of minister who simply "goes on tolling the bell as long as he is a monk"? We want fervently to retain our first fresh and lively dedication. The question now arose, however, as to whether I had taken the wrong road after all.

Several years have passed since that trip to Beijing. It is most gratifying to see that the church has recently made big strides on the road to a new life. With the advance of both motherland and church, we begin to see the significance of our work and delight in it all the more. "Why do you still want to be a preacher?" I would like now to give my fellow workers an answer based on my own experience.

In preaching the gospel we preach the truth. It is a priceless treasure; it alone can fill the aching void in people's hearts. People in all times and in all areas need the gospel. The truth will certainly manifest itself, provided we can purify it of the non-gospel elements with which it has become adulterated over the past one hundred years and more.

"As a hart longs for flowing streams, so longs my soul for thee, O God" (Ps 42:1). The soul's thirst cannot be measured, classified or explained. But we know that the truth of God's gospel can meet the need of our starved souls, just as brook water can meet the need of thirsty deer. St. Augustine prayed: "Lord, you have put a restless heart within me, so that I can never have peace until I rest in you" (*Confessions of St. Augustine*, Book One). We know from our hearts that this is exactly how things are.

"Come to me all who labor and are heavy-laden and I will give you rest" (Mt 11:28). Is this not the call we hear in the depth of our souls? Is this not the joyous rest we find after accepting God? God's communication with us is described in the words of the psalmist as "deep calling to deep" (Ps 42:7). The Holy Spirit speaks to our life's innermost depth of God's existence; of God's omnipotence, wisdom, glory, majesty, holiness, love and justice; and of our sin and rebellion. This is food needed in all times and in all places; it is in keeping with the hope within our souls.

Christianity does not monopolize truth, nor does it reject truth. In human history there are innumerable developments, including many scientific achievements that conform to the truth. Nevertheless, some of us take the wrong road. We try to find the shortcomings or faults of those who do not believe in God, instead of thanking God for their achievements. Why do we take this attitude, so devoid of kindness and love? Christians should not hesitate to welcome persons, events and movements that are close to the truth. There is only one God, from whom comes everything in the universe that is true, good and beautiful.

There is a well-known painting in which Adam and Eve are in the foreground; in the background an angel bars their way back into Eden. But beyond all expectation Adam and Eve look not in that direction but at a cross shining against the dark sky! This painting illumines the truth of the gospel: Whenever we sin God will be bearing the cross at that moment to do away with sin. The Christ on the cross is no less than "the Lamb that was slain" from "the foundation of the world" (Rv 13:8). This is the work of preaching: To help people recognize the cross, to call to them, "Behold the Lamb of God, who takes away the sin of the world" (Jn 1:29). Only a savior such as this can meet the need of our starved and thirsty souls.

It is a joyful thing to be a minister in new China—not just because we preach the eternal truth of God, but also because God shows special grace to us. The truth of God is unchangeable, but our comprehension of it is deepening. Today the Holy Spirit moves in on us and suddenly we see truth in a new light. Then we realize that our eyes and our minds have been dull and clouded. In the past we thought that Christians should not be concerned about national affairs. As a result, many passages in the Bible concerning love of one's country were closed to us. We must realize that the

Hebrew people were intimately acquainted with the possibility of both serving the Spirit and loving the nation. These two loves are entirely in harmony. Jerusalem is the place of longing—there stand both the Temple and the throne of David, or, in other words, the centers of religious and national life.

Centuries before Christ Isaiah compared Jerusalem to the loving arms of a mother:

> Rejoice with Jerusalem, and be glad for her,
> all you who love her;
> rejoice with her in joy,
> all you who mourn over her,
> that you may suck and be satisfied
> with her consoling breasts;
> that you may drink deeply with delight
> from the abundance of her glory (Is 66:10).

When the Israelites, returning to Jerusalem after the Exile, saw from afar the city walls and the pinnacle of the holy Temple, they excitedly broke into song.

> Our feet have been standing
>   within your gates, O Jerusalem!
> Jerusalem, built as a city
>   which is bound firmly together,
> to which the tribes go up,
>   the tribes of the Lord,
> as was decreed for Israel,
>   to give thanks to the name of the Lord.
> There thrones for judgment were set,
>   the thrones of the house of David (Ps 122:2-9).

Elsewhere we find passages that show the common people's concern for the peace and prosperity of Jerusalem (Ps 126:1-6); explicit love for their country (Ps 137:4-6); and grief for the nation's distress (Lam 2:11; 4:12; 5:11-12, 15).

In Luke 19:41-45 two graphic events are juxtaposed: When Jesus came within sight of Jerusalem, he wept in grief for the city, knowing that enemies were coming who would plunge the people into misery; then, going into the Temple, he drove out those who did evil there. These two events, coming together in the narrative, tell us that, for Jesus, honoring one's country and people, and honoring God and the church, are harmonious and complementary actions.

The apostle Paul, called to preach in foreign lands, was still concerned about his compatriots in Israel. For their sake, he said:

I am speaking the truth in Christ, I am not lying; my conscience bears me witness in the Holy Spirit, that I have great sorrow and unceasing anguish in my heart. For I could wish that I myself were accursed and cut off from Christ for the sake of my brethren, my kinsmen by race (Rom 9:1-3).

Judging from these texts, the Bible has never asked disciples not to love their country. The statements in the Bible are clear enough. It is simply that we were blind to them before. Today God wants us to see them.

We may easily miss other truths in the Bible that reflect God's truth. Jesus said to Peter, "What I am doing you do not know now, but afterward you will understand" (Jn 13:7). He also said, "I have yet many things to say to you, but you cannot bear them now" (Jn 16:12). "But the counsellor, the Holy Spirit, whom God will send in my name, will teach you all things, and bring to your remembrance all that I have said to you" (Jn 14:26). God knows that the vessels we received are too small. We can only handle a small portion at a time. God nourishes us gradually, in accordance with our differing needs each day and each hour.

Preachers have a glorious mission — to make the church worthy of its name, so that it becomes the dwelling place of God. A good church will be loved by the people and will match the progress being made in other fields by the people of the motherland. Will it be a sin if the church sees eye to eye with the people on some matters? Does glorifying God require the church to do things unworthy of the country or objectionable to the people? Absolutely not. True, Paul wrote about not simply trying to find favor with people or just trying to please them (Gal 1:10). From the context, however, we see that Paul here referred to sham disciples who were confusing the faith of the believers. With reference to the common people Paul urged us "to abound in love for one another and for all people" (1 Thes 3:12).

If we sincerely love the church, then, we certainly want to make of it a community that is holy, pure, glorious and beautiful, enjoying the love of the people. To this end we must work to dispel the darkness inside the church, to purify it of all objectionable characteristics, so that it may glorify the Lord and guide the people to God. This is what is meant by the phrase, "to be worthy of new China." Won't God be glorified if the church, taking on a new look and courageously forging ahead, keeps pace with the building of our motherland? Won't this also bring honor to the church in the eyes of the country?

Think about it. Precisely because of the darkness inside the church and the bad conduct of ministers, many of our compatriots begin to doubt or reject religious belief. It is a matter too serious to be ignored. Think how many more believers we will have in our country if our preachers practice holy and righteous conduct and clearly distinguish between right and wrong action! Let us therefore begin at once to live as new persons in these glorious times. Let the light of the church shine before the people so that they can see our good works and give glory to God in heaven.

In the past our church—controlled, manipulated and corrupted by the imperialists—duplicated the bad example of churches in Western countries, turning its back on beliefs, ideals and love. We need not be discouraged, however, for "a bruised reed God will not break, and a dimly burning wick God will not quench" (Is 42:3). God wants us as coworkers to reconstruct the church, making it clean, bright, beautiful and lovable, as dignified as countless other new structures in new China. Take the church in Nanjing, for example, where an unprecedented spirit of fellowship has been established between ministers and lay people. Two neighboring seminaries, which for the past fifteen years have held fruitless union discussions, have now not only voluntarily come together, but have also united with ten seminaries in east China. Coordination and cooperation among the various churches have developed to a point where they help supply each other's needs and share each other's heavy burdens: Half the amount needed to repair a church in the city, for instance, was donated by other congregations, an action inconceivable in the past. We do not claim the glory for ourselves, but praise instead the Lord who loves the church.

To be a preacher is a worthy thing then. But let us not be proud. Present-day demands are stringent. Negligence or slackening in the calling of any one of us—whether in church work, political studies, or morality and values—could lead to exclusion, a most tragic end for a pastor. We should ask God to give us genuine humility, engendered by a sense of honor about our holy duties. Only when we are conscientious and eager to make progress can we ask God to pare down our unworthiness. In the end the knowledge that our work is of use to God, people, church and country will be our high reward.

THE NATURE OF WITNESS (1953)

In the post-liberation years the church in China has never been subject to discrimination on the grounds of its past association with imperialist forces. Under the protection of the people's government we have been able to shatter the shackles of imperialism and truly become a church. For this we offer thanks to God who has given us a role to play in a new China filled with hope.

After such drastic historical change, though, how do we witness to Christ? How do we nurture the saints? I would like to share with you the results of my prayer, bible study and meditation on these questions.

First of all, we need to establish a basic premise: To witness to Christ is the church's mission, the cause of its being and the reason for its formation. Christ himself commanded us to witness. This is the duty of every believer.

Witness involves both the worship of God and the proclaiming of salvation. To proclaim God's salvation is to spread the gospel and to participate in the work of God's saving plan for the world. We need not know the day of the coming of the kingdom, nor should we make plans for its coming. This much, however, we do know: There is a close relationship between its coming and the church's witness here on earth.

The Holy Spirit is a spirit of freedom. We should not limit our perception of the Spirit—its methods can change according to people, time and place. "The wind bloweth where it wills, and you know the sound of it, but you do not know whence it comes or whither it goes; so it is with everyone who is born of the Spirit" (Jn 3:8). But there are some who insist that personal witness is the only means through which the Holy Spirit can work; others that the Spirit is at work only in huge evangelical gatherings. Both attitudes manifest stubbornness. What we ought to do is live in obedience to the Spirit's choice of methods, accepting that these may be manifest in different circumstances to different persons.

God may resort to some fairly "unorthodox" tactics to spread the gospel. On the surface it might look as if the door to evangelism is closing. In actual fact, God may be preparing to open even more perfect doors. Such is the working of the Holy Spirit. In the apostles' time, for example, the Holy Spirit was free to work through the church to bring in three-thousand converts on one single occasion, and on another five thousand. These were tremendous doings indeed. But we can see times even during those days when the work of the Spirit was not at all earthshaking: "And they went through the region of Phrygia and Galatia, having been forbidden by the Holy Spirit to speak the word in Asia. And when they had come opposite Mysia, they attempted to go into Bithynia, but the spirit of Jesus did not allow them" (Acts 16:6-7).

For Paul to have the door shut in his face like that must have made him feel that he had come to a dead end, not through any human intervention but through the Spirit itself. But in this way Paul was readied for a better and more beautiful thing—to hear the cry from Macedonia. So, with one door apparently closed, another could be lightly pushed ajar to allow the gospel to enter Europe. What tremendous impact that event had on the church and the world. At the time, however, Paul must have fretted and fumed about the impasse he seemed to have reached. In China today the door is still open, so that we should not think of our situation as an exact parallel to Paul's. Still, from scripture we can glean at least this ray of truth: The Holy Spirit employs many methods to open doors to evangelism. Stirring assemblies or still, small conversations—both are familiar doors. In addition there are those that remain unseen and ignored.

If we admit that huge gatherings for evangelism and revival may not be God's choice for today, we must then understand that we need to withdraw a little in order to learn lessons in Christ. Because of the deep influence of imperialism on our thoughts, we need to discipline ourselves to learn how to love our country; we dare not act rashly or be self-willed. God reminds us, "In quietness and in trust shall be your strength" (Is 30:15).

Our first lesson is to learn how to love the people. If we are serious about preaching the good news we must get close to them and become one with them. Even God, to give us the good news, took the route of the word, and became flesh in order to be one of us. Only in the solidarity of love, thus exemplified, could the transmission of the good news take place.

As citizens of China we should love our country and be at one with its people. To be worthy of the trust of the gospel we need to think what they think, love what they love, hate what they hate. Our Lord Jesus acted thus; Paul acted thus. If we keep our distance, however, God will not be able to use us to spread the good news. If there is no common ground, how can the gospel, no matter how beautiful it is, make any sense to those whom we want to reach?

Love does not only take the form of cheerful smiles and friendly joining of hands; to bring the good news requires that we truly love and care for a person. At the same time true love is sharing without reservation the highest and best of ourselves including, naturally, the gospel and the life that comes from God.

My fervent wish now is that as believers—who are Chinese *and* Christian—we set aside spiritual pride and enter with open hearts into the midst of the people. Then, whether it be in lifestyle, in learning, in work, even in study and literacy activities, there would be true joining of hands. When we have real love for the people, the Lord will put words into our mouths and we will be able to bear living witness. Our witness then will not simply be religious slogans, sounding gongs, or clanging cymbals. It will be lively and powerful, penetrating deeply into people's inmost selves to show forth the Lord.

God is showing us today how we should witness through our action. The Lord Jesus has pointed out that it is through action that the disciples should lead others to a knowledge of God and to glorify God: "Let your light so shine before people, that they may see your good works, and glorify your Father who is in heaven" (Mt 5:16).

Christians believe that all have fallen short before God and that people cannot rectify this by themselves. Justification by faith is a crucial doctrine: Only by trusting in the redemptive work of Christ on the cross can we hope to become righteous. But if we ignore the totality of Christian doctrine, uplifting and exaggerating "justification by faith" to the exclusion of "works," we may fall into error.

First, we may be tempted to regard the ordinary people's achievements as worthless simply because they do not believe. "Justification by faith" is then turned into a weapon against the people. In fact, it does not demand that we treat all those outside the church as "lost beasts of the flood" or "overflowing with evil." Instead, we should give thanks to God, wherever appropriate, for their virtuous nature and their great achievements; for scripture has told us that every good comes from God (Jas 1:16-17).

Second, under the rubric of "justification by faith" we may overlook sinful actions of the church. Certain people may be imperialists, or they may constitute harmful elements in society, endangering the nation. But once they appear in the guise of believers we tend to count them as righteous, condoning even their evil or criminal doings. Beloved workers in the Lord, not only should individual Christians witness for Christ in pure conduct; the church too should lead a communal life of purity and holiness. Only so can it lead others to Christ.

Since liberation, under the banner of the Three-Self Movement, Chinese Christians have shown their anti-imperialism by their conduct. The spirit of unity within the church is stronger than it has been at any time in the past. People in general sense something new about the church. Earlier attitudes, formed in imperialistic times, have undergone substantial change. This change is greatly beneficial to the work of evangelism. Is this not the fruit of concrete action on the church's part, my fellow workers?

Dean Hewlett Johnson did not hold any evangelistic meetings when he was in China. Nor did he often preach. When he did, it was only to those within the church. But because of his tireless action, aimed at world peace and a better future for humanity, many people who did not believe in Christ changed their attitude toward the church. How helpful this has been for our witness. Preaching, apart from action, is powerless to lead anyone to Christ. To assess whether an evangelist is truly of God, it is necessary to find out whether his or her actions manifest a love of God, of people, of country and of the church.

Witnessing, preaching, uniting people with the body of Christ—this is not all. Every letter that Paul wrote is directed to nurturing believers and pastoring the church. To the church at Ephesus he said that God's gifts were such that "some would be apostles, some prophets, some evangelists, some pastors and teachers, for the equipment of the saints, for the work of ministry, for building up the body of Christ" (Eph 4:11-16). To the church at Colossus he said, "As therefore you received Christ Jesus the Lord, so live in him, rooted and built up in him and established in the faith, just as you were taught, abounding in thanksgiving" (Col 2:6-7). Here Paul sets out the standard of pastoral teaching and nurturing for each minister of the gospel. He requires of us great eagerness and patience to work this out step by step. Empowering disciples and building up the body is a work of sweat and tears—there are no shortcuts. It requires patience, long-suffering and unremitting, uncomplaining toil.

There are many facets of pastoral work to be considered. Even in the church people often need friendship. The pastor is one who can share burdens as well as moments of grace. The minister must spend a great deal of time in prayer. It is in times of kneeling in sweet communication with God that everything concerning the congregation comes to the surface. A preacher cares about the flock as a parent or older sister or brother. As

Paul once declared, "Is there one that is weak and I am not weak, or one who stumbles and I not worry?" (2 Cor 11:29).

The church is a community of worship. Once we decide we want to worship God, how can we not employ all that is representative of the highest, the most beautiful and the best of all humankind? From this perspective there is no "excessiveness" in the way Christian workers prepare and study for worship and liturgy.

Another task is to educate the saints, so that they continually deepen their knowledge of things spiritual. We must take care not to let some lag behind, still steeped in reactionary thought. We need to help such persons become Christians who love God, nation, people and church; to become at the same time staunch supporters of the Three-Self Movement in the church. In this way the minister's work will be aided, not hindered.

To meet the manifold demands of our task we must strengthen and raise the quality of ordination and ministry. We need to recall our resolve to devote ourselves, through study, reflection and research, to a high level of pastoral ministry. Those of us who have been called to take part in building up the body of Christ in China are excited yet tremulous. We are challenged to be humble and repentant—to nail our old self to the cross, together with the sins of old China. Thereby a new self is released that God can use without reserve.

Who dares say that the nurturing work of a pastor is not worth doing? Three times the risen Lord asked of Peter, "Do you love me?" Each time Peter answered, "Yes, Lord, I love you." Although Jesus knew there was no comparison between Peter's love and his own love, he still trusted Peter, saying, "Feed my sheep" (Jn 21:17). Let us answer, "Yes, we will." Let us add, "Be thou our shepherd too, O Lord."

TOWARD UNITY (1956)

Nanjing Theological Seminary prepares candidates for the ministry and for other forms of Christian leadership. Its training is recognized by almost all the non-Roman Catholic churches in the country. About one hundred fifty students, including those attending refresher courses, were enrolled this spring [1956].

During a recent rural tour in Zhejiang province I visited eleven parishes, attended retreats and conferences with colleagues in several places and confirmed about seven hundred people between fifteen and eighty-one years of age. The diocese of Zhejiang today has over seventy churches in the full-time care of clergy. Services in the rural churches that I visited were not necessarily ordered or beautiful, but congregations were big, the spirit warm and the singing hearty. Our clergy were generally held in high esteem in the parishes. All these churches have gained from the restoration of peace, the ending of inflation, land reform, the movement toward co-operative farming and the introduction of advanced methods of agriculture.

The peasants now enjoy a better livelihood and have an interest in cultural life.

Significantly, our members no longer think of their church as belonging to a foreign mission or even to the clergy. They see her now as the church of God, belonging to us all. The minister of the rural town of Tatuan told me that the annual meeting in his parish used to consist of a small handful of people, passively listening to reports and assenting to elections. But now more people are taking part in the everyday work of the parish; all want to put their views forward. At the annual meeting small groups give everyone a chance to have a say on problems of church life, and the conclusions they reach genuinely represent the opinions of the whole congregation. It is understandable, then, that more young men in the rural churches now think of the ministry when they come to decide on their vocation.

For students at the Nanjing seminary life is simple and full. There are few rules, but plenty of mutual love and respect within the community. While the seminary provides an admirable environment for retreat and study, the seminarians also find opportunities in the city—fast becoming a cultural center—for wider academic, artistic and cultural activity.

As for curriculum, visitors from abroad are surprised that we have not given our faith a "new look." We think this would be wrong. We have repudiated unscrupulous efforts to place the church, Bible or theological teaching at the service of colonialism, racism, aggression or anything else that contradicts the true nature of Christian faith. But we are not aiming at revision of divine truth. Our stand is to take the Bible and the historic faith more seriously than ever.

Our newly won freedom is freedom indeed, because in it the truth essential for salvation is not sacrificed or diluted. On the contrary, with untruth exposed, truth presents itself in greater purity and fullness. It calls us to love it more dearly and bear witness to it more faithfully. Thus we do not apologize for our traditional theological education.

On graduation our students find varied opportunities. Recent graduates have mostly taken up pastoral work. Some have been called to Christian literature, work among children and youth, religious art and drama, sacred music, theological teaching and the sale of Bibles. One even helped produce a movie musical for Christmas. Many contribute to denominational periodicals. The seminary publishes the *Nanjing Union Seminary Journal* (mainly a forum for the faculty), *Fellowship With One Another* (the students' own magazine) and an alumni bulletin. Our professors devote much time to preparing courses and textbooks. We aim to do theoretical work on subjects relevant to the church in present-day China.

Throughout the church in China there is a new emphasis on reconciling theology with devotion and worship with life. A heightened sensitivity to the manifold brilliance of the Bible message also brings a healthy influence to bear on the theological and spiritual condition of the church. Our union seminary is a venture in cooperation, drawing personnel at all levels from, among others, Presbyterian, Anglican, Baptist, Methodist, Lutheran, Congregational, Pentecostal, Apostolic Faith and Seventh Day Adventist churches. The special characteristics and needs of each denomination are given due respect both in the preparation of the curriculum and the planning of worship.

We feel that our seminary can truly be a meeting place because we have all received one faith, we all serve the same Lord, and it is God's will that we should be one. We have some differences; we do not ignore them. We serve in mutual respect and esteem, entering as deeply as our humility can take us into the riches that are in Christ. This is something new. Compared with the spirit of competition and even hostility that existed between some of the church bodies in the past, we see it as nothing short of an act of God.

CHURCH'S MANDATE (1983)

People in the West assume that atheism is very much in the air in new China. We have not found that to be the case. Chinese Communists, as Marxists, are of course atheists, but the propagation of atheism does not enjoy top priority in their program. What they want above all is to unite everyone in building up new China and making her prosperous. They know, perhaps better than anyone else, that this is a task no group or party can monopolize. For unity, the special characteristics of all minority groupings need to be respected, not antagonized. Why deprive Christians of freedom when it is is clear that we want national prosperity and are working for it just as much as other citizens?

Since the end of the Cultural Revolution we have seen a return to a correct implementation of religious policy. There are complaints and grievances here and there to be sure. But now that this policy has gone into the national constitution, these problems can be aired before the proper authorities and a settlement found. For the church to flourish and bear Christian witness, however, a state policy of religious freedom is not enough. We need to build up a theological self-understanding that can guide us in all our decision-making, so that we move toward greater self-realization as the church of Jesus Christ in the midst of the Chinese people.

We have great admiration and respect for the epistemology and hermeneutics of praxis, and for the Christological insights others have to offer us out of their own struggle. We affirm their upholding of the Egypt/Exodus motif, their stand against developmentalism and reformism, and their support for efficacious love and structural change in society—in all this we gratefully and penitently see something that we as Chinese Christians ought to have recognized in our pre-liberation days. Chinese Christians do not, then, stand in opposition to the liberation theology of our fellow Christians of Latin America.

From our own experience, however, we have to say that socio-political liberation is not an adequate expression of our theology. The message we send out centers on reconciliation in Jesus Christ between God and humanity, a message just as valid in our post-liberation stage of history as in any other. The contradiction between rich and poor is certainly an important one that no Christian can ignore. But to make it the focus of Christian theology seems to us a relativization of biblical revelation and a departure from the totality of the historical tradition of the church. There is also the danger of absolutizing revolutionary justice for the poor just because they are poor, something we are familiar with from the ultra-leftism of the Cultural Revolution in China.

Locality, nationality, particularity—all these are focal to the relationship between the church universal and its parts. Indeed, the concept of locality is an important feature of the New Testament doctrine of the church. In order to insure the growth of a truly Chinese church, we have to raise a protective wall against internationalism, which does not give due respect to rightful national aspirations. Small, weak or old cultures, in which some great beauty resides, are struggling to prevent themselves from being pushed toward oblivion by a dominant technological society that is creating a sameness throughout the world. Under these circumstances it is natural that Christians want to express love and support for their nation. This is not any narrow nationalism of the "my-country-right-or-wrong" kind.

China-watchers in church circles abroad alarm us by purportedly discovering something salvific in the claims and intentions of our revolutionaries; they accuse them of usurping God. Revolutionaries in China have not advanced any soteriological program or promised the making of the new person in the Pauline sense. Their aim is simply to educate the people so that they have the welfare of others at heart, and the socialist motherland in mind, when making personal choices. We do not think the success of Christian evangelism depends on the failure of the socialist experiment in transforming the country and its people. On the contrary, our success depends on the identification of ourselves with the people who are the focus of that experiment. We cannot endorse the intervention of religious groups abroad, who refuse to honor the lessons of history and instead rally Western Christians' support for their "reoccupation" of China. We cannot allow them to restore a foreign image to our church.

The church does not think that the only good Christians are those who break entirely with their culture and milieu, as if these factors were outside the domain of the risen and ascended Christ, untouched by his grace. In consequence, we feel that to warn of the dangers of syncretism only makes us fearful and unable to communicate the gospel. In fact a much greater danger to evangelism than any threat of syncretism is our intransigence; the absoluteness of God's revelation in Christ should not lead us to absolutize our own inadequate understanding of it. Evangelism not only brings Christ to men and women—it brings Christ out of them, so that people at both ends of the line of communication are receivers of the gospel. Furthermore, the *logos spermatikos* idea and the notion of the cosmic function of Christ are gaining ground in the thinking of Chinese Christians, enlarging our understanding of the incarnation.

In China today many ideas contend with one another. We need to listen and discriminate among them, bearing in mind that there can be no good evangelism if we lump all ideas from non-Christian sources together on the assumption that they are all of a piece. Nevertheless, we should be sensitive to any slight approach or approximation to the spirit of Christ and any movement Godward that we can detect.

In an overwhelmingly non-religious country such as China, to see in Christ a great teacher or lover, a great liberator, the Tao, or the logos or savior — these are all welcome steps Christward. In the country of Confucius, where the ethical approach is so deep-rooted and where to serve the good of the people becomes the common people's understanding of Marxism, to approach God ethically rather than ontologically is entirely natural and acceptable. People want to know how a Christian views goodness and where resources for a good life may be found. With the thought content of over ninety-nine percent of our people having nothing to do with Christianity, we welcome all positive views about Jesus. They are all fruits of evangelism, not quite so countable as heads of individual converts receiving baptism, but possibly more important in the long run.

We resist any pressure that forces us into a Christian ghetto. We participate in People's Congresses and People's Political Consultative Conferences on national, provincial and local levels; we are in the university world and in other walks of life. Our presence makes people raise questions about Christianity; that is evangelism. The Chinese policy of the United Front also opens up opportunities for us in turn to learn from others.

As far as numbers are concerned, a present conservative estimate of baptized non-Roman Catholic Christians in China would be around two million, three times the number estimated for 1949 and already larger than our work of Christian nurture can cope with. But to pray "thy kingdom come" is to ask for something much wider than the mere extension of the church. The church is only that part of the world that acknowledges the ascended Christ's presence and work; it wants to help more people to see and accept him. The church, as leaven, must transform the whole mass of dough into bread, not just produce more leaven. In other words, its own growth cannot be its only goal.

Within a socialist system no private group, least of all the self-supporting church, could maintain medical and educational institutions at a level equal to those run by the state for the general public, unless it made exorbitant charges and thus catered only to the elite. Stripping down, or travelling light, should not be a cause for depression in the church. Today we find the church fulfilling — if as yet in a small way — a fourfold mandate: worship, nurture, concern for the welfare of the people and witness. In one sense, yes, the church has lost power — but it has always evangelized best out of powerlessness.

Part 3

CONFRONTING
THE WORLD

The writing in Parts 1 and 2 has shown us that Christians in China, as exemplified by K. H. Ting, did not somehow become completely politicized by the dramatic social changes of the Chinese revolution. We witness a persistent commitment to understanding and embodying Christianity in a way that was valid for China and to carrying out the Christian mission of service and evangelism in a flexible, creative style that was in synchronization with rapidly changing events. The pastoral role of the church was not neglected nor was the theological task, insofar as resources and energy were available.

On the other hand, the church in China was "involved in politics." It would be missing the point to ignore the harsh political realities that Christians in China had to face. In North America, especially in the United States, socialism and even liberalism have become taboo again, reminding us of the McCarthy era of Communist "witch hunts" in the 1950s. Chinese Christians in the 1950s were very much on their own in the task of discerning where and how the Western fear of socialism functioned as a cover for imperialist goals that had nothing to do with the gospel.

For China, the victory of socialism marked the return to independence from foreign intervention and the end of degradation and humiliation at the hands of foreign powers. It also meant the rehabilitation of addicts and prostitutes, the return of order and a new dignity for workers and peasants. China had arisen. Ordinary Christians in China were "mostly members of the working classes. They did not have much to lose in the liberation but a lot to gain" ("Theology in Socialist China").

Chinese Christians suddenly found that the ideological anti-communism of the West had misled them. They needed to find a way simultaneously to affirm their faith, their love for China, their appreciation of the "dreaded" Communist Party, which had led China out of the morass, their willingness to participate in socialist reconstruction and their sense of identity as both Christian and Chinese. This required a break with many of the political presuppositions of Western Christianity. In the Western world today, when ideological anti-communism and anti-socialism are again on the rise in the church, it is all the more important that we listen to the prophetic message that comes to us out of the experience of the church in China. K. H. Ting can say, "I have many Communist friends who engage in self-criticism more constantly than we engage in our devotions and prayers" ("Prophetic Challenges"). Can we hear and understand?

Jonah and the elder brother of the prodigal again symbolize for Ting disgruntled evangelists who do not really love the people around them ("New Initiatives"). In contrast, Ting can calmly state that "the Communist is a child of God for whom Christ died" and is "worthy of redemption. If we have faith, we have no fear. We can talk with Communists, learn from them, and try to evangelize them." Such statements, in the 1950s, fell mostly on deaf ears in the West.

In the writings in Part 3 we are called to ask ourselves whom we serve in our scientific endeavors ("Knowledge and Service"), whom we serve in our search for peace and human solidarity ("The Call of Peace"), and whom we serve in our proclamation of the gospel ("Prophetic Challenges"). These are difficult choices for us, as they were and are difficult choices for K. H. Ting and the church in China. Not all knowledge is used for good ends; not all development is helpful; evangelists can be corrupted; peace can be unjust.

The gospel continually calls us "to take a new road, no longer serving but subverting Herod" ("The Journey of the Magi," above). Herod represents imperialism with its armies and its religious servants. Christians in the West cannot both serve Herod and help China. This is true in the present as it was in the 1940s ("American Interventionism").

K. H. Ting's clear stand against imperialism surfaces throughout these writings. What also comes across strongly is that China will be defined by the Chinese and not by the West, although Western concepts and contributions may be accepted where useful.

Christians do not have to look at a world polarized along a belief-unbelief axis. Ting sees a shift away from this antithesis "to an appreciation of the unity of the whole creative, redemptive and sanctifying process in the universe and of what God is doing in history." In this faith stance it is not necessary to worry overmuch about atheism or unreligious governments. In fact, the image of Herod appears again as a symbol of governments that use religiosity to cover oppression. An officially atheist government such as China's has the advantage as far as Christians are concerned of not misusing religion ("Theology in Socialist China").

Even though all may be sinners from the perspective of Christian theology, nevertheless we have to distinguish between the perpetrators of injustice and those who suffer the injustice ("The Call to Peace"). There are echoes of this theme in Ting's 1979 sermon "The Sinned Against," above. K. H. Ting refutes the theological error that claims all are equally sinners, that the whole world is sinful, and that therefore Christians do not have to make political choices. The church is called to solidarity with the victims, the sinned against, and to have the courage to make judgments about evil powers in the real world of social and political policy. At this point Ting may be closer to liberation theology than some of his disclaimers would suggest.

7

CONSCIENCE AND CHOICE

The first selection in this subsection, "Knowledge and Service," is from an article written in 1947 when K. H. Ting was working in Toronto. It appeared as "The Dilemma of the Sincere Student" in the SCM publication *The Canadian Student.* "Knowledge and Service" is a reflection on the relationship of sincerity and technical skill that raises searching questions about technological development and the mission of the university. The right way for China will be sought in development and education. Technical knowledge is not as important as "knowing that the right person is going to use that knowledge." For a university to be "true to its highest calling," it must move its students "to relate their life-purpose to the world community."

After his return to China in the 1950s Bishop Ting was active in the Christian peace movement. In 1961 he attended the All-Christian Peace Assembly in Prague, where he delivered a speech in the Bethlehem Chapel. "The Call to Peace" is taken from this speech. It is the only article included in this book from the 1960s.

The third selection, "Prophetic Challenges," is excerpted from a speech given in Vancouver in 1979. It deals with the need to be discriminating in development work; not all new things are necessarily good things for China. Bishop Ting reminds, scolds and warns about the role of Western churches in China. The prophetic voice of the Chinese church calls us to repentance, respect and humility. China has learned some hard lessons, he points out, from which we also may benefit—if we are willing to listen.

Near the beginning of the talk Ting mentions the constitution of China and his problem with the phrase "free to propagate atheism," which he saw as "ultra-leftist." In a subsequent revision of the constitution, after consultation with religious groups, this phrase was removed.

KNOWLEDGE AND SERVICE (1947)

Doctors and medical students may be tempted to assume that as long as they are curing the sick they are doing the right thing. But in this "one world" can they, or any others, rightly undertake a job without thinking of the implications that their work may have on other people's lives?

In "The Cross and the Arrow" (Maltz, *The Cross and the Arrow*, Boston: Little, Brown, 1944) we are told of a house owned by a group of Nazi army officials, in which twelve women were kept. A doctor was also in the house for the protection of the officials; his job was to ensure that the women were free from disease and infection. The doctor did his job wonderfully well. None of the twelve suffered from venereal disease. The Nazis could use them in any way they chose. After a little while, however, the women could not bear it any more. They all became insane.

Can one really cure disease without taking into consideration men and women as total personalities? In the case of the doctor in the story, is he in any way responsible for driving the women to insanity? Is he treating them as things to be used or as persons? In the small hours, when he examines his own conscience, can he consider himself a "good" doctor?

In "The Soldier Who Has Not Yet Died" its Japanese author talks about his own struggle in the war years:

> We are restoring people to health, one by one, through a very careful and slow process. But look at the mass production of death and of maimed bodies by war and social injustice.

Every sincere and thoughtful medical student must at times experience similar feelings of frustration. Indeed people in all specialized fields have this dilemma. There is the social worker who finds that the world is producing more cases in one day than the whole profession can possibly handle in a year; the engineer who sees bridges and highways and residences, built for the benefit of fellow citizens, destroyed overnight in war; the pastor who realizes that political, economic and military forces are undoing, on a much larger scale, the work of the gospel that he is trying to build up.

Since the making and use of the atomic bomb, more and more conscientious scientists are wondering whether there can really be such a thing as the "amorality" of science—whether they have the right to limit themselves to "pure science." Science in fact can no longer be "pure" or "neutral" in the present-day world. It has to serve some cause. The question is what or whose cause we make it serve.

Skill and knowledge cannot simply be sold to the highest bidder. We have to ask to what purpose our work will be put. Will it serve to enrich a few individuals and endanger the welfare and peace of the whole world? Or will it be for the benefit of humanity in general? We dare not face the tribunal of our conscience if, in our absorption in technical science, we unwittingly contribute to making the world more miserable. The scientist, then, is coming out of the laboratory, and wants to find out what is happening in the world.

Norbert Weiner is a mathematician whose ideas played a significant part in the war-time development of guided missiles. In an article entitled "A Scientist Rebels" he expresses great indignation at being asked, less than two years after victory over Germany and Japan, to supply certain information that would perfect the atomic bomb. He goes on to say:

> In the past the comity of scholars has made it a custom to furnish scientific information to any person seriously seeking it. However ... to provide scientific information is not necessarily an innocent act, and may entail the gravest consequences. ... The scientist [may put] unlimited powers in the hands of people whom he is least inclined to trust with their use. ... I do not expect to publish any future work of mine which may do damage in the hands of irresponsible militarists.

Technical knowledge is important—but not as important as knowing that the right person is going to use the knowledge. I may be anxious to test the sharpness of a knife, but I am much more anxious to know in whose hand it is to be put. If an education merely imparts certain information or skills, it is like sharpening a knife without ascertaining the sanity of the person who is to handle it. In the same way we must know and define the ends for which we live, so that we will dedicate our knowledge and skill only to the right cause.

That leads us to the question of the purpose of receiving a university education. Is it a good university education if it just gives technical competence in a particular field? Should it not also help students consider the question of what they are going to do with their skills?

There are universities that seem to exist only for the production of technical workers. With the growth of technology and departmentalization, they are no longer universities in the true sense of the word. Graduates in engineering from such an institution, for instance, are hypothetically good engineers. But how good, really, are engineers whose technical development is achieved at the expense of those interests and abilities that further the rich and universal cultural purpose of human history? Should slide rules, T-squares, thumbtacks and reinforced concrete take precedence over the conscience of the individual and the concerns of society?

A university is true to its highest calling only as it moves its students to seek a more abundant life and to relate their life purpose to the world community. Ultimately they must locate themselves in the family and scheme of the eternal Creator. It is here that the Student Christian Movement is both a witness and a help. As a fellowship of men and women, who want to make the most of their university life together as Christians, the SCM helps the university to fulfill its true mission.

THE CALL TO PEACE (1961)

So when they had dined, Jesus said to Simon Peter,

"Simon, son of Jonas, lovest thou me more than these?" He said unto him, "Yea, Lord, thou knowest that I love thee." He saith unto him, "Feed my sheep." He saith unto him the second time, "Simon, son of Jonas, lovest thou me?" He saith unto him, "Yea, Lord, thou knowest that I love thee." He saith unto him, "Feed my sheep." He saith unto him the third time, "Simon, son of Jonas, lovest thou me?" And he said unto him, "Lord, thou knowest that I love thee." Jesus saith unto him, "Feed my sheep" (Jn 21:15-17).

Here Christ is revealed in both his expectation and his concern for the church. Christ puts before the church the image of the shepherd—protector, encourager, friend. But at the same time he is worried that it may fall short of this expectation, leaving the sheep uncared for, unable even to prevent the wolf from molesting them. Out of his high expectation and his uncertainty, he asks repeatedly of Peter, "Lovest thou me?"

How is the church to love Christ? If we turn the question around and look at Christ's love for the church, we are struck by the importance of his work of cleansing and sanctification.

Christ loved the church and gave himself for it that he might sanctify and cleanse it with the washing of water by the word, that he might present a glorious church, not having spot or wrinkle, or any such thing, but that it should be holy and without blemish (Eph 5:25-26).

The primary characteristic of the church is necessarily its holiness. The holiness of the church lies in its separation from the sins and evils of the world and the setting apart of itself for the service of love and justice and truth. Unity, if it comes of the Holy Spirit, promotes the true catholicity of the church. But a unity that tries to transcend or ignore the distinction between right and wrong, one that distorts or blurs the issues of good and evil, may make destructive inroads upon the life of the church. Thus separation can sometimes be a principle for the church just as unity is at other times.

As we assemble here in Prague to seek the course of peace, we are required to distinguish between right and wrong. The search for holiness implies the giving up of moral nihilism.

Sometimes, when the root cause of a particular tension in the world is under discussion, we are tempted to assume a "common guilt," calling everybody indiscriminately to "repentance." Before we know it our sound Christian teaching is used in such a way that issues vital to the people are glossed over, responsibility for international lawlessness and tension is shifted from where it rightly belongs to rest on all alike, and injustices to the masses of the people are allowed to stand as something indistinguishable from justice!

Archbishop Nikodim has said that "the peace which Christ brought to earth presupposes not our being reconciled with evil and the forces of sin on earth but, on the contrary, our victory over evil and the liquidation of sin by means of unflagging struggle against them . . . a bitter, obstinate fight." When the wolf is attacking the sheep, the shepherd's responsibility is to protect them. What sort of shepherd is the person who, in the name of fairness, puts the wolf on a par with the sheep? In the same way, how dare we make an ambiguous, equalized judgment between victim and oppressor?

We have held this All-Christian Peace Assembly in the native land of the great John Hus. We have heard about the continued suffering of our African brothers and sisters under colonialism; we have been told about the invasion of Cuba. We know that the struggle for peace goes on all over the world. All this inspires us to make common cause, as Hus did in his day, with the large majority of people everywhere in their fight against the forces of sin and aggression. This is God's call to us today. To answer it is our responsibility before history.

In this chapel we are praying and praising God just as John Hus once did centuries ago. We recall how Hus, seeing the degeneration of the church under the influence of foreign political power and the control of reactionary domestic autocrats, bravely unfurled the banner of holiness. It was not an empty, passive holiness, standing for nothing in the world of realities, but a holiness with content — a true concern for the suffering and the aspirations of the people, a search for their welfare and a resolute fight against sin and evil. On the wall of the Czechoslovakian National Museum of Literature these words of John Hus have been inscribed:

> Woe unto me if I remain silent. For it would be better for me to die than not to take a stand against great wickedness, as this would make me an accomplice to sin and hell.

Now, is this dividing of the right from the wrong, this taking of a side, contrary to our Christian faith? Far from it. This is exactly what faith demands of us. Is it a sign that we do not love Christ? By no means. A true love of Christ requires that we make a choice. And is this self-righteousness? Certainly not. This is precisely what St. Paul meant when he said, "And this I pray, that your love may abound yet more and more in knowledge and in all judgment, that ye may approve things that are excellent, that ye be pure and blameless till the day of Christ" (Phil 1:9-10).

PROPHETIC CHALLENGES (1979)

Even during the years of the Chinese Cultural Revolution a number of people became Christian, mostly through contacts they had made in the work place. I have not been to any of the services in recently re-opened churches in Shanghai, but some American friends of ours, who happened to be in the city on the day Mo En Church was re-opened, went to the service and observed that there were over a thousand people and that about twenty percent of them were young people. I would remind you that the Communists think that churches will wither away in three or four hundred years—but of course we don't need to be in a greater hurry than they are!

With regard to religion our national constitution states that all Chinese citizens are free either to believe or not to believe; they may also propagate atheism. I can see why the right not to believe is in the constitution, because in certain parts of China, especially in areas where the minority nationalities are dominant, the authority of parents and religious leaders is still so strong that young people do not have that particular freedom. We feel, however, that the present wording is not helpful because the two freedoms (concerning religious belief and atheism) are not put in a balanced way. The constitution says something about the freedom to propagate atheism, but nothing about the freedom to propagate theism. This wording reflects something of the ultra-leftist line during the years of the Cultural Revolution when this particular article was drafted. An official proposal has already been made to simplify the article, so that it would give all Chinese citizens the freedom to believe in religion or not to believe in religion. This solution has received the support of many non-religious intellectuals as well as cadres in the government. We are optimistic that this article will indeed be revised along these lines.

Opening China to the West means opening it—though not unrestrictedly—to the science and technology of the West. Our leaders and our people are careful to discriminate. We are not accepting Western things blindly. Some of you may be thinking of Coca Cola, which has gone to China. Coca Cola has been imported into China entirely for foreign consumption. It is only to supply the needs of tourists. I know that many Western friends are rather anxious that China should avoid some of the pitfalls they visualize, and we appreciate very much their goodwill.

Although individual missionaries went to China with the best intentions, for these people to go back today *as missionaries* is a denial of the whole spirit of our Three-Self Movement, which we have worked so hard over the last thirty years to promote. We certainly hope that Western Christians will honor the desire of Chinese Christians to make the churches in China Chinese and look for alternative ways of giving help. Through the Three-Self Movement we have been trying to overcome the denationalizing or uprooting effects of the missionary movement. Let us suppose a missionary goes to China and Christians there ask if he or she supports the Three-Self Movement. Now if the answer is yes, then this missionary should not be there; and if the answer is no, Chinese Christians surely cannot accept such a person.

The whole movement to promote self-government, self-support and self-nurture, to make the churches in China Chinese, is something extremely prophetic. To be prophetic does not necessarily mean being opposed to the government. If a government is in a true sense the people's own, and if the people have sacrificed much to bring that government into being, it would be quite mad for us to work against it. This would be acting contrary to the nature of the prophetic church. Christians are serving in the People's Congresses and in the People's Political Consultative Conference on the national, provincial and local levels. There are many opportunities for us to voice concern and criticism of government personnel and policies. This is prophetic. But we are not prophetic in the sense of standing against this government. We think of this government as our own—and we want to defend it.

In North America and in Europe the various religions engage in dialogue with each other. In China Christians and Buddhists and Muslims, and even Protestants and Roman Catholics, still stand in isolation. We do have more contacts now, however, made almost entirely in the context of the People's Political Consultative Conference. This organization draws its members from all walks of life—peasants, workers and soldiers, youth and women, religious and nationalist minorities, Communists and Democratic Party members, professors, teachers and students and performing artists. Questions concerning domestic and international policies are discussed in the conference. There is a special sector that looks at religious matters, where, naturally, we go more deeply into the policy of religious freedom and its implementation. The official proposal that I spoke about earlier emerged from that sector of the People's Political Consultative Conference.

In China today Bibles are in very short supply. During the Cultural Revolution a lot of Bibles were burned as a revolutionary act. We have had only two printings of the Bible since the liberation, one in the 1950s and one during the 1960s. I know of young people who have copied the Bible word by word into their notebooks; that is one reason we are planning a new publication of the Chinese Bible. We certainly do not want to have to import a Chinese Bible from a foreign country because that gives no credibility to Chinese Christianity.

As to persecution, it is true that Christians suffered during the Cultural Revolution, though less than many revolutionary cadres, who have sacrificed themselves in the revolutionary cause for several decades. Many intellectuals and professors also suffered under the ultra-leftist line. Since the downfall of the Gang of Four, all those wrongly condemned, including Christians, are being rehabilitated and reimbursed for their material losses. Similarly, more and more Buddhist temples are being repaired and reopened and that is also true of Islam and of Taoism.

In China freedom of religion includes freedom to evangelize. That has been emphasized in many of our newspapers, as, for instance, in a recent article in our *People's Daily*. Before the liberation, however, missionaries would take Christians to Buddhist temples—especially on festival days when there were big crowds of worshippers there — to preach and evange-lize. Today we regret these things because that certainly was not evangelism. That was exploiting Westerners' privileges in order to impose something on Buddhists, even in places they considered sacred. We no longer need this kind of evangelism, for evangelism is not merely a process by which we bring Jesus Christ to other people. It is also to bring something of Christ, in the revolutionary for instance, out of him or her. Evangelism also means that we ourselves come to a deeper understanding of the gospel of Jesus Christ. I would consider evangelism or at least an important preparation for it, the work of the Three-Self Movement, which improves communication between Christians and the rest of the Chinese people.

We have a lot to learn from the Communists, especially in their consci-entious execution of all the tasks of revolution. They are most self-sacrific-ing, putting the welfare of the people before everything else. They know that any mistakes could cost the revolution a lot, and therefore they are very self-demanding. I have many Communist friends who engage in criti-cism and self-criticism more constantly and drastically than we engage in our devotions and prayers.

Siu May and K. H.
Verdun, Quebec, 1947

K. H. Ting
St. Margaret's Bay, Nova Scotia, 1947

K. H. Ting
Nanjing Seminary, 1964

**K. H. Ting and faculty members,
Nanjing, 1964**

**Siu May and K. H.
October, 1978**

K. H. Ting with Ruth Sovik
World Council of Churches, Geneva, 1988

K. H. Ting and grandson

8

ENCOUNTERS
WITH IMPERIALISM

"American Interventionism" is from an article entitled "American Aid to China" published in the Canadian journal *The Anglican Outlook* in April 1947. Some of the content is very time-specific, but the total analysis is both informative and consistent with Ting's later positions. The opening critique of American churches, which both support policies of the United States hostile to China and at the same time try to carry out missionary work in China, is a clear forerunner of the later critique of those who try to serve "Herod" and those oppressed by "Herod" at the same time.

Madame Sun Yat-sen, to whom reference is made, was one of the famous Soong sisters—another being Madame Chiang Kai-shek—widow of the leader of the 1911 revolution. She stayed on in China after the Communist victory in 1949 and was active in welfare work for many years. Also mentioned is Feng Yu-hsiang. He was often called the Christian general, having been converted to Methodism by John R. Mott. Many people would agree with the assessment that American intervention aided the Communist victory by rallying the people against a common enemy.

An analysis in 1948 of China's internal conflict, "Civil War in China," is from an article that appeared in a progressive Anglican journal, *Bulletin of the Society of the Catholic Commonwealth,* in January 1948. The original article was entitled "The Sociological Foundation of the Democratic Movement in China." It provides a useful description of the forces at work within China and the problems of American foreign policy at the time. Ting still felt that a coalition government, rather than one controlled by the Communist Party, would emerge from the struggle, a not unreasonable prediction at the time.

Excerpts from a speech to the Standing Committee of the Three-Self Patriotic Movement were published in *Tian Feng*, a Shanghai-based Chinese church journal, in March 1955; "Unity Against Nuclear Threats," the final selection in this subsection, is taken from this; the translation was done by Ms. Cheng Musheng. Although the movement against atomic weapons is an important point in the speech, it also takes a consistent stand against imperialism. We also get a glimpse of the dissension within the Chinese church and the effort made to arrive at a common policy.

AMERICAN INTERVENTIONISM (1947)

The churches of the West continue their missionary work in China [in 1947]. But in China people are wondering how so many missionaries can honestly preach the gospel of peace and reconciliation, supposedly representing the goodwill of the West toward China, while at the same time giving unquestioning support to the hostile policy of the American government. That government would like the people to believe that only its actions (including military support for the Nationalist government and encouragement of civil war) prevent a Communist takeover in China. This argument is not only unsound but insulting, because it does not respect China as an independent nation responsible for its own decisions. The presence of American troops in China may also offer a pretext for the Soviet Union to intervene in China.

The present urge in China to reform the country into a strong, prosperous and modern democratic nation is so widespread that China simply cannot be an instrument of any other country, whether it be the United States or the Union of Soviet Socialist Republics. Any power that ignores this fact is bound to meet severe opposition from the awakened people of China, even though that power may temporarily secure the cooperation of China's autocratic and militaristic leaders. The only way to secure a mutually beneficial and constructive relationship with China is to pursue a policy that takes into account every level of society. At present the government of the United States is losing support among Chinese national industrialists, as well as liberal and democratic elements. The industrialists are now fighting on the side of the anti-American demonstrators. No wonder the American government has to rely upon conventional "Red-scare" tactics to counter the opposition it meets on this continent and in China itself.

The Chinese Communists have a leading role in the peasants' movement to secure the reduction of rents and a more equitable system of land distribution. It is an indigenous movement, and there is no evidence whatsoever that it is receiving any outside help—except from the United States, whose elaborately mechanized equipment (enough to arm seventeen divisions of troops) fell into the hands of the Communist troops when the Nationalists laid down their arms because they could see no point in continuing to fight!

As soon as the government of the United States ceases to aid the reactionary Nationalist one-party dictatorship, the influence of the fascist and militaristic clique within the party will immediately weaken. Then its more liberal elements (Madame Sun Yat-sen, Marshal Feng Yu-hsiang and others) will be permitted to have more say. The way will be opened for the establishment of a coalition government composed of Nationalists, Communists, members of the Democratic League and many others who do not belong to any party.

China is not going Communist. She will settle her own problems and emerge as an independent, democratic nation—*if* the American government immediately cuts off its supply of war materials, which only intensify the people's suffering by prolonging civil war. But the present conduct of the government of the United States is destroying precisely its own purpose and making enemies of four hundred fifty million people who have hitherto been its friends.

CIVIL WAR IN CHINA (1948)

The general economic state of present-day China is analogous in many ways to that of western Europe at the time of the French Revolution or of Russia in 1917. China, for instance, is primarily an agricultural nation whose great mass of peasant-farmers are sharecropper tenants on the vast estates of a relatively small class of landholders. The oppression of the peasants is aggravated by mountainous debts in the hands of Chinese moneylenders, a class of financial operators practicing a traditionally corrupt and ruthless exaction of interest.

This double burden of the Chinese peasants—sharecropping rents and high-interest debts—points to the connection, so familiar in the West, between the landlord class and the urban financial-commercial groups. But the over-all solution proposed by the Chinese Communist Party is not that of the West, where both Russian and European Communist strategy has been primarily concerned with urban and industrial laboring classes. In China a mixture of conscious planning and development of strategic opportunity, together with historic necessity, has led to a far different type of Communist revolutionary policy.

In the early twenties the Chinese Communist Party cooperated fully with the reforming party headed by Chiang Kai-shek. At this time the Chinese Communists' attention was focused primarily upon the organization and political education of the urban industrial proletariat since, in the southern areas of China, and in Canton and neighboring regions, it appeared to be an important factor in the promotion of social progress and the development of a democratic regime.

When Chiang extended his influence to encompass Shanghai and Nanjing, the Communists were forced to withdraw their cooperation. For in these great northern cities English, American and Japanese capitalist interests were powerfully ensconced. And to these influences were added a native Chinese capitalist class, now growing up lustily under an alien capitalist tutelage.

These powerful business interests, eager to exploit an as yet "undeveloped" country, sought the abandonment of the "Three People's Principles" of Dr. Sun Yat-sen, which were viewed as far as too radical and democratic for the purposes of a nascent but predatory capitalism. Chiang himself had at first been looked upon with fear and trembling as a Communist by the northern financial interests. But on his arrival among these capitalists Chiang sold out, turning upon his former Communist friends, and with foreign funds and equipment eventually driving them from the southern provinces.

In 1934 the Communist Eighth Route Army in an illustrious march westward and northward — one of the great sagas of world history — reached the northern Shaanxi area where it took possession of an overwhelmingly rural area. The leaders accepted the region as their destined field of work. Here the Chinese Communist Party, under the continuing leadership of Mao Zedong, has concentrated on developing an agrarian reform program; its work to date has been crowned with brilliant success.

Eighty-five per cent of China's four hundred fifty million people are peasants. Yet they possess less than twenty-five percent of the cultivatable land. The landlords number only one third of one percent of the population, but they own over fifty percent of the arable land. As sharecroppers, the peasants have been compelled to turn over at least half their crop to the landlords. They are also burdened with taxes and various extracontractual obligations. Consequently, although China is an agriculturally fruitful nation, the peasants are so poor that they can scarcely feed themselves. In many areas it is not uncommon for these wretched people to be driven to eat grass and weeds, or to fill their stomachs with clay to allay the pangs of hunger.

The policy of Dr. Sun Yat-sen, the founder of the Chinese Republic, included the distribution of land to those who tilled it. The Chinese people, however, know that when it comes to the enforcement of this principle nothing whatever can be expected from the Nationalist government, since it basically only represents the landlord class. On the contrary, it is the Communists who can now come before the people with the obviously well-founded claim that they are the true heirs of the policies of Dr. Sun Yat-sen.

During and after the war against the Japanese the Communist-enforced agrarian program was relatively mild. Landlords were permitted to remain in possession of their estates, and the Communist administration contented itself with reducing rent demands made upon the peasants. Rents, formerly ranging from fifty to sixty-five percent of the peasants' total harvest, were now reduced to around thirty percent. But with the return of peace the peasant farmers are no longer satisfied to be mere tenants. Furthermore, a large number of the landlords have been exposed either as wartime collaborators with the Japanese invaders, or as supporters of the Kuomintang civil war currently being waged against the people and their policy of agrarian reform.

In their development and application of agrarian policies the Communists have learned a lot through trial and error. At first, it must be admitted, there was much ruthlessness in driving out or "liquidating" landlords and dividing their estates. Present policies toward landlords are more temperate. They are no longer liquidated; neither are they forced to flight or impoverishment. On the contrary, they are allowed to take up farming on allotted holdings of from one to ten acres—according to local circumstances—and in every case on an equal footing with their former peasant tenants. Sometimes they are encouraged to set up as industrial producers in villages and towns.

The Chinese Land Act of October 1947, systematizing the agrarian program, is enforced in all the rural districts of the Communist-led liberated areas. Over one hundred fifty million people are involved in this historic movement for social change in China.

Today the Communist Party is the most popular political organization in all China—popular in the root sense of attracting the allegiance of people everywhere. This circumstance stems directly from its determination to redistribute land among the peasants. Communist leaders understand the strategically important role that the abolition of landlordism and sharecropping tenancy has played in the industrial advance of other modern nations. They know that agrarian reform is a key factor in preventing foreign exploitation and aggression and in eliminating a homegrown oppression of the people that perpetuates their poverty. Only a successful agrarian reform policy will open the way for democratization, industrialization and genuine national independence—as opposed to colonial subordination. Then, on the basis of prosperity, we may achieve dignified and free international cooperation.

Because the Chinese Communists seem to represent the best interests of the peasants, the Communist leaders have less difficulty, and less hesitancy, in putting their program into effect. In the Communist-liberated areas a new enthusiasm has been generated among the peasants for the defense of what has now become their own land against the re-encroachments of landlordism under the leadership of Chiang Kai-shek. In Nationalist China young men snatched forcibly from their homes to serve in the Kuomintang armies have to be roped or even chained together, because they would otherwise desert. These men, violently inducted into Nationalist armies, can see no point whatever in fighting for Chiang. But in the liberated areas young men themselves explain to recruiting officers why they ought to be allowed to join up rather than remain (as is sometimes necessary) to perform essential civilian tasks. Thus on the Kuomintang side the peasants see themselves as conscripts, fighting not only for the hated landlords against their own obvious interest, but against their fellow peasants as well. On the Communist side the war appears as a consistent and intelligent effort to overthrow landed oppressors whose successful return would restore the vividly remembered misery of old China.

Chiang Kai-shek relies strongly on the support of Washington. The enemies of Chiang, and of that reactionary feudal oppression for which he now so clearly stands, rely on the people of China. And the events of the last two years have proved that the people of China may solidly be relied upon. In spite of significant American support during this time, Chiang's position has deteriorated in every way—politically, economically and militarily. Chiang's armies are losing increasing numbers of men, many of them with American training and equipment, to the Communist ranks. It would seem that Chiang's days are definitely numbered and his downfall cannot be too long postponed, no matter how much outside help he may receive. The Chinese people have taken their country's fate into their own hands, and Washington can no longer decide it for them.

But Washington warmongers and American imperialist adventurers still credulously anticipate successful intervention on behalf of the reactionary forces of China. They now plan to give additional aid to Chiang Kai-shek. But we in China know that, despite all American efforts, the basic situation in China is not going to change. Furthermore, American adventurers of this sort would be well-advised to consider whether such action might not relieve the Soviet Union of its present Kuomintang treaty obligations. Indeed the Soviet Union might instead begin sending material aid to the Chinese Communists in the interests of the people's freedom. The United States will then appear as a powerful enemy of the people.

A fully socialist economy in China may well require a matter of some fifty years for its achievement. All the potential commercial and productive forces of the country must first be organized, built up and put into operation. China must be able to supply goods to her own producers and consumers before the entire economic structure of the country can be socialized in a thorough-going sense. At this time Czechoslovakia, rather than the Soviet Union, would best serve as an economic model for China.

With the fall of Chiang and the Kuomintang government, and after the defeat of contemporary Chinese reactionaries who now rally around Chiang, a democratic coalition government will be formed in which Communists, Democratic Leaguers, progressive Nationalists and members of other anti-reactionary parties will all participate. What Americans think of as a Communist dictatorship is not in the wind for China's future. Nevertheless, those responsible for fomenting civil war, in an effort to put down the people's democratic movement, will most certainly face eventual punishment meted out by the people's tribunals.

UNITY AGAINST NUCLEAR THREATS (1955)

Millions of people all over the world have set their signatures to protests against atomic weapons. By signing we are saying: If you have any reason on your side, sit down and talk with us. Since in fact you can't put forward any reasonable ground for your actions, we won't allow you to strike out at people. The imperialists want to scatter the seeds of death far and wide, but the people of the world have great strength. We will answer them with the words of the prophet Isaiah: "The treaty you have made with death will be abolished, and your agreement with the world of the dead will be cancelled" (Is 28:18).

At a time like this—when imperialists are stepping up their aggression and would be only too happy to see our ranks fragment—we suddenly find that a handful of Christians are fomenting disunity on the basis of differences in belief. What exactly are these differences? We believe in the same God and the same Bible; we have all been saved by Jesus Christ; we are all guided by the Holy Spirit. Of course each denomination has its own distinctive features in matters of faith, daily life and organization, but this only serves to prove the richness of Christianity—a cause for thanksgiving, not an excuse for divisiveness.

My experience has been that the Three-Self Patriotic Movement, in its respect for special features in the faith of each church, lays down a principle sufficient to guarantee for each the preservation of its faith. Moreover, wherever one Christian finds another there ought to be joy. Instead, there are those who, finding another, not only fail to thank the Lord, but rather search out and exaggerate points of difference, entirely obliterating the unity we should maintain in faith and anti-imperialist patriotism. I cannot find in them the least thanks, the least love, the least heart to glorify God's name, but only coldness and hate.

Even more heart-rending is the fact that some Christians have gone so far as to label others arbitrarily as unbelievers. What kind of action is this? Since they have been saved by belief in Christ, Christ has already died for them; in refusing to acknowledge our sisters and brothers we seek to slander and condemn them before God, calling for them not to be saved but instead banished from the kingdom of heaven. Who among us dares to bear false witness before God? "Who are you to judge the servant of someone else? It is his own master who will decide whether he succeeds or fails. And he will succeed because the Lord is able to make him succeed" (Rom 14:4). When people in the Corinthian church criticized Paul, saying he did not belong to Christ, he replied: "Examine yourselves, to see whether you are holding to your faith . . . I hope you will find out that we have not failed" (2 Cor 13:5-6).

9

SOLIDARITY WITH SOCIALISM

The first article in this section is from 1957; all the others are reflections from the 1980s. "New Initiatives," which appeared in *Student World* as "The Church in China Today," provides a useful theological analysis of the changes taking place in the 1950s and helps us bridge the long silent period in the 1960s and 1970s before the communication with the churches opens again in the 1980s.The tone of simplicity and clarity so characteristic of K. H. Ting's theology is sounded here. Bad religion is worse than no religion. Ting's social thought reflects some influence from William Temple (1881-1944), Archbishop of Canterbury, who was a social activist, theologian and leading ecumenist.

The second selection, "Insights from Atheism," was published in 1980 in *China and Ourselves* (Toronto) as "A Chinese Christian's Appreciation of the Atheist." Ting has a delightful sense of assurance when dealing with atheism. "We have no reason to be afraid of truth that comes from sources other than Christianity." Communists have much to teach Christians, and Christians have something to offer to the revolutionaries. William Temple is echoed again, "a wrong notion of God is actually a worse thing than atheism."

"Theology in Socialist China" is from a lecture delivered to students and faculty of Toronto School of Theology in October 1979 and published in *China and Ourselves* under the title "Religious Policy and Theological Reorientation in China." The reflections in this article on the atmosphere in the Western and Chinese churches in the 1950s are instructive. The figures given on the number of Protestants in China have been greatly revised since 1979 as access to more information in the post–Cultural Revolution period has revealed a more vigorous rural church than had been supposed (see the figures in the following article, "The Church Endures"). The Dr. Kraemer referred to is Dutch theologian and missiologist Hendrik Kraemer (1880-1965). The Social Gospellers' comment is related to some Christians involved in particular reformist efforts and is not a general comment on the Social Gospel as it developed in various contexts (the following article spells out in a bit more detail the kind of Social Gospel under critique).

The last excerpt in this subsection, "The Church Endures," is from a speech given in Denmark in 1987 and was provided by K. H. Ting. It is a reflection on the problems and difficulties faced by the Chinese church over the twenty-year period since the start of the Cultural Revolution. It portrays a church that not only is enduring but is growing in numbers and in self-understanding, very much at home in the context of socialist China. The future may be unclear—"We do not see what the next step is which God wants us to take"—but there is a quiet confidence that comes from having seen the church nearly die yet rise again. This selection provides a transition to Part 4, which concentrates on the emergence of a truly church Chinese.

NEW INITIATIVES (1957)

What is God teaching the church in China? A revolution is something very complicated. But how has God made issues clear and simple to us, thanks to the revolution? What are some of the points of our repentance, and of our thanksgiving?

First of all—and most important—we are faced with the bankruptcy of all pragmatic Christianity and the subsequent emergence of a Christocentric theology. In the past, pietistic people gave us Christianity as a ticket to heaven. Others tried to tell us that Christianity was a means to save society, to save our country or to save a certain civilization. There were those who told us that Christianity was a means to make people good, honest and industrious. Still others wanted us to believe in Christianity as a good way to get peace of mind or to overcome an inferiority complex.

Now we know that all of this is really bad religion. What Archbishop Temple said is very relevant here: "Religion itself when developed to real maturity knows quite well that the first object of its condemnation is bad religion, which is a totally different thing from irreligion, and can be a very much worse thing." He also said, "If your conception of God is radically false, then the more devout you are the worse it will be for you. You are opening your soul to be moulded by something base. You had much better be an atheist" (*Nature, Man and God*, London: Macmillan, 1935, p. 22). The kind of Christianity he was talking about was once very popular in China.

In new China things have changed. In the past people may have joined the church in order to obtain a free education, but now there is practically free education provided by the state, so why should they continue to be Christian? In the past, perhaps, people became Christian to gain certain material benefits, but now the standard of living has improved, so why should people remain Christian? Christianity was once recommended as a means of making people honest, but now there is a high moral level in society anyway, so what use is Christianity to us?

We should not, of course, prize the gospel for any aspect of its "useful-ness" but for its "uprootingness." Christ does not merely provide an answer—he challenges the very foundations of our questions. This movement away from different kinds of pragmatic Christianity to faith in Christ, to knowledge of him as king and Lord not only of the church but of the world, is the most important development in our life of faith. In the past, when we preached a pragmatic Christianity, although we brought many people into the churches, we were only converting disobedient non-Christians into disobedient Christians. And that we cannot really consider as evangelism.

To proclaim the kingship of Christ does not imply at all that the church should seek worldly privilege and power or a ruling position in the world. In the "good old days" the Chinese church enjoyed worldly wealth and prestige under the patronage of both domestic and foreign authorities. We had political and financial backing from abroad and were protected by discriminatory treaties. In those circumstances we were very happy when government leaders sought baptism and became church members.

Because we felt secure we did not realize the extent of our own alienation, from God and from our own people. We were building our church not on a firm foundation but on sand. To use another metaphor, we have come to realize that the path of our church should not be that of the church of Laodicea, of which it was said, "Thou sayest I am rich, and increased with good, and have need of nothing," but Christ had to tell it, "Thou knowest not that thou art wretched, miserable, poor, blind and naked" (Rev 3:17). Today we feel that our path should resemble that of the church of Smyrna, to which Christ said, "I know thy tribulation and thy poverty, but thou art rich" (Rev 2:9). In other words, we have a completely different standard by which to measure the success and failure of the church. We realize that Christ's strength is perfected in our weakness.

Even now we are still not satisfied with the results of our policy of self-support. Some of our ministers have only a meager livelihood. But many of our clergy know, in a way they did not know before, the freedom and the richness of poverty when it is borne in Christian faith and love. When a church has had that experience, it can never be the same again. I say this in all humility. Certainly Chinese Christians have not all of a sudden turned into saints. God has put us in such a position, though, that we must face the task of self-support. A church that has lived through this experience knows that self-support is less a financial than a spiritual necessity.

The evangelistic consequence of self-support is something we can never exaggerate. In the past we were called "eaters of foreign religion." Today we are referred to as "believers in Jesus Christ." That, of course, is a very important difference, and it stems from our achievements in self-support.

Our friends ask us, "Is the church in new China still a witnessing and evangelistic community?" The answer is definitely yes, even if the reference is only to the maintenance of old evangelistic practices with their predictable results, such as increasing numbers. But numbers can give us no ground for complacency. We must seriously consider whether our understanding of evangelism is adequate for the age in which we live.

Evangelism can only happen in love. God loves the world, that is, the whole of humanity. Can we say we truly love the people around us? Or are we indifferent to them? Do we even secretly hate them?

Too often our attitude is like that of the elder brother in the parable of the prodigal son, who hated the younger, or of Jonah, who felt ill-will toward the people to whom he was sent. As long as this is the situation, we are of no help in the work of witness. In the last few years Chinese Christians have come to see how much we really lacked love. To love people calls for more than just being "nice" to them. It is to understand and sympathize with them, to give due recognition to all their points of excellence, to see them as persons worthy of redemption, to enter into the depths of their thinking and feeling, their joys and sorrows.

Love does include all of these, and only as we love someone with this love will we realize that person's need for the gospel of Christ, and what that gospel means in concrete terms. It is only as we love with this love that a foundation emerges upon which the gospel can be communicated to our people.

The mission of evangelism is a very weighty one. We need to ask ourselves how much goodwill there is in us toward the person we seek to win for Christ. When we observe certain sins and failings, do we feel them to be our own sins and failings? Or are we instead secretly happy at having discovered them?

Most books on Christianity and communism that have been published in the West are of no help to us, because their authors are too much in bondage to the political atmosphere of hatred current in their own society. Their writings are just theological buttressing of their own political views. Their utterances do not rise above the words of Jonah or the elder brother of the parable.

We know that only judgments in love can have the power to convince people of sin, and to witness to the one true gospel of salvation in Christ. If you do not really love people you cannot really want to evangelize them and if you do not want to evangelize them, God cannot put the word in your mouth. Your own speech, then, will be just a clever way of saying things. And to the people whom we do not love, the clever things we say do not seem worth saying.

Christians from abroad have questioned our apparent lack of concern to create "indigenous forms" of communicating the gospel. Although indigenous forms of communication are important, we consider that it is love that is the essential factor. With love, we ourselves become part of the gospel. If we have love people will not mind coming to a Western-style building to listen to what the church has to say to them. But without love no amount of Chinese "native forms" can really be of much help in preaching the gospel. In fact, we would be deceiving the people.

Although we offer our thanksgiving to God for the increase in the number of new converts in these years, we do realize that in many cases they have come in spite of our efforts, or without knowing what these efforts were doing. We must always bear in mind that this is a period in which we are being prepared by God; as we ourselves are re-evangelized, and the church is cleansed and built up, we learn the lesson of love. Only Christ is the true evangelist, and only the Holy Spirit is the true worker of conversion. We must constantly put ourselves at the listening end of the gospel, so that Christ can remake us and change us from being a hindrance to evangelism into being a help.

Love of our brethren is also important. There are some sixty or more denominations in China. Even within one denomination we could not love one another in unity. Take my own church, for instance. The Holy Catholic Church of China, that is, the Chinese counterpart of the Anglican Church, was formed in 1912. In fourteen dioceses we have been using eight versions of the Book of Common Prayer. It is only now that the Anglican Church is producing a common version of the Book of Common Prayer.

The church must be a reconciled society in order to do the work of reconciliation in the world. Disunity has indeed been a very great handicap in our work of witness. Apart from the Roman Catholic Church, however, all the denominations are now very closely associated. Our five theological colleges (for all non-Roman churches) are examples of how Christians of many different backgrounds can work together. The special characteristics of each denomination are not challenged but mutually respected.

Our Student Christian Movement is another example. Many of the members of the SCM would have belonged in the past to such an organization as the Fellowship of Evangelical Students. But today we can have conferences and bible study together. That is something no human power could ever have brought about.

In the West our Three-Self Movement has been represented as a sign that Chinese Christians have yielded to Communist pressure. Sometimes it is taken to mean that Chinese Christians are trying to make an assertion of human self-sufficiency. Now, it is very important for Christians to understand the Three-Self Movement spiritually and theologically; "not that," as St. Paul said,"we are sufficient of ourselves to think anything as of ourselves, but our sufficiency is of God" (2 Cor 3:5).

The Three-Self Movement represents God's act of great mercy in giving Christians a new chance in China. It is simply a movement to make the church in China truly Chinese. It is not a nationalistic movement—though we do not feel we need to apologize for wishing the church in China to be a national Chinese church.

One of the goals of the Three-Self Movement is self-propagation, or the assumption by Chinese Christians of responsibility for evangelism, witness and every aspect of the life and work of the church including theology. We often heard in the past that the Chinese have no talent for theology. For this reason the theology of other countries, devoid of any concern for its relevance to the Chinese situation, came to dominate the church in China.

Because of economic backwardness and political subordination, intellectuals in a colonial country are likely to develop a cult of the West. They become detached from the culture, aspirations and struggle of their own people, even developing an attitude of contempt for them. They become denationalized cosmopolitans. In China the people used to caricature intellectuals of this sort, saying that for them even the moon shone more brightly in a Western country.

This mentality was quite common in church circles in China. Whatever was practiced in the West was regarded as orthodox; all else as wrong. This certainly stifled all theological creativity. In our seminaries we read a lot of Western books, but the more we read them the farther we were from our own people and from the problems in our own church. In those days we were like a group of people who know nothing about football, but have to listen to a game over the radio, cheering for a particular team.

The People's Republic of China is under the political leadership of the Chinese Communist Party. Now, the Communists have definite views about the non-existence of God and the complete irrelevance of Christ. They do not have any conception of humanity as standing in need of redemption—for them religion itself will eventually wither away. Of course we do not pretend to agree with these views. In fact, in Nanjing we very often debate these matters with Communists. The discussion is always very interesting to me, and I believe not without some effect on them.

Further, I must admit that under the leadership of the Chinese Communist Party the People's Government of China has done many essential things for the people, which had never been done in the past. I must also state that the Communists' spirit of self-criticism and their humility in admitting that their work may still be improved is something very moving to us. Freedom of religion is guaranteed in our national constitution, in whose planning all religions, classes and races participated. While the Communists do nothing specifically to help the church, they certainly do nothing to interfere with its life. If you know how backward China was and still is in many ways, and if you know the things that have been done to overcome that backwardness, then you will take a more sympathetic attitude to what Chinese Christians feel. Many Chinese Christians see the liberation of their country by the People's Liberation Army, and the new socialist order itself, not as God's punishment or judgment, but as an act of God, showing God's love for China.

When Christ wanted to teach his disciples about loving one's neighbor, he used the parable of the good Samaritan. At its end he said, "Go thou and do likewise" (Lk 10:37). Seeing what the Chinese Communists have done and are doing, and what many other people under their influence have done and are doing, we feel humbled. We thank God for them, and we want to learn from what they do.

Christ, however, did not tell us to "believe thou likewise." We can best serve our people by maintaining the integrity of the Christian faith. In the early days of liberation a few Christians thought it their mission to establish a theological synthesis between Christianity and Marxism. We know that this is a mistake, because Christianity has to do with Christ, a person, and there can be no satisfactory common denominator between him and any historically evolved ideology.

Are we Chinese Christians too naive? Are we ignoring the "essence" of the Communist, as our Western friends have sometimes worried? I think we know that essence: The Communist is a child of God for whom Christ died, as being worthy of redemption. And if I must err, I much prefer to err on the side of naivete rather than on the side of cynicism.

We feel rather uneasy when people speak constantly about the clash between Christianity and communism, as if Christianity clashes only with communism. In fact, we would much prefer to think not in terms of clashes but in terms of Christian evangelistic engagement in the world. The pathological preoccupation with "clash" is really a reflection of our lack of faith in our own gospel. If we have that faith, we have no fear. We are truly free. We can talk with Communists, learn from them and try to evangelize them.

There are a small number of missionaries, now outside China, whose speeches and writings reveal very bitter opposition to the People's Government. Of course the Three-Self Movement goes on unhindered by them. But their statements present an obstacle to the normalization of Christian fellowship between the Chinese church and churches in other countries. They also prevent many good Christians in the West from understanding how best to pray for Chinese Christians. We only hope that they will cease to do these things and take a more constructive attitude toward the present-day life of Christians in China.

INSIGHTS FROM ATHEISM (1979)

It may seem odd for a Christian to affirm positive things about those who deny the very existence of God. But this is exactly what I am going to do because the subject, paradoxically, is important for its spiritual dimension.

I find it impossible to put all atheists in the same class. For our present purposes, atheists may be grouped into at least three categories.

First, there are atheists who are moral bankrupts. Their life is so selfish, so irresponsible and so chaotic that they simply cannot afford to believe in the existence of a God who would certainly disapprove of them and thus be liable to interfere in the conduct of their life. Yet these atheists are sometimes cynical enough to want to patronize religion. There have always been politicians who use the garb of religiosity to further their unspeakably selfish ends. Like King Herod, they claim to want to worship the newborn Christ, but the real intention is to put the child to death.

Second, there are atheists who take the concept of God seriously, but honestly find it impossible to be anything but nihilist and agnostic. With human injustice, alienation and evil all around us, it is really hard to accept the Christian claim that God is both almighty and loving. It is so much easier to feel that we are standing in a cold, silent, unfeeling cosmos, unaided by any purposeful power beyond our own resources. So there are atheists who try hard to take the question of God seriously and whose honest doubts and unbelief deserve our sympathetic understanding.

Third, there is the atheism of the revolutionary humanists. They reject God because the God they have been told about does nothing more than maintain the status quo, opposing any revolution in structures or values and protecting a moribund and unjust social order. This is a God who takes the side of the oppressor/exploiter class, and who, for that reason, must be rejected.

Why do Chinese revolutionaries in particular reject the God of the Christians? Because Christians the world over stood on the side of Chiang Kai-shek, the enemy of the Chinese people. Because in 1949, when the People's Liberation Army was about to cross the Yangtze River in pursuit of the forces of Chiang Kai-shek, it was missionary-led Christians who prayed that God would perform a miracle and drown the soldiers of the People's Liberation Army. Similarly, a few weeks after the liberation of Shanghai, the leader of a Christian sect signalled from the ground to planes that were sent by Chiang Kai-shek to bomb the city. It was also claimed that this man could not sin, even when committing acts that in themselves were evil, because being regenerated he was no longer under law. From this viewpoint, if you profess faith in Christ, everything is permitted. This is antinomianism. It presents a God who permits Christians—and Christian nations—to do anything.

Now, if our God is so reactionary in political matters, what right do we have to expect our revolutionaries not to be atheists? Here we see how a wrong notion of God is actually a worse thing than atheism. What the atheist denies is not so much the reality of God as the adequacy of the believer's ideas about God.

Atheism of this kind has some positive content in its emphasis on the human factor. It inspires men and women to take their destiny into their own hands and to protest against fatalism and defeatism. This protest is exactly what is needed in a society that has been stagnant for thousands of years. In their denial of God, in their rejection of false notions of God, we hear the human cry for liberation and dignity.

There is something sublime in this sort of atheism. That we are destined by nature to engage in creative work; that alienation from each other is not natural to us but is imposed by a social order at odds with itself; that our lives are meant to be free; that we realize ourselves in creative labor; that labor in the new social order will express the workers' care for the people and will assume an honorable and humane character—all these profound convictions of our revolutionary friends are based on anthropological and social premises that are ultimately theological.

We are fascinated by the story of Prometheus as narrated by Aeschylus. He is the legendary monument of resistance and defiance. He stole fire from heaven to help humanity in its struggle against nature. He angered Zeus, who chained him to a rock and sent a vulture to prey on his liver — submission to his tormentor would have ended his suffering. But he preferred to serve his vulture and his rock. This is what he said:

> Be sure of this. I would not change my state of evil fortune for your servitude. Better to be the servant of this rock than to be faithful boy to Father Zeus (*Prometheus Bound*, lines 966-969).

Now the revolutionaries whom we meet in large numbers in China are the Prometheuses of history. Understandably they will not listen to the defenders of Zeus, whose deity they reject.

The atheists of today are lovers of humanity, ready to sacrifice everything for the welfare of their fellows. The most important mark of the revolutionaries is not hatred but love. True revolutionaries are guided by strong feelings of love. As Chairman Mao said, "All people in the revolutionary ranks must care for each other, must love and help each other" (Mao Zedong, *Selected Works*, Vol. III, p. 178). In a revolutionary situation there is indeed a lot of hatred, but the revolutionaries hate because they love. Their love for humankind makes them hate the forces that alienate men and women and make society inhumane. Their passion for justice results in their impatience with injustice. I think there is much truth in a remark made by Archbishop Temple: "The atheist who is moved by love is moved by the Spirit of God; an atheist who lives by love is saved by his faith in the God whose existence (under that name) he denies."

These revolutionaries can also make mistakes. But they know how personal mistakes bring harm to the cause of revolution and are most strict in self-discipline and self-criticism. They take their mistakes and the task of personal remolding seriously so as to insure that they transcend selfish interests. It is really quite misleading to call that brainwashing. It is something altogether conscious and conscientious.

Can we not try to get inside the mind of revolutionary humanists, recognize the honesty of their search, and appreciate their proper fears about the social consequences of the content of much that we preach about God? We should join with them in the quest for a social system in which love would be made available to the masses of the people. In so doing we shall not be losing our faith in God but preparing ourselves to become evangelists to the revolutionaries. At the same time we shall make progress in our own spiritual pilgrimage.

Unfortunately there are Christians today who need to dwell on other people's moral bankruptcy and spiritual vacuum in order to strengthen their own religious faith and missionary enterprise. But as Christians in China, we long ago gave up trying to boost ourselves by finding fault with the revolutionaries—rather we are greatly moved and humbled by their dedication. It is important that we see God at work in people of conscience, even though, finding no meaning in the word *God,* they may themselves deny that God exists. There is, however, something spiritual in them for me to embrace, and indeed, for Christianity to annex.

It is under the leadership of many of these truly consecrated revolutionaries that the Chinese people have been liberated and their material and cultural life greatly improved. Today almost a quarter of the population is being fed on one-seventh of the available arable land. For thirty years now the price of basic foodstuffs has remained steady. Nobody needs to starve or eat the bark of trees anymore. One quarter of our whole population is being educated. We now have a much more just society in China, and the way has been prepared for the Christian conception of God, the God who is at once all-loving and all-powerful, to be made comprehensible.

The question has been raised as to whether Christians can be fellow travelers with these atheists. My answer is yes! Jesus Christ is much greater than our conventional conception of him. In the New Testament we meet the Christ we are yet to know in full. In the Gospel of St. John, in Ephesians, in Colossians, we encounter the cosmic Christ, the crown and fulfilment of the whole of creation, the clue to the meaning of God's work. This Christ is the logos who teaches all people. At the end of history he will receive the work of all men and women—believers and non-believers alike—not to be destroyed but to be transfigured, perfected and offered to God our common Creator. The Christian gospel does not discard other insights. It makes room for multiple manifestations of truth.

We have no reason to be afraid of truth that comes from sources other than Christianity. There is no truth but truth. God lets different people achieve their several provisional unities of truths. These we can observe with joy and thanksgiving because they illuminate us and point toward the ultimate unity in Christ that is the promise of his revelation.

I believe there is something in Christ's revelation that speaks even to the Chinese revolutionary. I would like to say to that revolutionary: Carry on your valuable work but gain a fuller sense of its meaning and importance by relating it to the ongoing creative, redemptive and sanctifying movement in the universe under what we call God, so that all your undertakings—in industry, agriculture, science and technology, art and music—get an even deeper grounding. Religious faith will not dampen your revolutionary spirit but will purify it, make it more sublime, more acceptable to God.

In other words, we do have an evangelistic task here. But that is only half of the picture. The other half is the purifying effect the revolutionary could bring to our church in all its oldness, its institutionalism and its immobility. I visualize a day when the two halves will meet and merge. Then it will be a new world and a new Christianity. A synthesis between the traditionalist's God "above" and the revolutionary's God "in front"—this is the only God whom we as Christians can adore in spirit and in truth.

So the revolutionary atheists are not necessarily the enemies of authentic Christianity. Too often in our churches contrasts are overemphasized and false simplifications made of complex problems. The Christian community has become a prey to arrogance in its relations with those it should be seeking to understand. We might well ask ourselves whether the church is not cutting itself off from potential allies against idolatry by ill-defined, ill-considered attacks upon atheists. Or is the church really too indistinguishable from the world for us to expect it to be different? An atheism that denies the kind of false gods who dehumanize people and bestow a blessing on bondage and injustice—is that not a good United Front partner for the church in its pilgrimage?

THEOLOGY IN SOCIALIST CHINA (1980)

The People's Republic of China is under the leadership of the Chinese Communist Party. Communists do not have a high opinion of religion, essentially viewing it as an indication of people's suffering and hopelessness—an opiate to numb the sense of pain. In any case, in a few hundred years, they assert, religion will have withered away. We have good reason to welcome this frank approach. The Communists' frankly anti-religious posture makes it almost impossible for them to exploit religion for their own purposes, and that is something we like.

Now the Communists' understanding of religion and their policy on religion are two different matters. We shouldn't get the two confused. To take the view that religion will eventually wither away is not the same thing as to desire the immediate suppression of religion. Today, indeed, they want above all to unite as many of the people in China as possible in the work of building up socialism. There is certainly enough common ground here for us all to work together, and the Communists know that the task ahead is so gigantic that no single group or party can monopolize it.

The Communists would like to see the majority of the Chinese people join together in a united front; thus it is important for religious faiths to be respected. This is the basis of the policy of religious freedom in the People's Republic of China. The prosperity of our country and a better life for our people is the purpose we share. We emphasize political unity even though we maintain our differences. This is the principle of the united front. The Chinese Communists believe that religious people can be good citizens and so can very well be a part of the united front. As to differences, they have to be tolerated and respected.

But for the churches to exist, we need more than religious freedom. We ourselves must be convinced—and we must convince others—that Christianity has a message vital enough for people to listen to. This is where all the theological reconstruction and transformation that we have been going through in the last thirty years becomes important.

Chinese Christians constitute a part of the world's Christian population that has entered a new and unique stage of history, the stage of doing away with exploitative systems and of building up socialism in a country hitherto subject to colonialism and feudalism. Our response to this transition may be just as momentous and significant as that of the Reformation during Europe's transition from feudalism to capitalism. Therefore, to Christians the world over who take seriously to heart the future of Christianity, our situation may be considered a sort of laboratory whose experiments they cannot afford to miss.

There are roughly three million Roman Catholics and seven hundred thousand Protestants, Anglicans and Orthodox in China. Before the liberation strong strains of evangelicalism, neo-orthodoxy and the social gospel coexisted within Protestantism. It may be helpful to those of you who are younger to know something of the international theological-political orientation of those days, because Chinese theology then was to a very large extent an outgrowth of that orientation.

The two quotations that follow are representative of the political-theological thinking of the early fifties, the period in which I returned to China from Europe. A study pamphlet, "The Responsible Society," published by the World Council of Churches Study Department in November 1949 declared that

> the conviction most widely held among the member churches of the World Council of Churches is that communism, a movement which has its base in the Soviet Union, and is seeking to extend its power throughout the world through Communist parties, should be resisted both politically and spiritually, and the churches in the countries associated with "Western democracy" should give moral support to their governments in their efforts to check the extension of Communist power.

Another statement was given by Bishop Dibelius of Berlin and published in the *Ecumenical Review* of July 1956: "Perhaps the ecumenical movement is the prelude to a general theological or non-theological mobilization of all the Christian churches against the materialistic ideology of the East."

These two statements give us some idea of the political-theological atmosphere of those days. There was also a lot of talk about the utter depravity of humanity and the diabolical nature of human collectivities.

Before I left Geneva for China in 1951, I was invited by Dr. [Hendrik] Kraemer to go to his study to have a heart-to-heart talk for the last time. I remember very well the last remark he made as he held my hand. He said: "Always put a question mark to whatever a Communist says and does." So I went home to liberated China with this question mark in my mind.

Aside from a small number of Western missionaries and Chinese church leaders who could see something positive in the people's movement for liberation and wanted to identify themselves with it, all schools of theological thought in new China were on the side of political reaction.

Christians were made to pray for Chiang Kai-shek, the model Methodist, and were sent to preach on the streets (wearing special clothes to make themselves noticeable), warning people of the imminent second coming of Jesus Christ who would destroy the world. Within that political setup, to destroy the world meant to destroy the people's liberation movement. We found that strong doses of original sin, of the fallen state of the world, of the meaninglessness and absurdity of history, of the complete separation and antithesis of grace and nature, of the so-called pride in human works and of justification by faith could very easily be turned into a sort of antinomianism. This in the name of faith gave blessing to any sort of political stance required by the Kuomintang and United States policy.

The rank-and-file Christians in China are mostly members of the working classes. They did not have much to lose in the liberation but a lot to gain. They found that the People's Liberation Army was a very disciplined army, entirely different from what they were told. So naturally they were unwilling to follow their reactionary church leaders. The Social Gospellers, although sometimes good at exposing a moribund society, could not advance any program for change except for a few reformist measures, and they seemed unable to hold the Christians together.

Roman Catholics were ordered by the Vatican not to support the war effort of the People's Republic in its assistance to North Korea. The sacrament was denied to those who took part in patriotic activities. Roman Catholic parents were not allowed to let their children wear red scarves, which were a symbol of the popular young people's group, the Pioneers. Even the buying of citizens' national bonds was condemned as a sin. Many dioceses were being run by Western bishops who, under such circumstances, had to leave. Since Rome refused to appoint new bishops for these vacant dioceses, in 1959 the Roman Catholic Church in China began to elect and consecrate its own bishops. The conflict was very severe.

So it became very clear to us in those days how political our theology really was. I myself began to apply the Kraemer question mark not just to the Communists but to many others too.

Chinese Christians, however, felt that there is something in Jesus Christ that makes us unwilling to leave him — "Thou hast the word of eternal life, to whom shall we go?" (Jn 6:68). Although we were greatly humbled by the revolutionaries in China, we felt that the gospel does give us some assurance of things not seen, but real to us nevertheless, no matter how vaguely we may express it. There lies the beginning of our theological struggle, a struggle to keep the Christian faith, but also to keep it from being used to buttress the status quo.

Now, to be very brief, there have emerged two main theological approaches. The first still revolves mostly around the axis of belief and unbelief. Here the world is essentially evil and Christ is somebody extrinsic to this world. Nevertheless this is a position that does allow some partial affirmation of what is happening in new China.

In the second approach Christians engage in more fundamental theological reconstruction. We think much more about how large the area of God's concern and God's care is. We shift away from the belief-unbelief antithesis to a greater appreciation of the unity of the whole creative, redemptive and sanctifying process in the universe and of what God is doing in history. Creation is not an act completed in the past, in six days or in six thousand years, but a continuing evolution. And the end purpose of creation and redemption is the emergence of a truly free humanity in the image of God. When we say "in the image of God," we especially have in mind the nature of God in its community aspect. If creation is an act of love, then God cannot treat any creature as a slave or pawn. This means that as partakers in the new humanity we will freely choose to live in community with each other and with God, and then we will be like God; that is the consummation of history. Creation is an act of God, but it is very much an educative evolutionary process.

This world is God's, not Satan's. Christ is not an intruder, alien to God, but the first fruit of all creation. He is unique, but also akin to us because he himself is the perfection of what we all possess as our human birthright, as children of God. He is unique not because he stands against the world process, but because he reveals the fullness of the nature and potentiality of the world. He unites himself to every man and woman in some fashion, and therefore you will find Chinese Christians not only adoring Christ as redeemer, but also as the cosmic Christ, the incarnational Christ, Christ as the crown and fulfillment of the whole creative process, the clue to the meaning of creation, the one whom we find in the New Testament—especially in the fourth gospel, in Colossians and in Ephesians. For this reason, many contemporary thoughts and movements may be interpreted not as contrasting with—or even as destructive of—divine revelation, but rather as illuminating that revelation. In looking at events in this way we are not diminishing the unique significance of Christ, but magnifying his glory and confirming his claims.

We are deeply impressed by the fact that Christ was profoundly interested not in sacred things but in the most familiar things of secular life. He spoke of lilies and birds, sowers and seeds, women and children, a father with two sons, people who fish, the baking of bread, a merchant seeking pearls. He used the natural order and the everyday world to enable people to discover in them manifestations of the truth about God.

Now a world that can be used so often to teach us about God cannot be an entirely fallen one. If there is a total disparity between us and God, then incarnation would not be possible. We think that to say that humanity has fallen is really to say that we are not at present in our proper state, the state to which we ought to belong, the state for which we are made. In China we read this verse with great understanding: "For if by the offense of the one man all died, *much more* did the grace of God and the gracious gift of the one man Jesus Christ abound for us" (Rom 5:15, emphasis added). We like to emphasize "much more." In other words, we are born not only in original sin but also in original grace. It is inconceivable that the incarnation of the son of God should make less of an impact on humanity than the fall of Adam. Too often we have made original sin universal but have narrowed redemption and divine grace, as though Adam succeeded in leaving a deeper imprint on humanity than Christ. We surely think that our human solidarity with Christ is more universal, more decisive, and more efficacious than our solidarity with Adam. The deepest word in the New Testament is not sin, not matter, not liberation; it is grace. Human life moves toward a new creation and the emergence of humanity in the image of God.

What humanity does in history is not going to be simply and totally destroyed or negated at the end of history. Our work will be received, sublimated, transfigured and perfected. In this way we see the worth of what our Chinese people are suffering and striving for.

In this light we see that the first theological approach (briefly delineated above) dominant in pre-liberation Chinese theology was a reflection of our alienation from our own people. Revolving itself around the axis of belief and unbelief it was very useful in bringing about enmity between Christians and revolutionaries (mostly non-believers). But today, after thirty years, we have to abandon the security of old conceptual frameworks, and turn more resolutely to the second approach. We must remember what Kierkegaard said: "It is good once in a while to feel oneself in the hands of God and not always and eternally slinking around the familiar nooks and corners of a town where one always knows a way out." That is the experience of many Chinese Christians as we discover the immanence of the transcendent God in history, in nature, in the people's movements and in our own collectivities.

THE CHURCH ENDURES (1987)

From 1966 to 1976 there was in China a ten-year period of anarchy and disorder, the Cultural Revolution, which turned out to be something thoroughly anti-cultural. Ultra-leftism was in control. The ultra-leftists persecuted all those whom they disliked — revolutionaries of the previous stage, high government officials, intellectuals, artists, scientists, educators, religious people. Universities suspended their classes and students went to the street to make revolution. Christian churches all over China were closed down and put to other uses if not dismantled. Our seminary in Nanjing became the headquarters of the Red Guards of the city, and we were all driven out of it. Many of our colleagues in the church had to suffer in all sorts of ways. These Christians mostly do not think it is good to take pride in the fact that they have suffered a little for the name of Jesus Christ, so they generally are not eager to describe what they have gone through.

Even in those days Christians did not forget the teaching in the Epistle to the Hebrews that Christians should not cease to meet. We met in homes. We got together once a week, or once in two weeks, or still less often, ten or fifteen or twenty or more of us. We would have tea together, say our prayers together, study the Bible together, and talk over together what we each got out of the passage. Nobody was the minister; we ministered unto each other. Ministers should not insist on their being ministers and be teachy, as they were just members of the group. There was sharing in depth, called communication, and that was spiritually fulfilling. We all had our bibles taken away from us, but many Christians could recite various passages from memory, and we all put them down in our notebooks. We developed simple ways to celebrate the Eucharist, the name given to it was simply thanksgiving, or breaking bread.

All that I want to say is that, although we have church buildings such as this one, which is historic and helps us greatly to worship God in the beauty of holiness, the church of Jesus Christ can exist in all sorts of places wherever Jesus Christ himself is with his disciples, particularly as he breaks bread with us. As the New Testament shows, Christians had been meeting in homes long before there were church buildings.

During the Cultural Revolution all our church organizations were disbanded. Like many of my colleagues I was quite isolated and did not know what was going on among the Christians. My assumption in those days was that the number of Christians would have dwindled greatly and that this fourth attempt to land Christianity in China was probably again going to be a failure; all that would remain would be groups of Christians here and there meeting in homes. It was only later that I came to know that Christians had been meeting in homes all over China in growing numbers and that in my own city of Nanjing there were as many as twenty-five such groups meeting regularly except in the first few months of the Cultural Revolution.

Today, while we have thousands of churches back and have built new simple ones, largely in the countryside, we still have tens of thousands of groups worshipping in ordinary houses, many in homes. It is a highly laicized form of Christianity that will remain as a mark of the church in China for many years to come. My mother, who was the one Christian in the world who prayed the hardest for me and who died a year ago at the age of 101, had one such group in her house once a week until she was not strong enough to carry it on.

The first few years after the end of the Cultural Revolution were spent in the political and material rehabilitation of our ministers and church leaders. It meant the restoration of their status as good citizens of China and the reimbursement of their financial and material losses. Only then were they in the position to return to the work of the church.

Since 1979 churches are being re-opened or built at the rate of at least one per day for the whole of China. It means that for the Protestants there are now over four thousand churches used for public worship.

The number of Protestants has grown in the last thirty-seven years from seven hundred thousand to three to four million. Chinese Christians are bearing witness to Christ with enthusiasm but, aside from this, the Three-Self Movement must be another important factor to account for this growth; a Christianity with a Chinese selfhood is much more likely to make the Chinese people want to know what it is all about.

There are some abroad who like to say that the number of Protestants in China is now thirty or fifty or even one hundred million. This assertion has much to do with their aversion to new China, to the Three-Self Movement and their need to raise funds for their own purposes. What I have to say is simply that we who work in China have not found conversion to be so easy, that we have good cause to thank God for an increase in the number of Protestants in thirty-seven years at least twice as fast as the growth of the Chinese population, and that figures must be given carefully and responsibly and only on the basis of facts, and not on any human need for sensationalism to bring about questionable effects.

As we look back we cannot but see how God gave the Chinese Christians the Three-Self Movement not only for the strengthening of the evangelistic potential of the church, but also for preparing us to survive the fire of the Cultural Revolution and to emerge from it ready to build up the church in unity and in full strength.

The Cultural Revolution was a time when Chinese Christians with the Chinese people as a whole went through the valley of the shadow of death. After going through and coming out of this valley, Chinese Christians see that the Lord is indeed our shepherd who restores our souls and whose rod and staff do comfort us as much as green pastures. From our own experience we seem to understand better the place of Christ's resurrection after suffering and death, and in the light of Christ's resurrection we seem to have found some substantiation of the resurrection truth in our own life. Resurrection is the word most descriptive of what we have gone through.

There have been changes on two theological fronts in China that provide a good basis for the unity our China Christian Council represents:

1. Before 1949 we had in China certain Christian intellectuals who took pride in adhering to what they called the Social Gospel, which taught mainly the Fatherhood of God, the brotherhood of man, Jesus as a moral teacher or model, the Sermon on the Mount as the most important part of the Bible, the achievement of the kingdom of God on earth as the task of Christians. In the course of these thirty or more years, some of them have left the church to join what they consider to be more effective social movements, while the majority have come to take over the logos and cosmic Christology of St. John's Gospel and St. Paul's epistles, as given for instance in the epistle to the Colossians. This is a very liberating experience – to be engaged in the daily work for a more prosperous, progressive and humane

society and, at the same time, rooted and grounded in a faith that gives us a transcendental perspective and enables us to see the meaning, value and work of what our hands do in relation to the Christ, who is upholding the universe with his word of power.

2. On the other hand, a very important change on the theological scene is that the theology of those who advocate fundamentalism and evangelicalism has in the last thirty years or more turned to be less harsh and less grim and more loving. They are willing to consider other Christians as brothers and sisters in Jesus Christ.

In order that your prayers for Chinese Christians will be more informed, I would like now to tell you some of our problems:

1. There is a big age gap in leadership caused by our inability to carry on adequate theological training for a number of years. There is a preponderance of older colleagues. This situation is going to get worse in five or ten years' time, before it can turn to the better.

2. Our churches are mostly full on Sundays but, unfortunately, our work of Christian nurture has to be largely on a massive basis. There is little personalized pastoral care for the building up of Christian spirituality. We need a ministry that can cope with the influx of new converts.

3. We have ten theological schools, but only one of them has a relatively complete full-time teaching staff. We lack trained teachers.

4. Because of the vastness of the country and shortage of workers, a number of groups of Christians meeting in homes are in isolation. This makes for wrong and even heretical teachings.

5. The People's Government on all levels has repeatedly affirmed and is doing much for the implementation of the principle of religious freedom, not because it has a high opinion of religion but because it wishes to unite the whole people, including religious people, in the building up of the nation, but there is still the lingering influence of ultra-leftism; this makes for a lack of enthusiasm in correctly implementing religious freedom here and there in some parts of China.

6. Denominational structures no longer exist and all non–Roman Catholic Christians are within our China Christian Council. In this sense we are post-denominational. But this council is not yet the future, united church of China. We do not see the next step God wants us to take. We need to wait for God's time and, meanwhile, avoid any human impulsiveness.

So, the church exists in China in the grace of Jesus Christ and with no lack of problems. Here are at least six problem areas we would like you to know and to remember when you pray for us.

Part 4

AFFIRMING
THE CHURCH

Almost all the material in Part 4 dates from the 1980s. The articles reflect on the renewal of the Chinese church after the victory of socialism in China. They tell the story of the emergence of a church truly Chinese, speaking with a prophetic voice against those in China and in the West who would ally the church with imperialism.

These essays offer a resounding no! to two questions K. H. Ting raises rhetorically in "The Empowering Spirit": "Does acceptance of Christ as Lord entail acceptance of the culture and nationality of those who come to proclaim the gospel?" and "Does belief in Christ imply severing relationships with one's own people and becoming stateless or semi-foreign?" The Three-Self principles are appropriate for Christians in any situation, but for Chinese Christians the chance to live these ideas came simultaneously with the socialist revolution. Ideological prejudice would have kept Christians from acting on the Three-Self ideals in the new situation.

Some Christians were incapable of appreciating the fact that China under the Communist Party had achieved liberation and autonomy as a nation. Imbued with Western ideological anti-communism they opposed the new government in principle, without giving it a chance. They also worshipped things Western and did not respect China. The Three-Self Movement was an attempt to overcome the "foreign" label attached to Christianity in China and to nurture among Christians a sense of self-respect and pride in what they could contribute to the world church and to their country. Christians did not have "to worship America" but could follow the Chinese precept *"ai guo, ai jiao"* — love both our country and our church ("A Pioneering Theologian").

Today it is difficult to recreate for ourselves the extent to which Christianity in China was dominated by missionaries and mission funds. Even harder to recall is the mentality of dependence, the controlling role of

Western theology and ecclesiology, and the power of the political assumptions of Westerners. Nowhere had "Third World theology" (or even the term *Third World*), liberation theology, black theology, feminist theology, or minjung theology even been suggested. With rare exceptions there was only theology as defined by European and North American schools with choices among variations such as the Social Gospel, neo-orthodoxy, Thomism and evangelicalism. Politically the Western churches of all varieties were overwhelmingly guided by ideological anti-communism.

The necessary break with the West was traumatic and uneven. Painful differences erupted within the Christian community. K. H. Ting and his mentor, Y. T. Wu (see "A Pioneering Theologian"), were among those who led the church through the 1950s' decade of church reorientation and reaffirmation. "Truth and Slander," from 1955, is a very pointed critique of Wang Mingdao (b. 1900), a well-known preacher and evangelist, and its polemical tone is an indication of the depth of struggle at the time. "Persistent Imperialism," written a quarter century later in response to renewed Western interference in the internal affairs of the Chinese churches, shows that the deeply rooted Euro-American imperial mentality continues. Under these circumstances the establishment of a Chinese church with a Chinese identity is a rising from the dead, a resurrection experience ("A Chinese Identity").

Y. T. Wu (Wu Yao Tsung, 1893-1979) founded the Three-Self Movement. A Christian leader ahead of his time, a forerunner, he stood at the pivotal moment of transition in China. K. H. Ting, in his reminiscences on Y. T. Wu ("A Pioneering Theologian"), reveals much about his own journey of faith. The way was not always smooth as new things were learned and old things unlearned (see also "The Empowering Spirit"). A sad note, not expressed, is that Y. T. Wu died without seeing the flourishing of church in the 1980s, which resulted largely from his pioneering efforts.

The church in China thrives partly because it lost its education and health institutions in the socialist transition and therefore was brought back to the simplicity of the gospel ("The Potential of Three-Self"). Protestant churches achieved a post-denominational unity. The denominations are irrelevant to China. They resulted for the most part from very particular Western historical events. *Southern* Baptist is a meaningless geographical term in China, for example, and is only a more obvious example of the national and cultural trappings Western Christians carried to China. China needs to chart its own future and travel new roads in developing a faithful response to the gospel ("Charting the Future" and "New Roads to Travel").

The church in China is also making a contribution to the world church. It is not acting in isolation, but merely recognizing that independence precedes interdependence and true mutuality. When visiting the World Council of Churches in Geneva Bishop Ting said, "As long as our Chinese people think of Christianity as something Western, there is no way to show that at its center is the universal and absolute claim on all men and women of Jesus Christ as Lord" ("Selfhood—Gift and Promise"). Chinese Christian selfhood is both a gift of God to the Chinese church and a sign or promise to the world church. It is a breakthrough in history that is significant for Christians everywhere. The power of institutions and cultural forms is not final or absolute. As the Council of Jerusalem decided (Acts 15), Gentiles did not need to follow Jewish culture in order to be Christians. Gentile churches were not subservient to the church at Jerusalem. Three-Self is a contemporary manifestation of that biblical teaching ("The Empowering Spirit").

10

CASTING OFF IMPERIALISM

"Truth and Slander" is from "A Response to Wang Mingdao," an article in the Chinese church journal *Tian Feng* in August 1955, and was translated for this book by Ms. Cheng Musheng. Wang Mingdao, who vehemently opposed the socialist revolution, was imprisoned for subversive activities. He is seen as a courageous opponent of communism by some foreign Christians and receives occasional overseas visitors today in his Shanghai home. Chen Chong-gui, who is mentioned, was a leading conservative evangelist known in English by the name Marcus Cheng.

The second selection in this subsection, "Persistent Imperialism," is from an article Ting prepared on his 1979 visit to Canada and the United States. It was published in *China and Ourselves* in Toronto as "Facing the Future or Restoring the Past?" It is a strongly worded critique of continuing imperial attitudes in the West. The paper being critiqued and its author, in Ting's view, provided an occasion to make the point; it is for this reason that they remained unnamed. In fact, the author of the paper was Father Joseph Spae. The paper was given in 1979 at Lutheran Theological Seminary in Chicago and appears in the proceedings of a conference held there ("Recent Theological Research on China and Future Church Policies," in *Western Christianity and the People's Republic of China: Exploring New Possibilities,* edited by James A. Scherer).

"A Chinese Identity" is from a 1981 speech in Jiangsu, published in the Chinese journal *Curriculum* and translated by Cheng Musheng.

TRUTH AND SLANDER (1955)

In the past few years Wang Mingdao has published a lot of his work. We would not object to this if he were really supplying spiritual food to believers. But clearly he is filled with hatred for China and is absolutely against rational assessment. Wang flatly refuses to talk about the crimes of aggression the imperialists have committed against China; instead he insists that the ideas and opinions of Chinese Christians on the one hand and of ordinary Chinese people on the other are *"on every point* opposite and antagonistic." In so saying he hopes to cause ill will between Christians and new China. He groundlessly compares the new China of today to Nebuchadnezzar's rule, and the condition of Chinese Christians today to the condition of the three young men who were thrown into the blazing furnace. At the same time, Wang ignores the criminal actions of imperialists in utilizing religion; standing truth on its head he says, "What you call the poison of imperialist ideology is nothing other than the truth in the Bible." He unscrupulously distorts the meaning of the church's self-governing, self-supporting, self-propagating movement in an attempt to cause Christians to misunderstand the Three-Self Patriotic Movement.

How impressive our five-year plan is! How grand our plan to harness the Yellow River! We shall see many factories, machines, schools, hospitals — all belonging to the people. The Yellow River will no longer be a periodic flood scourge to tens of millions of people, but will become a source of wealth for our descendants. Let us look also at a serious social problem. In Shanghai alone, before liberation, there were reportedly more than four thousand registered prostitutes. After liberation, cured of disease and restored to health, they gained literacy and production skills, acquired the habit of working and were set forward on a bright road. When Christians see something good, we should say it is good; why should we feel ill at ease when we see the good works of others?

Wang wants us to believe that new China is oppressing religion. Today Wang is writing in the *Spiritual Food Quarterly*, calling on everyone to "be ready to give up your life," "at all times risk the danger of death," "give no thought to personal safety," and "prepare to die today." If such calls are considered spiritual food, then only those persons hiding on the mainland, plotting to sabotage new China, will find it to their taste.

In Beijing, at the Huai Ren Tang [a conference hall], not far from where Wang lives, Pastor Chen Chong-gui spoke at a meeting of the National Committee of the Chinese People's Political Consultative Conference. He talked about belief in God, the resurrection of Christ and the hope for eternal life; about bible study and prayer; about himself, now over seventy years old, still spreading the word of Christ; and about the satisfaction found in love of one's country and of the church. Brothers and sisters, the Huai Ren Tang is the place where we consult about important affairs of state. Pastor Chen's testimonial was heard by hundreds of the most representative and important figures of the whole country; it was also published in the *People's Daily* the following day, so that it was widely available. How then can we say that new China oppresses religion? Wang, however, has such a strong dislike of new China that the more freedom of religion there is the higher rages the fire of hatred inside him — even in his tone of voice he cannot hide his extreme antagonism for the people.

At the Geneva Conference in 1954, American imperialists spread the rumor that Wang Mingdao and twenty-eight other pastors in Beijing had been executed by a firing squad. If Wang had come forward to refute the rumor, wouldn't that have been most honest? But Wang refused to do so. How did this manifest his godly virtue? What is this attitude if not antagonism toward the people?

In the spring of 1955 the people of the world launched a petition opposing the use of atomic weapons, but Wang refused to sign. Brothers and sisters, how does this refusal manifest his godly virtue? How does it witness to a saving grace? This attitude clearly shows intentional antagonism toward the people in refusing to cooperate with them.

If we are so lacking in love toward our own people, how can we expect them to be willing to listen to the gospel? Paul always extended fellowship to the people he was among in order to spread the gospel. If the elderly Pastor Chen had been full of hostility toward the people, would he have had the opportunity to witness for the Lord at the Huai Ren Tang and in the press? The Lord said, "Your light must shine before people, so that they will see the good things you do and praise your Father in heaven" (Mt 5:16). In the disciples' time Christians were not opposed to the people "*on every point.*" The believers "praised God, won the love of the people, and the people the Lord saved were added to them every day." It would be good if we heeded their example. Today the best thing that could happen to Christians is for them to take part in the patriotic, anti-imperialist movement.

Wang Mingdao also hates, to the very marrow of his bones, the Three-Self Patriotic Movement. Brothers and sisters, the Three-Self Patriotic Movement is not just our work—it is the work of God.

Since liberation our church has been going through a period of necessary uprooting and replanting; this is also a cleansing process. Only after passing through this stage, predestined by God, can the church be renewed as a place to glorify the Lord and bear a living witness. Therefore, all those who really love the church are bound to welcome the Three-Self Patriotic Movement.

Recently there was an exhibit showing proofs of American crimes against China (in parachuting spies into our country). Brothers and sisters, if people can hang crosses on their bayonets, what is to stop them from putting bayonets on their crosses? In fact they have already done so. Imperialists have used the church in their aggression against China—this is an undeniable fact. Under the guise of preaching religion "missionaries" came to China with all kinds of political, economic, military and diplomatic baggage, and closely collaborated with the reactionaries. They themselves admit this. A student here told me that Wang's "Western friend" a so-called free missionary, wrote that the war criminal Yan Xishan, the "local emperor" of Shaanxi province, gave him a subsidy for his work there!

It is an indisputable fact that the imperialists used religion to commit aggression against China. Either we must admit this fact, and then draw a clear line of demarcation between the church and imperialism, carrying through the policy of the Three-Self Patriotic Movement, or we must deny this fact, supplying sufficient proof to convince others and ourselves.

Wang completely avoids the question of whether the imperialists made use of religion and whether Wang himself intentionally or unintentionally served the imperialists. He was, however, thrown into confusion when others pointed out how the imperialists made use of preaching and books and periodicals to distort religious doctrine and spread their poison. In reply Wang trumped up a false counter-charge against the Three-Self Patriotic Movement, saying, "These disciples of Judas Iscariot call the truth in the Bible the poison of imperialist ideology." This is a lie, an utter slander against the Three-Self Patriotic Movement.

The aim of the Three-Self Patriotic Movement is not to change anyone's beliefs or to criticize the Bible. All churches must preach according to the Bible. Both the Old Testament and the New Testament were written at the quiet direction of God; they contain only truth. It is just because we treasure the Bible that we will not allow imperialists to utilize and distort it, and that we must strive to rid ourselves of the poison that the imperialists have poured into our minds. Only then will our spiritual eyes and ears be clear and bright, eager for bible study.

For example, in Revelation we read of two horses with riders: the rider of the red horse wants to eliminate peace from the face of the earth so that people will be at war with each other; the rider of the white horse has a bow and is given a crown, going from victory to victory. Some have said that the red horse is the Soviet Union, the white horse the United States. We hold that this is an imperialist distortion of the Bible. Is it possible that even today Wang still believes in this interpretation as biblical truth? Another example: the Genesis story of Shem, Ham and Japheth is sometimes represented as biblical sanction for white people to enslave yellow and black people. Is it possible that Wang thinks this is not distortion? Again, in 1948, at the Wuhu Christian Youth meeting, Wang said, "The Kuomintang is our real mother; the Communist Party is our step-mother." We think such a statement is completely outside the scope of the Bible, representing the view that naturally results when the poison of imperialist ideology has seeped into the mind. Obviously Wang is exerting all his effort to launder imperialism, trying to temper Christian hatred for it, so that we will continue to swallow the poison, thinking it to be spiritual food.

In the past imperialism utilized Christianity against China for its own aggressive ends, a process still under way. When we look at the disaster Wang has brought upon the motherland and the church all these years, we understand the great importance of the Three-Self Patriotic Movement. This movement, blessed by God, is necessary for the church and has the sympathy of the people. Why is Wang trying so hard to disrupt it?

We know the Lord wants us to be of one mind and one heart so that we may make the gospel flourish. Jesus commanded us, "If you have love for one another, then everyone will know that you are my disciples" (Jn

13:35). Those who love the Lord should yearn day and night for love and unity among the disciples.

On the foundation of anti-imperialism and patriotism let us unite, neither obliterating nor exaggerating our differences in belief, and thankfully accepting all that is held in common. As for where we differ, we will not enforce uniformity but respect each other, so that no one feels wronged in matters of faith.

When we hear talk about different factions, we cannot help thinking of the pitiful scene in the church in Corinth. There they could speak in tongues, they had "become rich in all things, including all speech and all knowledge," they believed in the second coming of Christ, they had received "the good news . . . on which [the] faith stands firm"—indeed they had "not failed to receive a single blessing" (1 Cor 1:5,7; 15:1). This was a church which seemed in truth to have the Holy Spirit. But Paul said to them: "I could not talk to you as I talk to people who have the Spirit; . . . you belonged to this world." Why? Because "there is jealousy among you and you quarrel with one another. . . . One of you says, 'I follow Paul,' and another, 'I follow Apollo'" (1 Cor 3:1-4).

If we are all in favor of anti-imperialism and patriotism, why can we not unite? We believe in the same God and the same Bible; we are saved by the same Christ and guided by the same Holy Spirit. It is true that different denominations have different features, but these differences can serve to show more clearly the richness of the gospel of Christ. How can they provide an excuse for fragmentation? In a family no member is exactly the same as another. Paul said: "There are different kinds of spiritual gifts, but the same Spirit gives them" (1 Cor 12:4). Why can we never accept this circumstance? In two thousand years of church history, there has never been complete uniformity in belief. The Lord gave us four gospels—not one—and in the New Testament we have not only the epistles of Paul, but those of Peter, John and James. Who are we that we should try to monopolize the Lord's truth?

The Three-Self Patriotic Movement is a Christian patriotic movement—not one single person in the movement has used it to spread personal opinions. The vast majority of members love the Lord; their faith is pure. There are so many ways in which they can guide and teach us. I absolutely cannot agree with Wang's slanderous statements that they are "false disciples who have wormed their way into the church," who "use respect and piety as the road to gaining benefits," and only want "their families to dress warmly and eat their fill."

A servant of the Lord once said that unity is not a matter of belief, but of love. This is so true. Sometimes, as in a family, there is discord among people within the church. Is this necessarily a question of belief? The problem is a lack of love. If there can be unity only when there is complete identity in belief, the love of Christ is all in vain. In truth, mutual respect is a test given us by the Holy Spirit: Do we really experience the love of God in our community?

Mutual respect means not only that we should expect others to respect us, but that we in turn should learn modesty, should learn to love, value, and respect others—look at others through the eyes of Christ. If I am conceited and supercilious toward others and consider their faith worthless, then I will not know how to respect them. Paul says, "Be humble toward one another, always considering others better than yourselves" (Phil 2:3). "Is there someone there who reckons himself to belong to Christ? Well, let him think again about himself, because we belong to Christ just as much as he does" (2 Cor 10:7).

Brothers and sisters, the purity of faith is very important. We should give thanks to the Lord for guiding us throughout all these years. But we should also bear in mind that "these three remain: faith, hope, and love; and the greatest of these is love" (1 Cor 13:13). "Love is not jealous or conceited or proud; love is not ill-mannered or selfish or irritable; love does not keep a record of wrongs; love is not happy with evil, but is happy with the truth. Love never gives up; and its faith, hope, and patience never fail" (1 Corinthians 13:2-7).

PERSISTENT IMPERIALISM (1980)

Chinese Christians have entered a new stage in human history; they are breaking away from exploitative systems and building up socialism in a country whose structures have hitherto been semi-colonial and semi-feudal. For Christians the world over our situation affords a sort of laboratory, whose experiments they cannot afford to ignore.

There is, however, a line of thinking in church circles that works against fruitful relations in the future with China. For instance, a recent paper written by a European Roman Catholic and presented at a Lutheran school of theology in the United States provides an illustration of statements that sound incongruous and misleading to a Chinese Christian. The author— incredible as it may seem to us in China—lauds the sublime motivating power and performance of American free enterprise: "All American values have Christian overtones," he asserts, since "America is a country which is a model of a rational and humane government"; indeed "its national ethos cannot be explained, let alone imitated, without reference to Christianity." More relevant to our purpose here, we are told that the American ethos "reminds the Chinese of the best in the Confucianist tradition," and that "there was no greater loss for China than the loss of America in 1949."

The author links the concept of "manifest destiny" with the New Testament concept of election and declares himself "a strong believer in its applicability to Chinese-American relations." He even thinks it appropriate for President Carter to tell China to supplement diplomatic normalization with what he calls "ideological normalization." The context shows that one of the ingredients of the latter is the solution of "the thorny question of an eventual return of foreign missionaries to the mainland."

In extolling the United States as a Christian nation the author mentions by name none other than Norman Bethune as the image of the self-sacrificing Christian. Is the writer ignorant of the fact that his saint was a full-fledged Canadian Communist and atheist?

The writer's Christianity reflects the positive pragmatic Christianity of an America made up of all things bright and beautiful. He does not seem to know Christ as negator, or Christian faith as the antithesis of human triumphant confidence. True, the American people have certainly made significant achievements. Nevertheless, no country can afford self-esteem at the expense of self-criticism. A people only defines its potential by first defining its limitations.

In writing about China the author does not recognize the claim of its people to their own will, aspirations, passion or struggle. Instead, they are just the object of evangelism: to be converted by a renewed Western and transnational missionary movement; to be won by a "worldwide prayer campaign," in effect, by political maneuvers designed to mobilize hate-China feelings on an international basis.

New China means liberation to the overwhelming majority of our people. They are now able to work and live in peace, with self-respect. There is a new sense of unity and hope for the future. The price of grain has remained steady all through the last thirty years. There are problems and mistakes and excesses in a revolutionary situation, but we have to allow our people to learn to do better. Why does our author care nothing for the feelings of the Chinese people? Why does he have nothing positive to say about Chinese achievements? All he wants is to influence international public opinion against us.

To the author the Chinese people are truly faceless. After thirty years of "theological research on China," the only lesson he has to impart to his fellows is that "the tone of our proclamation of Christ was too low" and "the force of our witnessing to his saving grace was too weak." Missionaries must therefore return to the old job and work even harder. All of this from one who claims expertise in understanding the theological implications of new China!

The author represents those whose only concern is to make Chinese Christians into anti-Communists and enemies of the people's state. It is of no importance how the Chinese people are faring, what they aspire to, what God is doing with them, or what the Holy Spirit says to them. Has the author even tried to see why the Chinese people, including Christians, say yes to our new social system?

Recognition of the historical relationship between the missionary movement and Western economic, political and military penetration of China is basic to any understanding of the church in China. Professor Paul Varg wrote in 1958 of pre-liberation China:

To draw a sharp line between the secular movement of imperialism and the religious movement of the missionary is hazardous. ... The missionary spirit was not an isolated religious phenomenon, it was the religious aspect of the broader socio-economic and political movement looking beyond the limits of national boundary. ... So strong and continuous was the antagonism toward the missionary that he could never have attempted to Christianize the country had not the Western nations with their superior force upheld their right to be there (Varg, *Missionaries, Chinese and Diplomats: The American Protestant Missionary Movement in China, 1890-1952*, Princeton University Press, 1958, pp. 82, vii, 31).

Unlike the author of the paper discussed earlier, many Western Christians today are sensitive to this historical interpretation and want to avoid any repetition of past mistakes.

Authentic witness requires us to struggle for a Chinese Christian identity, a selfhood that is definitely not crypto-Western. The development of self-government, self-support and self-nurture (or self-propagation) is the reflection of our struggle to overcome the denationalizing and alienating effects of the missionary movement. As a result, those of us who are Christians now stand much closer to the people and are more readily accepted as their fellows. But our first author has not made a single reference to this achievement. The people's exercise of power under the leadership of the Chinese Communist Party so dominates his consciousness that he can see nothing but Communist maneuverings. As to Chinese Christians, it seems that we have not been part of Christianity for thirty years and are only now to be readmitted!

Chinese Christians would find most arrogant and insulting those summary judgments in the paper that divide them into a "patriotic church" (collaborators) on the one hand, and a "martyred church" on the other. How easily the cap of martyr is dug up for reactionary political ends. I wonder if the author can produce the name of just one of those "martyrs recently set free" who was jailed not for subversive political maneuvers but for religious belief. And was not Rome, in the fifties, responsible for inspiring those same acts of subversion? Similarly, the insinuation underlying the use of the word *collaborators* only reveals the author's deep hatred for the People's Republic of China and his longing for subversion of the national cause.

In any human grouping there are always concentric circles—leaders at the core, then enthusiastic activists, then warm supporters, passive supporters, neutrals, and lastly those with various misgivings. There is nothing strange in finding Christians in China who either lack political enthusiasm or even actively dislike our socialist system. Do such people really constitute a martyred church? To us it is a question of patience and education, but to our author it is a cause for rejoicing and thanksgiving—he has found evidence for his two-church hypothesis!

Let me call the reader's attention to an alarming and dangerous matter. For thirty years groups abroad, opposed to new China, have never ceased to foster separatism within Chinese Christianity. They may talk ecumenism and oneness but in reality they are determined to undermine our unity. Money, secret messages and instructions, radio programs—all are used to promote opposition to our work and fragmentation of our membership. Theirs are certainly the best-paid martyrs in church history. And as they foster division they talk at the same time of "reconciliation between both churches." What Machiavellianism!

Chinese Christians today meet in churches or in their homes. They are all citizens of the People's Republic of China. Those meeting in homes are self-governing, self-supporting and self-nurturing—just as much a part of our movement as the big crowds found in the churches, whom in fact they sometimes join in worship. They would be furious to find themselves named an "underground church."

We are always ready to engage in any international Christian contact that is beneficial. I appreciate the relative frankness of the paper in question, but must say we are not open to the "future church policies" it advocates when they constitute a complete denial of what we have worked for in the last thirty years. Fortunately many Christians and Christian leaders abroad give high priority to friendship with China. They welcome the new life and the new spirit of the Chinese people and respect the desire of Chinese Christians to be more closely identified with their fellow citizens. In the West, then, there are really two distinct and opposed lines of approach to China and to Chinese Christianity. I find that situation, at least, encouraging.

A CHINESE IDENTITY (1981)

Christ was nailed to the cross; he died and was buried and on the third day rose from the dead. For us as Chinese Christians resurrection has a personal meaning: In relying on our risen Lord, we turn our backs on power, wealth, real estate and other forms of worldly enterprise. The truth of resurrection is this: Through suffering, misery, loss and death, you will obtain life. As the Lord said, "a grain of wheat remains no more than a single grain unless it is dropped into the ground and dies. If it does die, then it produces many grains. Whoever loves his own life will lose it; whoever hates his own life in this world will keep it for life eternal" (Jn 12:24-25).

In the nineteenth century foreign countries relied on their cannon, gunboats and favorable treaties; their missionaries brought Christianity to China. Even though Western missions had sizable amounts of money and personnel, there were never more than seven hundred thousand Protestants in China, many of whom were bread-and-butter Christians. After liberation, under the socialist system, the state took over church-run schools and hospitals, apparently curtailing the influence of Christianity. In its visible form Christianity seemed to disappear almost entirely during the Cultural Revolution. We had few opportunities to spread the gospel; only a few of us could meet together, so that we appeared very weak. But in fact current statistics show that Chinese Protestantism is growing and sending down roots. This manifests the important spiritual truth of resurrection. Paul says, "Although punished, we are not killed; although saddened, we are always glad; we seem poor, but we make many people rich; we seem to have nothing, yet we really possess everything" (2 Cor 6:9-10).

In the ten-year holocaust our experiences may have differed one from another, but on one point they were all the same: The Lord led us to realize more clearly the great power and truth of his resurrection. Now we must build up the church using that knowledge and that experience.

During the past thirty years we have been concerned about the policy of freedom of religious belief. This policy is an important part of our socialist democracy and our legal system and a legitimate concern of all Christians. But we cannot simply lie back at our ease on this policy. The Chinese church must work to establish its own special features. A movement of this kind has in fact been going on for thirty years; it has encouraged Chinese Christians to love their country and has turned Chinese Protestantism into a church belonging to the Chinese people.

At the Yuhuatai Martyrs Exhibition Hall are recorded the words spoken to the students by the president of Jin Ling University on May 9, 1924 (the Day in Memory of National Humiliation): "Since you are studying in a church-run school, what national humiliation can there be?" Another university president said to his students, "Since you have enrolled in a church-run school, you should sever your relations with the country; there is absolutely no room for the word, *patriotism*." Obviously before liberation the Christian church was not telling the people to be patriotic; it was telling them to be unpatriotic, to forget national humiliation. How can we expect the Chinese people to have any good feelings for a Christian church that urges people not to be patriotic?

When the Jin Ling Union Theological Seminary [Nanjing Theological Seminary] was established in the fifties, a policy of religious freedom was in effect, but though respectful, people were still cool toward us, perhaps considering us semi-foreigners. Now things are very different; many people come to look us up. When Chen Zemin, Vice Principal of the Theological Seminary, gave a lecture at Nanjing University on the topic "Talking About Christianity," the hall was filled to capacity. If it were not for the Three-Self Patriotic Movement, this audience would not have wanted to hear what Protestants had to say.

The Chinese church has a lot of nurturing work before it. The Three-Self Patriotic Movement stresses that the church must be organized by

Chinese Christians themselves, not by foreigners or by the government. And we must do a good job, caring for it and preaching the gospel, so that the Chinese church matures as Christ himself matured. This was the idea behind the Three-Self Movement when it was launched by Dr. Y. T. Wu and others—Three-Self not just for its own sake, but for the sake of the church.

Today many people gather in churches, while many others meet at home. The majority of us love the Lord and love our country. Everybody wants the fullness of spiritual life, without which the church will fall into heresy. To fulfill the needs of spiritual life, the correspondence course office of the Theological Seminary is organizing teaching materials; we hope to improve the quality in the future, and all your suggestions are welcome. No matter where believers meet together, we hope the Lord will allow us to be of some guidance in their spiritual life, whether it be in bible study or prayer. Orders for one hundred thirty-five thousand copies of the Bible are now being met, and we are preparing for a second printing. Our goal is for every Chinese Christian to have a Bible and read it regularly. We are now in the process of putting out a special publication on preaching, hoping it will be of some help and inspiration to fellow-Christians throughout China.

11

TAKING A STAND

Y. T. Wu (Wu Yao Tsung) died in 1979, just as the church was beginning to emerge from the Cultural Revolution period. "A Pioneering Theologian" is an important reflection on the life and work of the founder of the Three-Self Movement. Ting wrote it in 1981 in Chinese; the English version is his own translation. The reference to Matthew 25 is to the story of the last judgment. The blessed ones who are called to salvation are surprised. Their salvation is not for any outward religious stand they took but because they fed the hungry and comforted the prisoners and the sick. This is the parallel drawn by Y. T. Wu to the Chinese revolutionaries—they do not claim the name of Jesus but they put love into practice.

A lecture given by Bishop Ting at Doshisha University in Kyoto, Japan in 1984 is the basis of "The Potential of Three-Self." The lecture was given in English. The opening paragraph mentions Zhou Enlai as a non-Christian Chinese who supported the Three-Self Movement. Zhou Enlai and Mao Zedong were the two leading figures of the Chinese revolution. Zhou became premier of China after the victory of the revolution in 1949, and in April 1951 held a historic meeting with Christian leaders in which he supported their efforts to develop the church without dependence on foreign support.

Matteo Ricci was one of the most illustrious missionaries in history. Born in Italy in 1552 he became a Jesuit and lived for twenty-eight years in China, dying in Beijing (Peking) in 1610. He is famous for his scholarly abilities and for his efforts to create a Chinese form of Christianity. History may have been quite different if missionary rivalry had not led to suppression of certain of Ricci's views on incorporating Chinese customs into Christian practice, such as honoring the souls of ancestors.

Reference to the Kiao-chow incident has to do with the German government's desire to seize the port of Kiao-chow in Shantung Province. Two German Roman Catholic missionaries were killed in 1897, and this provided an excuse to take the port as "compensation."

"Christians in Solidarity" is based on a 1979 lecture given at McGill University, Montreal.

A speech given in English at an international meeting in Nanjing in 1986 is the basis of "Selfhood and Sharing."

A PIONEERING THEOLOGIAN (1982)

Y. T. Wu's passing was a big loss to Christianity as well as to China itself. Chinese Christian theologians down to his time were on the whole a prejudiced generation, unable to shed the shackles acquired from their domination by Western capitalist culture, or to deal with the demands made by the fact of the Chinese people's liberation. A leaf put before one's eyes, as we say, is enough to blot out the view of the Taishan mountains. These intellectuals proceeded on the assumption that the West represented the mainstream of human history, and that only Western ideas were high-caliber, axiomatic and vital. They deemed the rule of the Kuomintang Party and government fit and proper, capable of giving the leadership necessary for national salvation, especially if polished with a veneer of Christianity. If there was any awareness at all of liberation, it was treated as a temporary aberration, of no consequence, not worth studying.

Most of these theologians claimed to take God, however, as the object of their studies, and felt themselves to be over and above the mundane world. As a matter of fact, their background and upbringing was all the while conditioning their more important judgments without their even knowing it. What they wrote and said had many political implications, usually echoing the views of Western powers and the Kuomintang. Theirs were voices of deception, bringing the people to passive acceptance of their state of bondage. There was also a small group, more blatant and violent, whose role was to vilify Communist and progressive forces.

But Y. T. was out of the ordinary. He gave importance to history, to the people and to popular movements. He looked at things in historical terms. As early as the 1930s, he saw the great significance of the people's liberation movement in China, attaching hope to it and adopting theological views that helped him to overcome his own alienation from it and to bring Christian youth into sympathy with it. It is important to see that Y. T. was always aware that, before God and before humanity, the theologian has to face the question of political accountability. He had to shout from the housetop, calling the church back to the standpoint of Christ and the prophets, to be on the side of justice without counting the cost. As a result he faced opposition from church authorities and from the Kuomintang. It was Y. T. who restored some old ingredients to our Christianity, enabling the church to achieve a new image in the eyes of the Chinese people.

My contact with Y. T. began in the middle of the 1930s, during the national crisis caused by the aggression of the Japanese militarists and their occupation of the provinces of the Northeast. As a pacifist, Y. T. would still refer to his opposition under all circumstances to taking up arms, but he had already ceased to want to propagate nonviolence. What he dwelt on most was the question of national salvation. He said that if as Christians we simply carried out our devotions behind closed doors or sought personal salvation and a place in heaven after death, we would still remain in bondage to selfishness. Only after the social system in China underwent a basic change would objective conditions emerge to make personal transformation possible. China needed a political restructuring so as to be streamlined to the requirements of the national struggle for liberation. He spoke out loudly for a united front of all patriots, particularly addressing the Kuomintang and the Communist parties, and for an all-out mobilization to resist the aggression of the Japanese militarists.

In his speeches Y. T. presented a Jesus who stood with the masses of the suffering people, ready to go through the torture of the cross and to shed his blood for their liberation. Y. T. said that he himself took this Jesus to be his Christ, from whom he received abundant life, and who now urged him to share that life with the mass of the people.

Even while listening respectfully to Y. T., I had in one pocket my lexicon on New Testament Greek and in another my textbook on the Thirty-Nine Articles of the Church of England. The education I was receiving led me to absorb myself in questions of Christ's two natures and of his place and role in human redemption. A Christology such as Y. T.'s, which placed Jesus in his own historical time as well as within the realities of our own national conflicts, struck a fresh, compelling note for me. It opened up a whole area I had not known existed and hence had never entered. But now it summoned me. On the one hand I felt myself to be above politics — indeed the world — but on the other hand I was quite dissatisfied with Chiang Kai-shek's non-resistance policy vis-à-vis Japanese aggression, which had resulted in the loss of the entire northeast. I was disgusted with many of my schoolmates, who were leading a life given over to wine and nonsense, some so lacking in patriotism as to be discussing which would be the best world power to take over China as a colony! Y. T.'s love for Christ and his concern for the well-being of China was a source of inspiration for me — I felt that a new direction had been given to my life.

In his vision of the immanence of the transcendent God in nature, in history and in people's movements, Y. T. was not only drawing on classical Chinese notions — which were therefore evangelistically important — but also playing, both theologically and politically, an enlightening and liberating role. He opened up a sluicegate, allowing many Chinese Christians to take their place in the movement for national salvation with their faith intact, as well as allowing intellectuals mindful of the nation's fate to take their place among Christians.

The change in my attitude to Marx, from blind animosity to respect, was also due to Y. T. All that I knew of the writings of Marx or Engels I had understood only indirectly. Marxism was monstrous, ascertained by one scholar after another to be nothing but trash. But Y. T. had assumed an

open-minded attitude toward Marxism. In one of his speeches to us he
quoted from Marx:

> Labor produces miracles for the rich, and yet sheer poverty for the
> workers. Labor creates the palaces, but at the same time slums for
> the workers. Labor creates beauty, but at the same time makes the
> workers deformed. Labor produces machines to take the place of
> manual work, but sends some workers back to barbaric labor, and
> turns the other workers into machines. Labor creates wisdom, but
> makes fools and idiots of the workers.

I was moved by this apt description of polarization in Chinese society.
The simple language also impressed me with its poignancy. And it came
from Marx. Shocked out of my unwarranted contempt for Marx, I now
became more sympathetic to victims of exploitation and oppression in our
society. Picking history up from the dust, looking at it from the people's
standpoint, finding in it the mission of Christianity and partners in the
fulfilment of that mission—this overall radical approach was what made Y.
T.'s work different in theory and in practice from that of other theologians
of his time. Y. T. was truly a forerunner in the evolution of a theology
relevant to the aspiration and struggle of Third World peoples, as they fight
to establish independence and democracy in the face of colonialism, feudalism and reaction.

It was not until May 1949, with the People's Liberation Army taking over
Nanjing and Shanghai, and Y. T. in Prague for a meeting of the World
Peace Council, that I had another chance to talk with him at great length.
We spent a lot of time together on the eve of the establishment of the
People's Republic of China.

On that occasion Y. T. told me what he knew of life in the liberated
areas, dwelling particularly on the spirit and the interpersonal relationships
that emerged as people became masters of their own destiny. Referring to
Matthew 25, he said that the Communists denied Jesus Christ but put love
into practice, while many Christians never ceased to profess Christ but,
lacking love for the masses, could not present him to the world.

If the government were to do away with religion, I asked Y. T., would
he still support new China? Y. T. said he was sure that in new China
problems and grievances of all sorts could be settled through a democratic
process of consultation. He spoke of the important place of the United
Front in the national life of new China, and of the theoretical and political
basis of the policy of religious freedom, pursued by the Communist Party
in the liberated areas and soon to be taken up by the National People's
Government. Local problems could not be finally eliminated without extensive and intensive education about the religious policy, not only among
adherents of various religions, but also among the general public and cadres
at all levels. As yet Y. T. had not realized that Chinese Christianity could

not depend for its survival solely on a government policy of religious freedom. In fact, if we were to have a footing on which to ground Christian witness to our fellow citizens, we had to go further, making the Chinese church self-governing, self-supporting and self-propagating.

On that occasion Y. T. also said that the coming of the kingdom of God was a hope beyond history, and that he would not equate new China with the kingdom or think of China as reaching in that direction. Y. T. stressed even more strongly that such a hope should not lead us into neglecting the tasks set for us within the limits of history. In all his remarks there was already a germ of the thinking that Chinese Christians later summarized with four characters: *ai guo, ai jiao*—love the motherland and love the church.

After liberation Y. T. paid greater attention to ecclesiology. That Christianity in any country should be self-governing, self-supporting and self-propagating and thereby become a religion with a national character of its own is a vision basic to the ecclesiology of any Third World church. Few churches have actually achieved complete selfhood. It took someone like Y. T. to make use of the whole trend toward independence in newly liberated China to lead Chinese Christians to take the Three-Self path on a national scale.

Over thirty years the Three-Self Movement has been responsible for significant changes in the church in China. Christians are no longer behind others in their love for the motherland. "One more Christian, one less Chinese" has become past history. Christians are contributing in many fields to national construction. Furthermore, Chinese Christianity can claim autonomy with regard to personnel and organization, as well as finance and policy-making. There is now a foundation upon which to build up a Christian church rich with Chinese characteristics. As a result of these achievements people in China are coming to take a more enlightened view of Christianity, no longer condemning it as a foreign religion. As the relationship with the Chinese people is normalized, the number of Christians increases.

The Three-Self Movement aims to make Christianity Chinese. In any country it is only as Christianity achieves independence from the influence of foreign political powers and the bonds of foreign historical traditions that the radiance of Christ shines through the prism of national culture with a brilliance all its own. The people will only feel at home in the presence of this brilliance, and Christians the world over will be strengthened in their knowledge of the riches that are possible in Christ.

The Three-Self impetus to Chinese Christianity is by no means over yet. The question of cultural transformation and building up is harder than that of political allegiance. When we think of the strictures and hesitation on our theological front, and when we note the persistence of Western tradition in our life of worship and devotion, so incompatible with the Three-Self ideal, we are aware that we are not fulfilling the original vision of

Y. T. and other forerunners. We hope that the next thirty years of the Three-Self Movement will witness an in-depth cultural development.

From the middle of the 1950s to the middle of the 1960s was a period during which I had many contacts with Y. T. We were often together, discussing questions of theological line or theological reconstruction, as we called them. Those were occasions for personal sharing between two Christians. To this day I associate them with eating together, in the Wu household, the Cantonese breakfast of salt fish and rice porridge.

In those conversations Y. T. unfolded his view of the role of Paul. Y. T. thought highly of Paul's missionary work. We owe it to Paul that the Christian gospel broke loose from its Jewish shell and became the treasure of all humanity. This breakthrough was of inestimable significance in the making of human history. Paul was a rebel with great courage and resolution. Justification by faith was expounded not in order to create division between those with faith and those without—it actually played down the contradiction between the circumcised and the uncircumcised. Justification by faith meant that circumcision was no means to justification. We may say that Y. T., in starting the Three-Self Movement, played a part comparable to that of Paul; they both prompted the Christian religion to rid itself of certain deformities and narrowness so that it could enter a new stage of history.

Y. T. often spoke of the poverty and misery of a religion that revolved around the belief-unbelief axis. In such a religion Christ is there only for a person's use and advantage, giving salvation and peace of mind as recompense for belief. This is a self-centered attitude, a negation of Paul's experience. If we listen to the sum total of the Bible, paying attention to its high point of revelation, we see that the realm of God's concern extends itself much farther than the circle of those who recognize God. Y. T. felt strongly that for people living in new China, who have at last gained political power, the New Testament references to Christ as the sustainer of the whole cosmos carry a special meaning and sense of reality fundamental to theological exploration.

Y. T. also stressed the Holy Spirit's work of sanctification. He recognized the Holy Spirit as the bestower of all values and virtues in humanity and the danger of setting limits to the Spirit's work of sanctification and renewal in all areas of the church.

We often went into the question of nature and grace as one of the areas in which the politico-theological line was drawn in Chinese Christianity in the early fifties. Y. T. was naturally adverse to juxtaposing the two. If nature were indeed so fallen and rotten—the enemy of grace—then there would be some dichotomy between the Creator and the Redeemer. For Y. T., to make grace a negation of every particle of truth, goodness and beauty in nature and history would be to deny anything in common between Christ and humanity and to alienate him from the life that he entered when he was born. That amounts, of course, to a virtual denial of true incarnation.

Y. T. was helpful to Christians theologically in broadening their perspective. He opened their eyes to the importance of the world and its history (hitherto held in some contempt); he brought them from alienation from humanity and a lack of concern for others to a loving and caring position. He also enabled us to find in the world not just the tension between belief and unbelief but that between good and evil. All of this plays a liberating role in the thinking of those who want to keep to the Christian faith and yet move toward love of the motherland and other realities.

Y. T. readily agreed to the assertion that religion often plays the role of opiate. But to use this metaphor as the approach to all religious phenomena was to him a dangerous oversimplification. For instance, it would not be fair to lump together as opiate both those theological voices that defend the Three-Self Movement and those that sang the praise of the Kuomintang. Narcotism is one of the roles religion sometimes plays, but not its only or major role.

I have put down here a few glimpses into Y. T.'s personal theology to show that even as he advanced in age he remained mentally as keen as ever. Throughout his life he was striving to bring his subjective knowledge into line with objective facts.

Y. T. and I had little direct contact during the years of the Cultural Revolution. When we met again in Beijing in 1975, the first question we got into after the long separation was whether from now on Chinese Christianity could do without church buildings and clerical professionalism. Y. T. was still the idealist he had always been. But neither in that conversation nor subsequently did we ever go into our personal experiences during the Cultural Revolution.

A person such as Y. T. necessarily had enemies and was sometimes misunderstood. As early as the 1930s he was labelled a heretic, an unbeliever, an atheist and Communist. On the basis of the title of one of his books, *No One Has Ever Seen God*, Y. T. was once attacked for propagating atheism. It was well-known, however, that the quotation (part of Jn 1:18) was used in order to emphasize the text that follows—"The only Son, who is in the bosom of the Father, has made him known," which was in fact the book's theme. Not only in that book but in his life Y. T. was trying to show that the nature of this God whom no one has seen was revealed in Jesus Christ. He wanted us to come, to behold and adore, and then to put into practice what we have seen.

Y. T.'s faith in Christ was of the most stable sort. He kept his own religious faith steady while conversing with atheist revolutionary comrades on the truth embodied in Christ. Cadres in leadership positions in party and government have spoken respectfully of Y. T.'s quiet conversations with them concerning his religious convictions, even testifying that Y. T. stimulated their interest in reading the Bible.

If by spirituality we mean belonging to the Holy Spirit, if we in accordance with Christ's teaching judge a person by the fruit he or she bears, and if holiness, integrity, justice, love, faith and hope are fruits of the Spirit, then we have to acknowledge that Y. T. was a most spiritual Christian. Hating darkness, he worked for its banishment; yearning for the brightness and joy of a new heaven and a new earth he strove to bring it about.

Y. T. used to tell his audiences that Christian prayer was not an attempt to change God's good and holy will or to bring about events or acts that violate God's nature. Prayer is instead a way of opening up the windows of our souls, allowing the light of God to shine into our inner darkness. As our stubbornness and prejudices melt away, our thoughts, feelings, words and deeds may be brought into harmony with the nature of God.

I think neither our traditional Chinese "good death at the end of a long life," nor the traditional Western "eternal rest in peace" can adequately mark the conclusion of the kind of life and witness exemplified by Y. T. Even though they may never have heard of Y. T., more and more Christians in China and in other Third World countries are taking up views similar to his, augmenting and amplifying them. So the cause Y. T. gave himself to is flourishing. I like to think that now, in a place much closer to the presence of God, Y. T. continues to search for truth and to practice truth as he sees it; that he continues in a life of adoration and dedication, and remains even now our co-worker, strengthening our endeavors on earth.

THE POTENTIAL OF THREE-SELF (1984)

I am especially glad to talk about the Three-Self Movement in Japan, in view of the fact that one of its non-Christian sympathizers and supporters lived and studied in Kyoto sixty years ago. I am referring to our late beloved Premier Zhou Enlai, whose memorial tablet we visited this morning.

To tackle the topic of local or national forms of Christianity—which is what Three-Self is all about—is to violate the views many people hold on the supra-national nature of the church. But remember that the question came up as early as the first generation of Christians: In becoming Christian should Gentiles adopt Judaism, since Christianity was a sect within Judaism, and the evangelists were themselves Jews? Should Gentiles practice circumcision, for instance, in order to be Christians? A conference in Jerusalem was held on this very subject. Its decision that Gentile Christians would not have to observe Jewish laws and customs was truly momentous for the future history of Christianity and of the world. The Pauline stress on justification by faith was liberating. It implied that Christianity, rather than remaining a sect within Judaism, was free to enjoy a flexible relationship with other cultures; thus it had the potential to become a world religion.

This world religion is not, however, a disembodied, cosmopolitan faith. In the course of its give-and-take history, it picked up local color wherever it was to be found. Alan Richardson points out that the fact of "locality" is a very important part of the New Testament doctrine of the church.

The church is not like a school of Stoic or Epicurean philosophers, whose existence in a given place is quite accidental. The catholic church is always a local church, the church of some city or country— locality, nationality and particularity are the essential marks of the universal church (*An Introduction to the Theology of the New Testament,* London: SCM, 1958, pp. 288-289).

Thus the liberation of Christianity from its initial Judaic context allowed it to express its faith in forms that were intelligible to the non-Judaic world.

The question of particularity emerged again when Western evangelists came to China four hundred years ago. Was Christianity to remain a purely Western phenomenon, in keeping with its evangelistic source? Would it be compromised if Chinese forms were adopted? Matteo Ricci worked for a Christianity that would incorporate native Chinese elements. In so doing he succeeded in making Christianity communicable to the Chinese intellectuals of his time. Kang Hsi, an early eighteenth-century emperor, was sufficiently sympathetic to the Christian faith, when presented in this way, to write a poem on the passion of Jesus Christ:

> With his task done on the cross,
> His blood forms itself into a streamlet.
> Grace flows from West Heaven in long patience:
> Trials in four courts,
> Long walks at midnight,
> Thrice denials by friend before the cock crew twice,
> Six-footer hanging at same height as two thieves.
> It is a suffering that moves the whole world and all ranks.
> Hearing his seven words makes all souls cry.

It seemed that conditions were ripe for the emergence of a Christianity that would be open to all that was true, good and beautiful in Chinese national culture. Under pressures from Rome, however, and anxious to guard against syncretism, missionaries soon developed an intransigent attitude toward Chinese national culture. Eventually they were ousted on the order of the emperor Kang Hsi himself.

It is worth knowing that the principles of Three-Self—self-government, self-support and self-propagation—were nevertheless long accepted in enlightened missionary circles. Henry Venn, the chief executive of the Church Missionary Society of England, was perhaps the first person to put the goal of missionary work in these particular terms. In a paper written in 1850, "Native Church Organization," he spoke also of the "euthanasia of mission," urging that missionaries act in such a way as to make themselves dispensable. In the 1920s Roland Allen, a missionary of the Society for the Propagation of the Gospel who worked in north China, was especially effective in showing that Paul's understanding of mission was to make churches independent and local rather than keeping them tied to the apron-strings of any mother church.

China was a country of early nationalist awakening. Anti-Christian movements in the nineteenth and twentieth centuries were not so much attacks on the content of the Christian message as opposition to a Christianity enlisted in the service of foreign powers anxious to gain influence in China. Political overtones made it difficult for people with national self-respect to hear the message itself. From the 1920s many independent churches, some organized on a national basis, emerged in China, advocating Chinese leadership and Chinese financial support. Thus the Three-Self Movement did not suddenly come into being in 1950. A good number of Western missionaries in pre-liberation China supported the Three-Self ideal and worked hard to establish an independent foundation for the Chinese church.

It is important for the church in any country to have a selfhood of its own rather than a borrowed identity; it facilitates effective evangelism, and it enriches understanding and worship in the church universal.

Let us look first at the question of evangelism. The gospel brings home to us our sin, and that is something we do not want to hear, human nature being what it is. Intrinsic to the Christian message then is a sort of stumbling block, a "scandal"; but we cannot simply do away with this obstacle without radically altering the gospel itself. In bringing the gospel to others, however, we should take care to add nothing else to make its acceptance even more difficult. As evangelists we must therefore rid ourselves of all that is "foreign" in our approach if we and our message are not to be rejected.

In 1901 Roland Allen highlighted "the political difficulty" that hampered the progress of missionary work:

> At present the Chinese commonly look upon the missionary as a political agent, sent out to buy the hearts of the people, and so to prepare the way for a foreign dominion, and this suspicion has been greatly strengthened by the fact that Western nations have, as in the case of Kiao-chow, used outrages upon missionaries as a pretext for territorial aggression (Allen, *The Siege of the Peking Legations,* London: Smith, Elder, 1901, pp. 1-13).

This admixture of cross and flag gave an ambiguous quality to the growth of Christianity. The frustration may easily be visualized, as missionaries sought to convince their listeners that the Christian gospel was something entirely separate from Western domination; and that, in spite of appearances, it embodied a universal call to men and women of all nations. Celso Constantini, the first apostolic delegate to China from Rome, astutely observed:

> The Apostles built Christian communities and placed at their head autonomous bishops. . . . Among all the accusations against [Christi-

anity], that of being a foreign religion is not found. . . . If the Catholic religion appears to the Chinese as a foreign importation, tied to foreign political interests, is it the fault of the Chinese?

His comments, however, were not to bear any fruit. In 1949 only twenty of the one hundred forty Roman Catholic dioceses in China had Chinese bishops.

Those opposed to accommodating national culture and aspiration within Christianity often elaborate on the danger of syncretism. As a result warnings about syncretism are now associated with a certain triumphalism and intransigence typical of colonial empires.

Here it is relevant to recall that Christianity, originating in Palestine and Asia Minor, took root in Europe only because women and men—in theology, spirituality and art—were bold enough to bring the gospel to each community in terms of its own culture. The irony is that now, as historic Christianity, secure in its own selfhood, moves to the modern world scene, local cultural factors are actually perceived as obstacles to the worship of a universal Christ and the preaching of his gospel.

China used to receive more personnel and funds than any other mission field, yet the number of converts was extraordinarily small. At the time of liberation in 1949 the number of Protestants was not more than seven hundred thousand. Today, thirty-five years after liberation and thirty-four years after the launching of Three-Self, the number is conservatively estimated at three million. The underlying reason for this growth is that the church in China has at last shed many of its Western trappings. Its Chinese identity is not only apparent in leadership personnel and fund-raising sources, but also in its art, thought and worship.

We do not emphasize medical or educational institutions; we are an evangelistic church. Christians witness at home and in the workplace. Now that the stigma of being a Western religion has been removed, men and women in various walks of life are more willing to hear what Christianity is all about.

Three-Self is not specifically anti-missionary. We thank God for the gospel of Jesus Christ brought by the missionaries and for all the good they did in China. We do want to distinguish, though, between obedience to the commission of Christ and political, economic and military expansion of Western colonialism. While there is a time for Christians to go out and preach the gospel in another country, there is also a time for them to let well enough alone, so that the church established there can come of age and be itself. Many former missionaries have recently returned to visit us, and we are glad to find they appreciate and endorse the Three-Self principle and are ready to join with us in thanking God for it.

As stated earlier, Three-Self is also important for the enrichment of the spiritual life of the church universal. It can be said that any local or national church has two poles—its universality and its particularity. We need to raise our consciousness of both. In 1982 the Archbishop of Canterbury said:

> The Three-Self Movement was known in the Anglican Church in the sixteenth century when the Reformers determined to have the Bible read and heard in English. They devised a liturgy in the language of the people and they established a Church which, while not abandoning Catholic doctrine, had local autonomy and self-government.

On another occasion he added: It is only if you cherish your identity and love your roots that you will have something to give to enrich the worldwide communion (Nanjing, January 8, 1982).

Any meeting between Christian universalism and cultural particularity best occurs in the local church. As Chinese we liken ourselves to a small procession, distinguished by its local characteristics, entering New Jerusalem as the church of Jesus Christ in China. We are no longer just a dot on the missionary map of other churches.

Three-Self does not imply isolation. We want to be rooted in Chinese soil, but we want also to affirm our unity with Christians everywhere. We hope to be nourished within the one, holy, catholic and apostolic church that extends throughout the ages and exists within all sorts of social systems and cultural environments. We cannot afford not to hear what the Holy Spirit says to other churches.

The breadth of catholicity embraces churches throughout the world, while its depth encompasses the fruits of the encounters of Christian faith with all cultures. To the fullness of catholicity, still to be realized, the Chinese church makes its contribution of Three-Self. The spiritual understanding of the church universal will thus be enriched in seeing what the gospel makes of the Chinese people as well as what the Chinese people make of the gospel.

The work of evangelism and church-building in China is the responsibility and task of Chinese Christians; no group outside China should undertake such work without first consulting the China Christian Council. This is a protective measure, taken to secure more favorable circumstances for the growth of Chinese selfhood and for evangelistic outreach. It is a plea to international Christianity to take a sympathetic attitude—or at least a Gamaliel attitude—to what Chinese Christians are trying to do and to be. Let us recall the words of Uchimura Kanzō:

> Jesus and Japan: my faith is not a circle with one center; it is an ellipse with two centers. My heart and mind revolve around the two committed names. And I know that one strengthens the other (*The Complete Works of Kanzō Uchimura,* Tokyo: Kyobunkwan, 1972, vol. IV, pp. 154-155).

In the same way we liken our faith to an ellipse with two centers—the two C's, Christ and China.

As to patriotism and nationalism we need to make a distinction. Nationalism gives its first loyalty to the state and upholds "my country, right or wrong." That is chauvinism, favoring an atmosphere in which just criticism of state policies is stifled and oppression and aggression justified. When the word *patriotism* is used by Chinese Christians, it is not used in that chauvinistic sense.

Patriotism is a form of nationalism that is born of the people's effort to resist foreign encroachment; it is manifested in defense of territory, culture and language when these are under threat, and must not be equated with the nationalism of the aggressor. These are circumstances in which Christians choose to take the side of their people and support a positive nationalism that makes for progress in history. Dr. Sun Yat-sen, a Christian, made a choice of this kind in his stand against Manchu despotism and foreign encroachment, and we are mindful of the support he got from friends in Japan.

Patriotism of this kind expresses itself in sorrow over national humiliation and in joy over the people's emancipation and achievements. We find examples of both in the Old Testament. Psalm 137, for example, expresses sorrow over national catastrophe:

> By the waters of Babylon,
> there we sat down and wept,
> when we remembered Zion.
> On the willows there
> we hung up our lyres.
> For there our captors
> required of us songs,
> and our tormentors, mirth, saying,
> "Sing us one of the songs of Zion!"
> How shall we sing the Lord's song
> in a foreign land?
> If I forget you, O Jerusalem,
> let my right hand wither!
> Let my tongue cleave to the roof of my mouth,
> if I do not remember you,
> if I do not set Jerusalem
> above my highest joy!

Psalm 126 is an example of joy and thanksgiving for the people's achievements:

> When the Lord restored the fortunes of Zion,
> we were like those who dream.

Then our mouth was filled with laughter,
and our tongue with shouts of joy;
then they said among the nations,
"The Lord has done great things for them."
The Lord has done great things for us,
we are glad.
Restore our fortunes, O lord,
like the watercourses in the Negeb!
May those who sow in tears
reap with shouts of joy!
He that goes forth weeping,
bearing the seed for sowing,
shall come home with shouts of joy,
bringing his sheaves with him.

Patriotism in China today affirms the achievements and self-sacrifice of millions of our fellow citizens, and pledges that we will work for material and cultural betterment and for greater justice and human dignity. That is a responsible love of country. For us, caring for China is our point of departure, the first stage in our love of humanity.

One result of Three-Self in China is that Chinese Protestantism finds itself in a post-denominational situation. In the early fifties, with the war in Korea, American funds for China were frozen. All the national and many of the provincial and diocesan denominational bodies, as well as the National Christian Council, were paralyzed. Under those circumstances Christians built relationships across denominational lines. Because of the shortness of denominational history in China, denominational loyalty was not an impediment to the growth of the spirit of unity among Christians under the umbrella of Three-Self. Today, while denominational structures no longer exist, their characteristics in matters of faith and worship, which Christians cherish, are honored and preserved.

Chinese Christians are faced with other problems; the big age gap between our present church leaders and their successors still in training; the inadequacy of pastoral nurturing; the existence of heretical teachings; and mistakes at the local level in implementing a policy of religious freedom. But we are aware that despite problems churches have always moved ahead. As we go forward on the path of Three-Self, prayers of support from Christians elsewhere mean a lot to us. We hope and pray that through exchange visits of Japanese and Chinese Christians a deeper, more sympathetic and loving relationship will develop between the Christians of our two countries, enabling us to strengthen each other in the work of building up the body of Christ.

CHRISTIANS IN SOLIDARITY (1979)

Ever since our defeat in the Opium War the Chinese have been asking how they can save China. The Fourth of May Movement of 1919 summarized the key answer in two words: science and democracy. With socialist modernization as the primary target in China, these two words are very much in the air again after a period of eclipse during the Cultural Revolution. Modernization requires the participation and involvement of the masses if it is to succeed. And without such democratization scientific initiative can make no solid contribution to modernization.

Practical democracy does not come naturally to China. Our people do not have the habit of questioning authority; even those who are politically conscientized tend to accept without comment the rule of the Communist Party and its cadres. Similarly those in leadership positions expect others to submit to their authority. But now, after the experience of the last decade or so, we have come to see how dangerous all of this can be.

At present we are struggling to bring about socialist democracy. We do need the leadership of the Communist Party, for it has a political philosophy oriented toward a just and humane transformation of our society. It also has the tools for a thorough and correct historical and social analysis; a clear perception of agents of change; and familiarity with the means of conscientizing and involving the population in a coalition or united front. It is also able to propose policies compatible with those ends. What is needed is organic integration of that leadership with the mobilization and democratic participation of the masses. So we are now in the midst of a struggle between democracy on the one hand and bureaucracy (entailing insensitivity and irresponsibility to the good of the people) on the other.

The United Front plays an important role in the struggle. The Communist Party constitutes only three percent of the population. The United Front is a coalition of all classes, nationalities and sectors that have a stake in the building up of a new China. The extent to which these elements are incorporated into it indicates the degree of democratization we are able to achieve.

An important organ of the United Front is the National People's Political Consultative Conference, with its provincial and local counterparts. It comprises representatives from all walks of life—workers, peasants, soldiers, youth, women, democratic political parties, minority nationalities, scientists, educators, artists, writers and religious leaders. In this conference all the important policies and appointments, both domestic and foreign, are discussed and investigation and consultation carried on. Buddhism, Lamaism, Islam, Roman Catholicism and Protestantism are represented in its religious section, providing a forum for airing views on such matters as the implementation of religious freedom.

There is little religious fanaticism in China, perhaps because Confucianism itself has a moralist emphasis. Almost all the important religions in China have been imported. Today, fifteen percent of the population at most professes a formal religious affiliation. Yet to non-believers the extent to which religion enjoys democratic freedom is a barometer of our struggle for democratization. So there is a genuine concern for the correct implementation of religious freedom as laid down by Chairman Mao Zedong and Premier Zhou Enlai. At the same time believers themselves are struggling for internal changes that will make religion more consonant with state independence and modernization. In this discussion I shall look only at what is happening in Chinese Protestantism.

New China marks an epochal break with the capitalist world empire as the people enter an unprecedented stage of post-colonial, socialist reconstruction. Drastic departures from the norm of Western Christianity are only to be expected. These changes may be seen as threefold.

First, there is a move away from the mission field to the establishment of a church that is instead self-governing, self-supporting and self-nurturing. Our church is to be thoroughly Chinese, not only in personnel and financial support but also in social and political orientation, that is, in its close identification with the people's cause of liberation.

Chinese people are gradually changing their view of the Christian religion, no longer seeing it as a foreign religion but rather as one to which all Chinese citizens have a right to belong. This development, largely brought about by the Three-Self Movement, has extremely important historic implications for the task of Christian witness in China. The fact that a Christian Center for Religious Studies now forms part of Nanjing University would have been quite unthinkable in the fifties and sixties.

Second, we are in the process of deinstitutionalization. As we look back over the history of Christianity we find that in the past faith was often replaced by a search for security. Institutional Christianity tended to exist for its own sake. This quest for self-perpetuity required collaboration with the powers-that-be, so the church inevitably sided with the status quo. It bound us to the dead past, becoming a symbol of identification with a social order that it was supposed to question. When Christianity sanctifies the cultural, social and political structures of oppression, it effectually denies the gospel it affirms. It gets in the way of our vital communication with Jesus of Nazareth and with each other.

Now the loss of our church-related institutions was a sad experience for many of us. It has been difficult and painful to part company with universities, colleges, hospitals and orphanages even though our socialist state and communities are running all of these in much larger numbers and on a much larger scale. With this connection severed, however, something apparently important died. And yet, through this death we may actually find a more intense and spiritually satisfying life. From our own experience we know that in institutionalized Christianity we make the enterprise of religion our god while with deinstitutionalization we make God our religion.

Third, we are working for theological reconstruction. The dominant pre-liberation theology, revolving on the exclusivity of belief, was a reflection of alienation. After thirty years, in the light of historical change, our theology has shifted to the pluralistic language of practice. Our focus has moved from non-believers to the non-persons mass-produced by our old society—we look for ways to help them. This shift has forced us to abandon those conceptual frameworks in which we once found our security. Christians are discovering the immanence of the transcendent God in history, in nature and in people's movements and collectives. God, who is worthy of our worship and praise, is not so small as to be concerned only—or mainly, or first of all—with a small fraction of Chinese who profess belief. God's concern and care is for the Chinese people as whole.

To believe that God is loving and at the same time almighty is difficult anyway, if one is serious about it. But because liberation in China has brought material and cultural improvement in people's lives, it is easier for them to visualize such a God, though only if adequately presented. We must carry our Three-Self Movement still further so as to make good Chinese of the good Christians. This means we must live down our historic association with the West, further altering the public perception of Chinese Christianity. Then a common language will emerge to enhance the dialogue between Christians and other people.

SELFHOOD AND SHARING (1986)

The element of self-support in the Three-Self Movement stresses that financial maintenance of church personnel, evangelism and nurture is our responsibility as Chinese Christians; we must not rely on missionary funds from abroad, no matter what buildings and other facilities they allow us to construct. We must realize that self-support is an important condition for our church in its struggle to become Chinese. It is only a church possessing a selfhood of its own that can truly play its part in the give-and-take of interchurch sharing—in other words, only as we overcome dependence and achieve independence is true interdependence possible.

Approximately four thousand Protestant churches and tens of thousands of Christians meeting in homes are self-supporting financially. Admittedly we benefit from a government policy of tax exemption. On the other hand, larger church organizations and seminaries still have to make do to some extent with rental accommodation, something that is not conducive to solid self-support.

We believe that genuine, disinterested love is possible between Christians of different nations; our adherence to the self-support principle must not be seen as outright rejection of this love. Christians from abroad are just as free to make offerings at church services as their Chinese fellow Christians. Other gifts and contributions will be gratefully accepted as long as those who give—individuals or organizations—are not hostile to new China and to our Three-Self principle. Similarly, the size of such gifts should not be such that it impairs our selfhood and the Chinese image of our church or forces a Chinese church group to become dependent or parasitic. This apparent rigidity on our part may suggest that we are depriving ourselves of many good things for church development, but in the long run only a church truly without privileges and materially close to its own people can take Christ's message to them.

The Three-Self principle does not mean that we are totally to refrain from giving to other churches. But in giving, within our limited means, we want to be sure that the act is truly one of love, respecting the integrity and rights of others, avoiding publicity and making no demand for accountability. Our own selfhood must not infringe on the sacred space that constitutes the selfhood of other countries and their churches.

Today, many individual Christians from abroad as well as church groups and church-related groups are establishing connections with non-church Chinese institutions for educational, medical and social welfare purposes, giving their support in the form of technology, equipment and personnel. As Chinese citizens and Chinese Christians we support in principle such links insofar as they do not trespass upon Chinese sovereignty but contribute only to China's modernization. While we are thankful that these links are being made, the fact that there are sometimes Christians involved on the Chinese side should not be taken to mean that the Chinese church has departed from its principle of self-support.

I would urge, furthermore, that these links not be used as cover for hostile infiltration of new China. Christians from abroad involved in these projects should be quite open about their religious identity. They are certainly welcome to participate in the life of local churches, though not to proselytize among the Chinese people or interfere in the internal affairs of the Chinese church.

Chinese Christian organizations appreciate the fact that many Christian and church-related groups from abroad who are working now with non-church Chinese bodies do inform us of their involvement. In turn we want to help them, whether in a consultative capacity or in any other way.

Our experience over the last thirty years and more tells us that Three-Self is not something that can be firmly established—let alone taken for granted—without the hard work put in by several generations of Chinese Christians. As contact develops between China and the rest of the world, it is admittedly possible to find Christians weak in their commitment to Three-Self who are tempted to return to "the good old days." We know that there are those outside China who are working only too hard to bring this about. Thus the struggle between principle and temptation is not yet over. Such circumstances pose a testing time for commitment to Three-Self, in China itself as well as among our friends abroad.

Recently, for instance, we heard an alarming rumor of the fragmentation of Chinese Protestantism; it is said that pastors within the China Christian Council and their provincial and local counterparts, out of their wish to receive missionary funds from abroad for church work, are turning their back on Three-Self organizations and thus on the basic principle of self-support. We are sure that pastors with any judgment at all will have no reason to join such a movement because Three-Self organizations, despite their shortcomings, mean so much to the very existence of Christian witness in China. Indeed it is the pastors themselves who give leadership at all levels to both Three-Self organizations and Christian Councils.

From a world and historical perspective Three-Self is an experiment carried out by Chinese Christians on behalf of the universal church. If successful it will mean the enrichment of Christians everywhere. And so, we make this appeal: Let those who have been our enemies drop their enmity, at least for a while, and become more objective observers; and let those who are already observers come forward to join us as friends.

12

TRULY CHINESE

"Charting the Future" is from a 1980 address given at the Third Chinese National Christian Conference. It was made available in typescript in English and was also published in English in *Ching Feng*, a Hong Kong–based journal, under the title "Retrospect and Prospect." Even at this date it talks of the need to rid Chinese Christianity of its "colonial nature." The fuller opening to the West since 1980 means the temptation of Western Christians to go back to old patterns is all the more present. The second selection in this subsection, "New Roads to Travel," is from the closing speech at the same conference. It was published in Chinese in the Christian journal *Tian Feng* in March 1980 and was translated for this book by Ms. Cheng Musheng.

"Building Community" is from "Christianity in China Today," originally published in English in the news weekly *Beijing Review* in June 1984. K. H. Ting's preface to the first issue of *Chinese Theological Review* (1985), an annual publication in English edited by Janice Wickeri in Hong Kong, is the source of "A Nurturing Theology."

In these articles Ting writes that the task of maintaining church unity, avoiding various Western splits such as that between evangelicals and ecumenicals, is not easy. Liberation theology is to be avoided since it would work against church unity in China. Supporting socialism is a political option exercised by Chinese Christians as citizens, but theology can and should be kept separate from politics. The theological meaning of liberation is not an issue of interest, according to K. H. Ting. This position is difficult for many Christians outside China to understand and future dialogue on it will be instructive.

"Selfhood—Gift and Promise" is from a sermon given in Geneva. An excerpt entitled "Sign for Something Beyond Itself" was published in the World Council of Churches' publication *One World* in January 1984. The final selection, "The Empowering Spirit," is from a sermon delivered at a service marking the 30th anniversary of the founding of the Three-Self Movement. An English translation of the sermon was published in *Chinese Theological Review*, 1985, as "The Holy Spirit and Us." These final two selections give strong prophetic witness to the mission of the Chinese church.

CHARTING THE FUTURE (1980)

In the four years since the downfall of the Gang of Four, and especially during the recent months of preparation for this conference, a great many pastoral workers and lay people around the nation have been looking to the future and pondering the question: What should the Chinese church be doing in the days to come? The Standing Committee of the National Three-Self Movement discussed this question in a week-long meeting earlier this year. Since the meeting's distribution of "An Open Letter to Brothers and Sisters in Christ Throughout China" on 1 March, a great number of opinions and suggestions have been put forward in response.

We now realize that this question is indeed a matter for our own decision—it cannot be answered for us by other people. The independence of the church is now an established fact. As we rejoice we acknowledge that the Three-Self Patriotic Movement is very precious to us, and we look for a bright future for Christianity in China.

We have been separated by great distances and have not seen one another for a long time; we have had many different experiences over the past years; and anti-China forces outside our country have never ceased to sow dissension. Yet it can truly be said that we are "of the same mind having the same love, in full accord and of one mind" (Phil 2:2). How would we have been able to achieve this unity of heart and mind without the work of the Holy Spirit, allowing us to communicate with one another in Christ?

I would now like to bring our opinions together in order to facilitate discussions over the next few days.

Feudalism, imperialism and bureaucratic capitalism long weighed like three mountains on the backs of the Chinese people. Although there were missionaries and Chinese church leaders who supported efforts for liberation, Christianity in general stood with the reactionaries rather than with the Chinese people. As a result of our affiliation with that kind of Christianity our national consciousness weakened; we were not of one mind with our own people and seemed to have become semi-Western. The clamor within the church against the Communist Party and the people was especially loud around the time of liberation. How could the Christian gospel be preached effectively when Chinese Christians and the people of the motherland lacked any common language?

Such a Christianity, backed by foreign power, lost its source of support after liberation. As it became isolated within China, Christianity faced a difficult situation. It was then that Chinese Christians discovered that God would not quench the dimly burning wick of Chinese Christianity but would allow it to shine forth. In God's providence two things came to our aid:

The first was the policy of religious freedom formulated by Chairman Mao and Premier Zhou; the second was the Three-Self Movement launched by Chinese Christians themselves. For us, these are signs that God has prepared for us a new opportunity and a new beginning.

While we are completely free not to accept the religious outlook of the Communist Party, this is not to say that we oppose all its points of view. For example, it would make no sense for us to oppose the Communist Party's proposal for the United Front. Like all other citizens, those who believe in Jesus Christ ardently desire a strong and prosperous motherland and look forward to the early realization of the Four Modernizations; it is only natural that Christians are part of the United Front. [The Four Modernizations was a campaign launched in 1975 to update industry, agriculture, science, and national defense.] There is freedom to maintain any religious faith, any worldview, under the principle of mutual respect. It is in this way that unity and stability, the formation of the United Front and the realization of the Four Modernizations are made possible. In the West there are those who persist in saying that the Communist Party wants to standardize everyone's worldview and that it does not permit people to believe in religion. This view is totally incorrect.

The Gang of Four was completely different from the Communist Party. The two should not be confused. The Gang of Four wanted neither the Four Modernizations nor unity and stability. They had no use for veteran cadres, intellectuals, religious believers or the United Front. Because they wanted to eradicate religion, they had no regard for the policy of religious freedom. They disbanded all the Religious Affairs Bureaus, whose duty was to implement at all levels the policy of religious freedom. It was precisely because the Chinese Communist Party had such a policy of religious freedom that Christians were protected by the state after liberation—even though we were not very popular with the people—and given an opportunity to continue to exist.

But for Christianity to continue in China and to serve as a witness to Jesus Christ, it would not have been enough only to rely on a national policy of religious freedom. It was also necessary to develop a common language with the Chinese people, so that a foreign religion could be transformed into one that was China's own. Three-Self is a patriotic movement of Chinese Christians. It encourages us as Chinese Christians to develop a sense of national self-respect, to love our motherland and to dedicate ourselves to the goal of national prosperity, walking and thinking together with our compatriots. With regard to the church in particular, it stands for self-government, self-support and self-propagation, advocating an independent Chinese church organized by Chinese Christians.

The Three-Self Movement has been—and will continue to be—an instrument for significant change. In particular there are three main aspects of its life that I would like to comment on now.

First of all, it has imbued Chinese Christians with a worthwhile sense of patriotism. Patriotism is the profound feeling of the people toward their motherland. This feeling reflects the self-respect and the self-confidence of the nation. It embodies the heroic commitment and struggle of a people to make the motherland independent, prosperous and strong. A patriot actively works to overcome the backwardness of the country, but without any accompanying feelings of inferiority or any wish to hurt national dignity or esteem.

We now see more clearly that Christianity does not ask us to look down on nationality, but rather to acknowledge it in good faith. The Book of Revelation tells us that Jerusalem will one day descend from heaven. Then there will be no temple; indeed many things that we have in today's world will be no more, including nationality. All these things will become one in Christ and Christ will become all in all. But today is not yet that day. Today, in consonance with divine providence, people belong to this or that nation and country. When the son of God became flesh, even he did not become a stateless nihilist. Jesus and many of his disciples were Jews among Jews. The gospel first took shape by uniting itself with Jewish life and culture. Paul also had strong national feelings, calling his compatriots "my brethren, my kinsmen by race" (Rom 9:3). We who are Chinese are not born so by choice—it is God who ordains it. To be good internationalists and confident members of the world family, we must first become patriots and stand with the Chinese people.

Christianity in China has by and large now rid itself of the control and exploitation of imperialism, bureaucratic capitalism and feudalism. It has become a religious community of self-government, self-support and self-propagation. It is no longer a dependent of foreign missionary societies but is organized by a part of the Chinese citizenry out of faith and love of Christ. It is more and more a Christianity with Chinese characteristics. While affirming the universality of our religion, we understand that Chinese Christianity cannot talk of making contributions to world Christianity unless it rids itself of its colonial nature and ceases to be a replica of foreign Christianity. We must not alienate ourselves from the Chinese people but join in their cause, plant our roots in Chinese culture, and develop our Chinese selfhood.

Chinese Christianity cannot change or cover up its history. Rather we have to accept fully the lesson of our past and go on to write new pages in our history. The Three-Self Patriotic Movement has brought Christianity, once rooted in old semi-colonial, semi-feudal China, into harmony with new socialist China. It has cleansed the church, enabling the light of the gospel to shine forth.

In consequence, more and more people understand that Christians too are Chinese citizens, capable of national self-respect, and that Christianity is a religion that Chinese citizens are fully entitled to believe in and to uphold by their own choice. The change in public opinion will ease the way for the policy of religious freedom. As we in Three-Self organizations work to implement such a policy we find many cadres and other people who understand that Christianity does not stand in the way of the Four Modernizations. They have goodwill toward us, respect our faith and firmly adhere to the policy in dealing with us. We deem it an honor that Christianity was not tolerated by the Gang of Four. The maltreatment they meted out to churches and individual Christians was unpopular precisely because we had carried out the Three-Self Patriotic Movement after liberation. The broad masses of the people knew that this treatment was not in keeping with the policy of the state. We had the people's sympathy, and that is very precious.

The Chinese Christian Three-Self Patriotic Movement represents a significant stage of development in the broad history of Christianity. As an Asian Christian leader recently said, "The Chinese experience of decolonization must be presented forcefully in front of the Asian Churches as one of the important exemplary models to be considered as they struggle to achieve their self-hood."

Chinese Christians are in this situation not because we have any special merits or attainments, but because of the particular place that China occupies at present in the historical process. Paul said to the Corinthian church: "Consider your call, brethren; not many of you were wise according to worldly standards, not many were powerful, not many were of noble birth; but God chose what is foolish in the world to shame the wise, God chose what is weak in the world to shame the strong" (1 Cor 1:26-27). We ought to recall these words often, so as to remind ourselves to remain humble, firmly grasping the will of God.

In spite of its various shortcomings the Three-Self Movement is just, reasonable and necessary. This has been proved by its great accomplishments. When we review the past, we thank God with all our hearts for raising up in our midst our dear Mr. Y. T. Wu, Bishop Chen Jianzhen, Bishop Z. T. Kaung, Rev. Hsieh Yung-ching, Rev. H. H. Tsui, Rev. Chia Yu-ming, Rev. T. C. Chao, Mr. Y. C. Tu, Principal Ting Yu-chang and others who led the way before us. Their faith, insight and courage continue to encourage us to go forward.

The second point that I wish to make is that while the Three-Self Movement has accomplished much in the past, its task is still far from finished. Its achievements must be consolidated, defended, enlarged and developed.

For a long time, the Three-Self Patriotic Movement has held high the banner of patriotism. It has helped us to distinguish wrong from right; to cherish the country and the church; to become good Christians and at the same time good citizens. The Three-Self Movement must continue to hold high this banner, helping Christians in political study and in making a contribution to our national task. We must safeguard national stability and unity; carry through the Four Modernizations; bring about the return of Taiwan to the motherland; and oppose hegemonism and aggression while safeguarding peace.

With the help of the Three-Self Patriotic Movement we must encourage fellow Christians, especially the younger ones, to care deeply for our motherland and the socialist cause and to be proud of the history and progress of our country. We must help them to observe the teachings of Christ, to increase the demands they make of themselves, to study and work hard, so that, no matter whether it be in the family, the neighborhood or the work place, they may bear good witness, shining forth for the Lord and their motherland.

There are anti-China organizations abroad that wantonly proclaim an underground evangelism in China and raise money for their own designs. They claim that they have established so-called underground churches in our country. Christians, however, are resolved to observe the laws as loyal citizens and to protect the name of the church. We will have nothing to do with anybody, inside or outside China, who humiliates the church, conducting, in the name of Christianity, illegal activities detrimental to the physical and mental well-being of our fellow Christians and to public order.

The third point to note is that we want to move from a self-organized church to a well-organized church. From its beginning Three-Self envisioned a well-governed, well-supported, well-propagating church of Christ growing up on Chinese soil. The Lord has shown us that in order for Christians to build up the body of Christ in China, we must model ourselves after the church of the apostolic age. We must obey the God who is revealed in the Bible. We must absorb the fine traditions and the solemn lessons of church history. And we must allow the Holy Spirit to show us a path that others may not have walked before, but which is appropriate for China. We must dare to leave behind the insights and symbolic representations of faith gained by other nations, other ages and other Christians and allow our own spiritual experience to blossom forth, so that the wisdom and stature of the Chinese church can grow together with the love of God, and of men and women for it.

We know that we should be humble and cautious in explaining the word of God. In dispensing Christ's truth we must be comprehensive and genuine. Christ's truth is falsely spoken if it loses its wholeness or if, when the people gather, the leader follows his or her own will. There are even those who do not hesitate to say whatever some people would like to hear in order to better their own position. Serving Christ becomes the path to riches, and the church is tarnished as a result. These circumstances are easily exploited by evil persons. Christians today hunger and thirst for the gospel. We must carefully watch over them, guide and train them.

Apart from work on the revision and translation of the Bible, leading up to a new version, we would all like to see the publication of periodicals that would help in introducing basic Christian doctrine, in studying the Bible, in cultivating the life of the spirit, and in raising the standard of our colleagues' work. Furthermore, we all feel that regular teaching at Nanjing Union Seminary should be promptly resumed in order to provide theological education appropriate to our situation in China and to the training of people for the Lord's use.

Christians are gathering together in meetings throughout the country, enjoying fellowship in Christ, helping and encouraging one another. But we are still relatively scattered. Because we don't receive the supplies, the interchange, the assistance that we need, we may sometimes be off the mark. We must find ways of improving communication so that all become part of the Christian community.

At the enlarged meeting of the Standing Committee of the National Three-Self Movement we sought God's guidance as we discussed the formation of a new national organization to carry on certain kinds of church work according to the principles of self-government, self-support and self-propagation. It was decided in the end to carry out the necessary preparations. As we hold this national meeting, we shall continue to seek God's guidance on this matter and to exchange ideas fully.

With regard to this new body, the National Church Affairs Organization, and its relationship to the Three-Self Patriotic Movement, we think it appropriate for both to exist at the national level, even though there may be some duplication of personnel. Both are made up of Christians who are committed to our national purpose: The former organization stresses the Christian aspect of our life; the latter the patriotic. They are comparable to the two hands of a body, joined in a relationship of intimate cooperation. It is not a case of one leading the other. With these two organizations, the scope of our unity is even broader. At the local level, however, each area must decide for itself if it wishes to set up its own church affairs organization.

Before I close I would like to speak for a moment about our international relationship. We are all happy to note that new China has friends all over the world, including a good number of individuals — some former missionaries — and groups in churches outside the country, who have shown friendship toward Chinese Christians as well. They are happy to see China's progress on all fronts, and they have no intention of interfering in the internal affairs of either our nation or our church. We do not speak of them in the same breath as overseas anti-China forces. Rather, we welcome their friendly attitudes and are grateful for their prayers and assistance. Chinese Christianity cherishes its own special path, but has no wish to exclude beneficial international contacts. To the best of our ability we are willing to develop mutual friendship and give-and-take relationships, within the body of Christ, with all churches and Christians who treat us as equals and respect our principled stand of independence and self-determination.

There are others, however, who fan the flames of antagonism. They exploit our ten years of turmoil in order to mislead Christian sentiment abroad and to lead an attack on the patriotic thinking, speeches and activities of Chinese Christians. They flatly deny the lessons of past foreign evangelistic activities in China. They ignore our expression of independence

and self-determination in the work of the gospel, and the justice, reasonableness and necessity of self-government, self-support and self-propagation. They look upon Three-Self as a thorn in the flesh, vainly attempting
to return Chinese Christianity to its colonial past. Chinese Christianity is
now more unified than ever, but they are striving to divide us. To deal with
this kind of outside meddling and infiltration all Christians in our country
must increase their vigilance, guard the fruits of the past thirty years and
defend the Three-Self path of the church.

The Three-Self Patriotic Movement has a political as well as a theological and spiritual significance. Its development must continue unimpeded.
At the same time all of us see clearly that tending the Lord's flock, the task
given to Peter after Christ's resurrection, is also the task that our risen
Lord has entrusted to us. Christians urgently need to be guided in a way
that enables them to cherish both the church and the motherland. They
are like the five thousand who came to hear Jesus. We cannot send them
out to search hither and yon, lest they be cheated. According to the Lord's
own instructions we should instead encourage them to sit down with him.
We should take up the five loaves and two fishes, presenting them to Jesus
to bless and distribute to all. In this way everyone will have enough to eat,
and the church will be able to develop in good health, benefitting not only
itself but all Christians and the motherland.

NEW ROADS TO TRAVEL (1980)

This meeting has discussed a number of important problems in our
church. For many of us this has also been a significant spiritual experience.
Here we seem to have come closer to God and to our brothers and sisters;
we have all made progress in nurturing our spiritual life. One fellow Christian has said this seems to be a spirit-building meeting. I certainly feel more
than ever before that God is omnipresent with us, loving, protecting and
guiding us. I believe more strongly than ever in the power of the believers'
prayers.

Some of us worship in small places; others come from big churches. What
is important is our increasing belief in God not only as truth, goodness and
beauty, but as a loving God, very near to us, ever guiding us. At the same
time we truly draw strength from the prayers of many believers both at
home and abroad. A large number of letters, telegrams and telephone calls
have come in telling us that over the past few months people have been
praying for this meeting. To use the words we recently put in a resolution,
they "have lifted up this meeting with their prayers." I think "lift up" is
better than "support" because the prayers of the believers in China and
the whole world have lifted us up so that we are closer to God.

Since we have not seen each other for twenty years, this meeting has
also allowed us to "synchronize our watches." It is as though each of us
were a watch; during the last twenty years some of us ran fast, others ran

slow, and still others stopped for a while. During this conference we have synchronized with God and with the people of the motherland; here we have had communication and synchronization among ourselves in preparation for the roads we must travel and the battles we must fight.

Over the last twenty years Chinese Protestants have made progress in patriotism. Our Three-Self Patriotic Movement has been realized and tested; a growing number of people and cadres have a new opinion of Christians and Christianity. The speech given by Minister Zhang at this conference is a sign that the Party even welcomes as special friends those who give them frank opinions.

As Protestants in Nanjing we have never broken off our worship at home. But yesterday was the first time since August 1966 that we have held a service in a church. I hear that several government cadres were there too. Of course they did not come to worship God but to see if we need their help in solving any problems. What moved me deeply is that, so I heard, when we stood up to pray or sing, they also rose to their feet. In the fifties it was not like that. We would invite cadres from the department of religious affairs to attend our meetings for consultation; when we rose to pray, they remained seated, even smoking cigarettes. We can conclude from their behavior yesterday that more and more cadres are beginning to realize what Protestantism is all about; and knowing that we Protestants are also patriotic they respect our faith more.

BUILDING COMMUNITY (1984)

The Three-Self Movement is not anti-foreign. Its aim is to achieve a solid Chinese identity for the churches in China. In fact we are quite open to international relations with all Christians and churches elsewhere who respect our Three-Self principle. We were most glad to host the Archbishop of Canterbury when he came to visit us recently with a delegation of twenty from the British Council of Churches. We have also welcomed delegations from national councils of churches in Canada, the USA, Australia and Japan. It was a joy when a group of Asian church leaders came to visit us. Our delegates have been to many countries as guests of churches there. Recently I was in the German Democratic Republic [East Germany] to take part in the celebration of the 500th anniversary of Martin Luther's birth. I took the opportunity to visit churches in Hungary and the Ecumenical Center in Geneva, Switzerland, as well.

Chinese Christians did not take to the concept of Three-Self immediately and uniformly after its introduction. But they have certainly come to realize the justice and necessity of the Three-Self Movement as a principle for churches in any independent country. And we do see that as our church has gained a Chinese identity, the people in general take a more friendly attitude toward it. More of them have become willing to hear what Christianity is all about.

The churches are now entirely under Chinese leadership with regard to personnel and financial management. Politically Christians are generally good, loyal citizens, taking their place by the side of the rest of the Chinese people and playing a role in building up the material and cultural wealth of our country. In worship, in church music, in art, in theological thinking and in education, we are also consciously working for the development of Chinese ways of expressing our Christian faith.

Chinese Protestants are united on a much wider scale than ever before in our history. We are now post-denominational; that is, structurally we have done away with sectarian divisions. Protestants of different theological views are working together in mutual respect within the Three-Self Movement and the China Christian Council. These two bodies are doing their best to serve all Christians, those worshipping in church buildings and those worshipping in homes and other meeting places. We do not see how a difference regarding the location for meetings can become a cause for contradiction or division, as some strong critics of new China are trying hard to make out in their propaganda. If they are really for the church of Jesus Christ, they should instead thank God for the love and unity that has emerged among us.

Not all Christians in China worship in churches. In the first place, China is so vast that the sixteen hundred churches now open are still not easily accessible to all Christians. Then, to meet in homes once a week or so has been the longstanding practice of many Chinese Protestants who do go to churches to worship. There are also a number of Christians—for instance those converted during the Cultural Revolution—who have had no experience of worshipping in a big congregation. They prefer the intimacy and fellowship of meeting in a less formal setting. But no matter where we worship, what unites us are our common faith in Jesus Christ and our common adherence to the Three-Self principle.

There are various considerations that may explain the recent increase in the number of Christians. If we try to relate the increase to a loss of faith in socialism, then we must remember that in old China people were certainly very dissatisfied with the Kuomintang rule. But the number of Protestants then was less than one-third of what it is today, in spite of the presence of thousands of Western missionaries and the millions of dollars that poured in each year to maintain mission universities, colleges, schools, hospitals and other institutions.

There are other points to bear in mind. The Chinese population has more than doubled over the last thirty years. The National Constitution mandates respect for people's religious faith: Discrimination against religious believers is not regarded as good but criticized and in serious cases punished by law. On top of that, Christianity has taken on a Chinese image, which the public welcomes. All things considered, it is not really so abnormal for there to be an increase in the number of Christians today. Chinese Christians do not see any incompatibility between cherishing the socialist motherland and affirming the political leadership of the Communist Party on the one hand, and proclaiming their love of God and the church on the other. In Shanghai, for instance, one out of every one hundred twenty five Protestants is an "advanced" or "model" worker. Thus we are at once adherents of the Christian faith and supporters of socialism.

The most serious obstacle to our work at present is ultra-leftism. We find it entirely possible to work with true Marxist revolutionaries who, while entertaining no high opinion of religion at all, do see the importance of the United Front in propelling society forward. They work hard to unite all Chinese, including Christians, in the common social and political task of making China prosperous. They are most serious in implementing the policy of religious freedom. But the ultra-leftists have no respect for the United Front, nor for religious freedom. We suffered from them greatly. We are glad that ultra-leftism revealed its true character more fully than ever before in the Cultural Revolution, and that it has now largely discredited itself.

As for the future of Protestantism in China, as Christians we will continue to be in political solidarity with socialism, which is the cause of the Chinese people. Of course this solidarity does not exclude but rather affirms our responsibility, as citizens of the People's Republic of China, to criticize and supervise government work. I do not think Chinese Protestantism will cease to be a minority religion in the foreseeable future. But thanks to the thorough criticism of ultra-leftism, the effective implementation of the policy on religious freedom, and the good work of the Three-Self Movement and the China Christian Council, I foresee that pastoral care, theological strengthening and evangelism will be put on a much healthier basis. This will be to the benefit of both our country and our church.

A NURTURING THEOLOGY (1985)

There are people abroad who try to make out that the Chinese church and its Three-Self Movement are opportunist, serving a political purpose and preaching a message not fully Christian. There is little ground for this accusation, which is based on a very condescending view of the members of our church. In reality our structurally post-denominational church and its bible-loving, bible-honoring and bible-studying Christians are not theologically so blind as to fall victim to false or misleading teachings.

On the other hand, I wish to react to the alarm and disappointment voiced by friends abroad when they fail to find in China anything approaching liberation theology—even thirty years after liberation! To them Chinese Christianity is still "pre-liberation" and "colonial," and Chinese Christians, being theologically conservative but politically pro-socialist, seem to lead compartmentalized lives, dwelling in two separate realms. While I do not want to write an apology for this state of affairs, I feel that a Chinese viewpoint may redress the balance of these judgments.

The separation between spirituality and secularism—the concept of two realms—has had a long history with strong theological underpinnings. It was a major element in the missionary teaching of the nineteenth and twentieth centuries, and as such it persists today. What has come to be a motto in the Three-Self Movement (*ai guo, ai jiao*—love the motherland and love the church) continues to sanction this separation, but in the post-liberation period compartmentalism has not proved itself to be such a harmful thing as before. Our observation in the last thirty-six years does not bear out the judgment that it necessarily leads us to be apolitical. Certainly Christians of this kind are no less participatory than other Christians or other citizens. Furthermore, their theology is always open to change, although the changes are not so spectacular as some of our friends would like them to be.

The Three-Self Movement and the more recently organized China Christian Council aim at uniting all men and women of Protestant faith. We want to avoid reproduction of a pattern abroad whereby Protestants are grouped into "ecumenicals" and "evangelicals." Faith, hope, love and experience combine to tell us that in our present reality it is possible to avoid that pattern. We want to ensure the growth of unity. The last thing we want is a split in the community.

In matters of faith, worship and theology, our policy is generally one of equality and mutual respect, not one of offending people's religious feelings. We do not give priority to steering Christians away from their compartmentalism toward theologies with articulate social and political content (or vice versa). Our priority is to work together on such things as printing bibles, reopening churches, publishing Christian literature, strengthening theological training centers, implementing a policy of religious freedom in political and theoretical fields, and improving Christian nurture both in churches and in groups meeting in homes. These are the things that unite us and help us discover and learn from one another.

Ours is a unity worth paying for. We have not found that this unity results in stagnation. Three-Self is newborn since liberation and independence; it is neither "pre-liberation" nor "colonial." It is a mass movement in which many Christians move forward together, though perhaps at a slower pace than some may expect.

With all the importance given these days to contextualization, it may not be fashionable to say that theology must dialogue not only with the social and cultural context of the church but also with Christians in the fold. A "contextualized theology," appreciated by socially conscientized intellectuals far away but foreign to its home church constituency, is an anomaly. We must always remember that we are supported spiritually and materially by Christians in China. Our first attachment is to them. To be true native sons and daughters is the glory of our theologians. We write first of all for domestic consumption, that is, for the nourishment and edification of Chinese Christians. We meet them where they are in ways they can accept.

We do not impose on them anything they are not ready for.

Dialogue with culture, with natural and social sciences, with philosophy and with the international community of theologians is valuable insofar as it can be channeled to serve the needs of rank-and-file Christians. We value the work of those theologians who can, without condescension, orient themselves to fellow Christians at their gate, learn from them, summarize their insights and help them reach a fuller knowledge of God's revelation. Chinese Christians support all the positive changes in our society brought about by socialism. Religious commitment and spirituality—whatever the theology—cannot really remain untouched by social and political stance, although in many cases the changes are just "touches" and nothing drastic. It is for theologians to be sensitive to these touches and to reflect them honestly and reverently in their work.

This new and unprecedented width of Christian unity—realized in the last thirty years as "ecumenicals" become more evangelical and "evangelicals" become more ecumenical—is the cutting edge of Chinese theological renewal. It deserves our attention and thanksgiving.

If all that I have said constitutes a defense, it is not on the behalf of compartmentalism. It is a defense of the right of Christians of whatever theological inclination to be treated as equals, of our responsibility to keep Christians of all sorts in the common bond of community, and of the importance of reflecting and molding the constituency given to us.

SELFHOOD—GIFT AND PROMISE (1984)

This child is destined to be a sign which men reject; and you too shall be pierced to the heart. Many in Israel will stand or fall because of him, and thus the secret thoughts of many will be laid bare (Lk 2:34-35).

As Simeon declares in his prophecy, Christ, who is ultimately the unifier, is first of all a divider. The incarnation of Christ lays bare what is in the hearts of men and women.

The New Testament shows that human beings who confront Christ reveal themselves to be in one of three categories. First, there are Christ's despisers and enemies: the Herods, the Caiaphases, the Pharisees, the Sadducees, who hate and reject him. Then there are liberals of various degrees, who choose to be noncommittal and refrain from making a judgment: the Gamaliels, the Pilates (and perhaps Nicodemuses). Finally, there are those who, in spite of the human, finite form of the Christ they see, recognize in him the son whom God made heir to the whole universe, through whom was created all orders of existence—the radiance of God's splendor and the stamp of God's very being, sustaining the universe by his word of power. In this Christ they see the vision of a perfect order, consonant with God's will, and to this Christ they commit themselves in praise, adoration and action.

A splitting into groups—despisers, liberals and friends—happens not only when we are face-to-face with the fact of incarnation. It happens whenever there are newborn things in history. Such divisions, as well as movement from one category to another, can also happen when there is new birth in the church. Throughout history movements representing the cutting edge of the church in the world have had to battle the forces of the status quo. Too often they have been captured by them and tamed into something docile, conventional and harmless.

Now newborn things are not often beautiful right from the beginning. There is bound to be some awkwardness, even faults and mistakes, which may provide some with a pretext for opposition and others with grounds for hesitation. But in judging a thing we need to grasp its essence, not its aberration. It is the essence of the matter that counts because of its relative stability and permanence. If virtue lay only in avoiding mistakes, the one who did nothing about anything would be the most virtuous person. Learning would then be entirely irrelevant and out of place.

As Chinese Christians we have come to Geneva for two reasons. First, our coming is an acting out—for Christians everywhere—of the oneness of the body of Christ and the relationship of the church in China to the church universal. We are not relaxing our efforts to make the church in China Chinese. As long as our Chinese people think of Christianity as something Western, there is no way to show that at its center is the universal and absolute claim on all women and men of Jesus Christ as Lord.

Furthermore, if we do not cherish our selfhood, we will have nothing to give to the church universal. Fostering our identity then is important to us. Nevertheless identity bears an inescapable provisionality, because it concerns only the form of our selfhood, whereas the substance and the justification for the existence of this selfhood are necessarily its being the church of Jesus Christ. And this substance we share and affirm with the churches of the whole world. We hope our visit can be a sort of actualization of this truth.

Second, we have come to plead for a serious evaluation of our Three-Self concept. Here we hope to find, as it were, a continuing spearhead of church venture, a continuing defender of experimental engagement in the world, and an incubator for a child born perhaps a little ahead of its time.

Might not Three-Self really be a child born in the household of God and destined to be a sign for something beyond itself? Could it be one of the really important breakthroughs in history, with a significant message for Christians everywhere?

We hope our visit here can mark the beginning of a process of give-and-take within the family of God, a process that will bring about better self-knowledge as we examine our aims and undertakings from new angles that you will provide.

THE EMPOWERING SPIRIT (1984)

The fifteenth chapter of Acts describes a meeting that Peter, James, Paul and the other apostles held in Jerusalem. This meeting was extremely important for the future of the church and indeed for human history. The Spirit itself was at work there, leading and inspiring the apostles, opening their ears to what Peter and Paul had learned of God among the Gentiles. They reached a decision: In proclaiming the gospel to the Gentiles, Jewish law should be set aside. A letter went out to the Gentiles saying, "It has seemed good to the Holy Spirit and to us"—note this extraordinary wording—"It has seemed good to the Holy Spirit and to us to lay upon you no greater burden" (Acts 15:28). The Holy Spirit and the apostles worked together at that meeting and reached a decision together. They upheld justification by faith and gained a great victory over those who would have bound newcomers to Christianity to observance of Jewish law. Gentile Christians everywhere could now organize their churches according to the guidance of the Holy Spirit. They were no longer appendages of the church in Jerusalem. Churches appeared in many places during the New Testament period. They were all under the care and guidance of the Holy Spirit, all localized, all with their unique characteristics and local color. In mutual support with the church in Jerusalem, they were also on an equal footing with it, free of any subservient or parent-child relationship.

Those who say that the term *Three-Self* cannot be found in the Bible are right. But we may ask whether Three-Self as a principle or as a task is to be found there. I believe it is. The fifteenth chapter of Acts deals with just this question. What Paul advocates on behalf of the Gentile churches is exactly the same selfhood that our Three-Self stands for. His point about justification by faith, and his opposition to the notion that one may be justified by keeping the law, allowed Gentile churches to cast off the burdens put on them by the so-called mother church and to find their own path.

No matter where the gospel has been proclaimed in the past two thousand years, the problem of how to follow one's own path has gone with it. Each ethnic group, each country, must ask itself two questions. Does acceptance of Christ as Lord entail acceptance of the culture and nationality of those who come to proclaim the gospel? Does belief in Christ imply severing relationships with one's own people and becoming stateless or semi-foreign?

There was a missionary in Africa who said he wanted Christians there to become in all respects just like whites—except for the color of their skin. Is this a good approach to mission? There are numerous independent churches in Africa today, independent in administration, financial resources and the work of evangelization. Is this wrong?

I myself did not understand or support Three-Self all at once. When Mr.

Y. T. Wu and other senior church leaders initiated the movement, I was still living in Switzerland. When I returned I wanted to look things over first, to find out something about it. My attitude was that of Gamaliel: "If this plan or this undertaking is of men it will fail; but if it is of God you will not be able to overthrow them. You might even be found opposing God" (Acts 5:38-39). Later I saw more clearly. I learned from the New Testament what the church's path ought to be. Three-Self was Paul's way; it came from the Lord himself. Once, when the risen Christ appeared to the disciples, John said softly to Peter: "It is the Lord." I seemed also to hear these words: The hand of the risen Lord himself was pointing the way. And I laid down my burden and began to support Three-Self.

One of our beloved senior church leaders, the Reverend Jia Yuming, also went through a wait-and-see period with regard to Three-Self. He waited upon the Lord, and received these words: "The source is unpolluted." He then resolved to support Three-Self. After that he was chosen to be vice-chairman of the national Three-Self Movement. But we need not be concerned so much with the persons involved—if we look to humanity, we will stumble. If we look to the Bible and to the source, we cannot go wrong.

Let us place the decision we made thirty years ago before God's altar. Let us place there also the future of the Chinese church and seek the guidance of the Holy Spirit.

> Where the church is corrupt, O Lord, cleanse it,
> where it is mistaken, correct it,
> where it is lacking, enrich it,
> where it is divided, grant it love,
> where it has lost the capacity to witness to Christ,
>   bring it back,
> where it is presumptuous and complacent grant discipline,
> where it has humility, goodness, unity and mutual love,
>   bless and strengthen it.
> All this we ask in the name of Jesus Christ, the head
>   of the church.

A GUIDE TO FURTHER READING

This guide is brief and selective. It is for the general reader who wishes to develop a fuller background on China and the Chinese church. The books listed, though scholarly, are for the most part readable and understandable without special background. Almost all these works are written by people from Western cultures, an important factor to bear in mind. With China, as perhaps with every culture, we are dealing with interpretations rather than "facts." The cultural background of the interpreter colors the interpretation. Some translations from Chinese sources are noted in the last section.

INTERPRETATIONS OF CHINESE HISTORY

Chou Ts'e-Tsung, *The May Fourth Movement: Intellectual Revolution in Modern China* (Cambridge: Harvard U. Press, 1960) is a well-written account of the cultural renaissance in China in the post-Qing period, focussing on the May Fourth Movement of 1919.

John King Fairbank, *The United States and China* (Cambridge: Harvard U. Press, rev. ed., 1972) does more than the title suggests. The book describes concisely traditional Chinese social and political organization, the impact of the Western world on China, the rise of modern revolution and reform, the development of "Communist China" and the basis of United States' China policy.

C. P. Fitzgerald, *China: A Short Cultural History* (London: Cresset Press, 1961) is a classic first published in 1935, providing a very readable interpretation of China's cultural development from pre-history to the end of the Qing Dynasty.

Kenneth Scott Latourette, *The Chinese: Their History and Culture* (New York: Macmillan, 1934, 1964) is an encyclopedic tome covering 3,000 years of gradual and rapid social change. Each chapter is followed by a substantial list of bibliographical references. Also of interest for its wealth of facts is his *A History of Christian Missions in China* (New York: Macmillan, 1929).

Sterling Seagrave, *The Soong Dynasty* (New York: Harper & Row, 1985) is a popularly written story of the family behind the Nationalist interlude. It is an incredible tale of ship-stowaway Charlie Soong, who made his way to North Carolina in the 1870s, where he was converted to Methodism and then returned to Shanghai to achieve wealth and political power. His children (including Soong Ching-ling who married Sun Yat-sen and Soong Mei-ling who married Chiang Kai-shek) were major players in China before liberation.

Jonathan D. Spence, *The Memory Palace of Matteo Ricci* (New York: Penguin Books, 1985) is a fascinating study of the interaction of high European culture represented by Jesuit Father Ricci and Chinese culture as he encountered it in the late sixteenth century.

Cynthia R. Whitehead, *The Optics of Imperialism: British Images, Actions and Interests in China, 1793-1840* (unpublished dissertation, Harvard University, 1984) is a useful description of the change in Western attitudes toward China in a very short period, from adoration to scorn.

WESTERN INTERPRETATIONS OF THE CHINESE REVOLUTION

Lucien Bianco, *The Origins of the Chinese Revolution* (Stanford: Stanford U. Press, 1971) is an excellent scholarly account of the social conditions and suffering that motivate people to join the revolutionary struggle. This book originally was published in French.

Stephen Endicott, *James G. Endicott: Rebel out of China* (Toronto: U. of Toronto Press, 1980) is the biography of a famous Canadian missionary who came to an early appreciation of the socialist revolutionaries and became an interpreter of new China to the West in a period when not many dared speak.

C. P. Fitzgerald, *The Birth of Communist China* (New York: Praeger, 1966) tells the story of the rise of the Communist Party and the People's Liberation Army and the conditions and strategies that led to their victory.

William Hinton, *Fanshen: A Documentary of Revolution in a Chinese Village* (New York: Monthly Review Press, 1966) tells how peasants in an ordinary village put socialist principles into action to transform their lives. The book gives an interesting picture of life in China in the years of transition immediately after the Communist victory.

David Milton, Nancy Milton, and Franz Schurmann, editors, *People's China: Social Experimentation, Politics, Entry onto the World Scene, 1966 through 1972* (New York: Vintage Books, 1974) is a good source for documents of the Cultural Revolution and comments from various Chinese and foreign sources at the time. A good balanced study of the Cultural Revolution in China does not exist. Serious analysis of the social origins of the Cultural Revolution is yet to be done. Interpretations written in the 1970s tended to be caught either in the spirit of radical hope that the movement aroused both in China and abroad, or in reactionary antipathy to "dangerous" people's movements. In the 1980s political needs still governed Chinese statements of the Cultural Revolution period and observers in other countries had no reason to be interested in apparently moribund revolutionary theories. One suspects that the next generation will evaluate the China of both the 1970s and 1980s in quite different ways. A good library will have shelves of books on the Cultural Revolution, but it is difficult to recommend any one in particular.

Edgar Snow, *Red Star Over China* (New York: Random House, 1938) is a justly famous first-hand account by a journalist who visited underground leaders, including Mao Zedong and Zhou Enlai, to hear their stories. He also interviewed ordinary soldiers and workers at the remote base of the Communist Party and army. The book had an impact on Western views of the struggle in China, and also became hot underground reading in China among those who could lay their hands on a copy or translation. Snow told the world for the first time the story of the Long March.

MISSIONARY INTERPRETATIONS OF THE RELIGIOUS POLICY OF THE PEOPLE'S REPUBLIC OF CHINA

Katherine Hockin, *Servants of God in People's China* (New York: Friendship Press, 1962) reflects on the transition in China after the victory of the revolutionaries. The author is a Canadian missionary who experienced the transition in China and was not embittered. She has wise insights into the ways of missionaries and Chinese Christians and their response to radical social change.

Francis Price Jones, *The Church in Communist China: A Protestant Appraisal* (New York: Friendship Press, 1962) is a very fair reflection on political changes taking place in China in the 1950s. Although the author is clearly unsympathetic with the means used by the revolutionaries, he is very tempered in his critique of the Christian leaders who supported the new order.

Donald E. MacInnis, *Religious Policy and Practice in Communist China: A Documentary History* (New York: Macmillan, 1972) is a useful collection of statements by political leaders and scholars, official documents and decrees, and other statements indicating that there was a plurality of views and interpretations of religious policy in the 1950s and 1960s. A revision, *Religion in China Today: Policy and Practice* (Maryknoll: Orbis Books, 1989), presents the basic documents establishing religious policy in the PRC and describes the implementation and practice of these policies since 1979.

David Paton, *Christian Missions and the Judgment of God* (London: SCM, 1953) is a description of the failure of the missionary movement in China and a theological reflection on the roots of the problem.

Robert Whyte, *Unfinished Encounter: China and Christianity* (London: Collins, 1988) first presents nearly two hundred pages on the history of Christianity in China prior to 1949, then about three hundred pages on religious policy and church practice since 1949 with reference to the theological issues facing Chinese Christians. An extensive bibliography is appended.

Philip L. Wickeri, *Seeking the Common Ground: Protestant Christianity, the Three-Self Movement, and China's United Front* (Maryknoll, NY: Orbis Books, 1988) is a comprehensive study of the variety of responses of Protestant Christians to the religious policies of the Chinese government. The book includes a useful bibliography.

CHINESE SOURCES ON CULTURE AND RELIGION

Theresa Chu and Christopher Lind, editors, *A New Beginning* (Toronto: Canada China Programme of the Canadian Council of Churches, 1983) includes a variety of materials from the 1981 Montreal church conference on China. About twenty presentations by Catholic and Protestant leaders from China make this collection a good source for Chinese Christian thinking.

William Theodore de Bary, Wing-tsit Chan, Burton Watson, *Sources of Chinese Tradition* (New York: Columbia U. Press, 1960) provides a convenient collection of translations from Chinese sources from the earliest times to the twentieth century. The reader is helped with introductory notes and explanations.

Mao Tsetung (Mao Zedong), *Selected Readings from the Works of Mao Tsetung* (Beijing: Foreign Languages Press, 1971) brings together in one volume some of Mao's most important essays. There are many other collections of his essays, as well as several anthologies of his poetry.

Wallace C. Merwin and Francis P. Jones, editors, *Documents of the Three-Self Movement: Source Materials for the Study of the Protestant Church in Communist China* (New York: National Council of Church in Christ in the USA, 1963) is a good resource book containing English translations of speeches and statements from Christian leaders and church groups from 1948 to 1962.

Raymond L. Whitehead and Rhea M. Whitehead, editors, *China: Search for Community* (New York: Friendship Press, 1978) fits under a number of the categories of this guide. The book includes interpretative material on the Chinese revolution and on the church in China. Interviews in 1976 by Eugene Stockwell with Siu May and K. H. Ting, and with educator Wu Yifang, give a glimpse of what Christians were thinking about at the close of the Cultural Revolution. It was a time of de-institutionalized Christianity when it was said, "We have discarded ordination entirely," and "We have done away with institutions and church buildings."

Janice Wickeri, editor, *Chinese Theological Review*. This annual review started in 1985 contains translations of articles and sermons by Christian scholars and church leaders as well as other materials such as art work and stories. It is available from the Foundation for Theological Education in Southeast Asia, 86 East 12th Street, Holland, Michigan 49423.

SOURCES OF ARTICLES
IN CHRONOLOGICAL ORDER

Knowledge and Service
"The Dilemma of the Sincere Student," *The Canadian Student* (1947).
American Interventionism
"American Aid to China as Seen by a Chinese Christian, unsigned article in *The Anglican Outlook* (April 1947).
The Simplicity of the Gospel
"The Simplicity of the Gospel," *The Canadian Student* (1948).
Civil War in China
"The Sociological Foundation of the Democratic Movement in China," unsigned article in *Bulletin of the Society of the Catholic Commonwealth* (Cambridge, Mass., January 4, 1948).
A Vital Vocation
"A Chinese Answers the Question: Does God Call Us?" *Student World* 41 (1948): 318-325.
Christianity in Tension
"Power and Its Denial on the Cross," *Student World* 41 (1948): 210-215.
Hunger, Food and Grace
"A Creative Experience for Chinese Students," *Student World* 42 (1949): 22-32.
The Task of the Church in Asia
"The Task of the Church in Asia," *Student World* 42 (1949): 235-248.
Realizing the Gospel
"Behold the Man," *Student World* 44 (1951): 148-155.
The Nature of Witness
"Spread the Gospel and Establish the Body," *Tian Feng* 390, 391, 392 (November 16, 23, 30, 1953), translated by Ng Kam-yan.
The Spirit of Wisdom
"The Spirit Who Grants Wisdom and Revelation to Humankind," *Tian Feng* 398, 399 (January 18 and 25, 1954), translated by Ng Kam-yan.
Why Be a Minister?
"Why Must We Still Be Preachers?" *Nanjing Seminary Journal* (April 1954), translated by Yao Niangeng.
Unity Against Nuclear Threats
"Excerpts from a Speech to the Standing Committee of the Three-Self

Patriotic Movement," *Tian Feng* 457 (March 28, 1955), translated by Cheng Musheng.

Truth and Slander
"A Response to Wang Mingdao," *Tian Feng* 477, 478 (August 15, 1955), translated by Cheng Musheng.

Wrestling with God
"The Man Who Wrestled with God," *Nanjing Seminary Journal* 4 (November 1955), translated by Cheng Musheng.

Toward Unity
"Chinese Christians: New Prospects, New Unity," *Student World* 49 (1956): 291-295; originally published in *China Reconstructs*.

New Initiatives
"The Church in China Today," *Student World* 50 (1957): 45-59.

Challenges to Faith
"On Christian Theism," *Nanjing Seminary Journal* 7 (August 1956), new translation by K. H. Ting, 1985.

The Call to Peace
"Sermon Preached in the Bethlehem Chapel," Prague, 1961.

The Sinned Against
"On Human Beings," sermon preached at Riverside Church, New York, 1979.

Christians in Solidarity
"Science, Religion and Democracy in China," speech given at McGill University, Montreal, 1979.

Prophetic Challenges
From an unpublished talk with question and answer session, Vancouver, 1979.

Insights from Atheism
"A Chinese Christian's Appreciation of the Atheist," from an address given in Vancouver, November 1979 in *China and Ourselves* (January 1980).

Persistent Imperialism
"Facing the Future or Restoring the Past?" *China and Ourselves* (January 1980).

The Cry for Bread
"Give Ye Them To Eat," sermon on Luke 9:12-17 delivered at Timothy Eaton Church, Toronto, November 1979, in *China and Ourselves* (January 1980).

Theology in Socialist China
"Religious Policy and Theological Reorientation in China," lecture delivered at Emmanuel College, Toronto, October 1979, *China and Ourselves* (May 1980).

Charting the Future
"Retrospect and Prospect: Opening Address Before the Third Chinese National Christian Conference," *Ching Feng* XXIII, Nos. 3 and 4 (1980).

New Roads To Travel
"Closing Address at the Third National Christian Conference," *Tian Feng* 2 (March 20, 1980), translated by Cheng Musheng.

A Chinese Identity
"Address at Third Jiangsu Christian Conference," *Curriculum* 7-9 (May 1981), translated by Cheng Musheng.

The Reality of Resurrection
"Address at the Lambeth Palace Chapel," London, China Study Project, 1982.

If Christians Speak Rightly
"Sermon on John 18:22-24, Jesus Before the High Priest," Uppsala Cathedral, 1982 (unpublished).

Changing Relationships
"The Church in China," Uppsala University, 1982 (unpublished).

A Pioneering Theologian
"Forerunner Y. T. Wu," in *In Memory of Y. T. Wu*, Shanghai, 1982; English translation in *Ching Feng* (April 1983).

The Church's Mandate
"Evangelism as a Chinese Christian Sees It," *China Notes* XXI, 4 (Autumn, 1983).

Selfhood — Gift and Promise
"A Sign for Something Beyond Itself: Sermon on Luke 2:34-35," *One World* (Jan.-Feb. 1984): 16-17.

Christian Selfhood
"Sermon in Sydney Cathedral," Sydney, Australia, 1984 (unpublished).

Building Community
"Christianity in China Today," *Beijing Review* (June 1984).

The Cosmic Dimension
"Theological Mass Movement in China," Rikkyo University, Tokyo, 1984.

The Potential of Three-Self
"A Rationale for Three-Self," Doshisha University, Japan, 1984.

The Empowering Spirit
"The Holy Spirit and Us: Sermon on Acts 15:28-29," *Tian Feng* 23 (September 30, 1984).

The Journey of the Magi
"Sermon on Matthew 2:1-13" (unpublished), translated by Cheng Musheng.

God's Love of Life
"Sermon on I Kings 3:16-28" (unpublished), translated by Cheng Musheng.

New Life
"This Your Brother: Sermon on Luke 15:32," India, 1985.

Resurrection and Liberation
"The Greater Christ: Sermon on Colossians 1:15-17," India, 1985.

A Nurturing Theology
"Preface" to the first issue of *Chinese Theological Review* (1985).
Selfhood and Sharing
Speech given in Nanjing, 1986.
The Church Endures
Address given at Lutheran World Federation meeting in Denmark, 1987.

Index